THE EARLY RECORDS OF THE TOWN OF

ROWLEY MASSACHUSETTS.

1639-1672

BEING VOLUME ONE OF THE PRINTED RECORDS OF THE TOWN

BENJAMIN P. MIGHILL

AND

GEORGE B. BLODGETTE, ESQ

HERITAGE BOOKS
2008

HERITAGE BOOKS

AN IMPRINT OF HERITAGE BOOKS, INC.

Books, CDs, and more—Worldwide

For our listing of thousands of titles see our website
at
www.HeritageBooks.com

Published 2008 by
HERITAGE BOOKS, INC.
Publishing Division
100 Railroad Ave. #104
Westminster, Maryland 21157

Other books by George B. Blodgette, Esq:

Early Town Records of Rowley, Massachusetts. First Record of the First Church, Copied and Communicated to the Essex Institute, Inscriptions from the Old Cemetery in Rowley, Massachusetts

International Standard Book Numbers
Paperbound: 978-0-7884-4897
Clothbound: 978-0-917890-41-8

To the Memory of

EZEKIEL ROGERS,

FOUNDER AND FIRST MINISTER OF

ROWLEY, MASS.

"He was a man of eminent piety, zeal, and abilities
With the youth he took great pains, and was
a tree of knowledge, laden with fruit,
which children could reach."

This Volume is Respectfully Dedicated.

ACTS

OF THE

General Court Concerning Rowley.

---

13 March, 1638 – 9

"Mr Ezechi: Rogers, Mr John Phillips, & their company had granted them 8 miles every way into the countrey, where it may not trench vpon other plantations already setled."

4 – 7 mo., 1639

"Mr Ezechi: Rogers plantation shalbee called Rowley."

13 May, 1640

"Rowly is granted two years imunity from publike charge in regard of their great losse, & charge by purchasing of land, & hinderance of planting the last yeare."

"It is declared, that Rowley bounds is to bee 8 miles from their meeting house, in a straight line, & then a crose line diameter from Ipswich Ryver to Merrimack Ryver, where it doth not piudice any former grant."

PROEM.

The book used for recording the general affairs of the town of Rowley from 1639 to 1672 is much worn, mutilated, and nearly illegible, many leaves are missing, so that nothing remains of record before August, 1647. The printed copy begins on page 51.

Another book, containing the record of the laying out of lands and division of fences, was begun in 1643. It appears herein on the first fifty pages and thence chronologically in connection with the first named record.

There is a third book, styled "Book No. 1" of the town records, into which some matters from the first book have been imperfectly copied. Records therein, not found in the other two books, appear herein in proper order.

A list of those who had house lots in the first division is here given with a brief account of each :

GEORGE ABBOTT. Death not of record. The will of his son Thomas, dated 5 – 7 mo., 1659, and a deed recorded with the Essex Deeds, 1 Ipswich, 625, show four sons old enough to have been brought with him in 1639.

WILLIAM ACY. Had wife Margaret and four children all brought with him 1639. His death is not of record. He made his will 22 April, 1689, "being very aged;" it was proved 30 Sept., 1690.

THOMAS BARKER. Had wife Mary; no children. He was buried 30 Nov., 1650. His will was proved 25 – 1 mo., 1651.

JAMES BARKER. Had eight children. Buried 7 Sept., 1678. His will, dated 3 – 7 mo. 1678, proved 24 Sept., 1678, mentions himself as "born at Stragewell, in Low Suffolk, in old England."

WILLIAM BELLINGHAM. No mention of wife or children. Death not of record. His will was proved 24 – 7 mo., 1650. He was brother of Gov. Richard Bellingham.

MATTHEW BOYES. Had wife Elizabeth; ten children born here. He went back to England, and in 1661 was of Leeds, and about fifty-two years old.

WILLIAM BOYNTON. About fifty-six years old in 1652. Had wife Elizabeth and seven children. Died 8 Dec., 1686.

JOHN BOYNTON. Brother of William above. About forty-eight years old in 1662. Had wife Ellen (or Ellenor) and seven children. Buried 18 Feb., 1670–1. His will was dated 8 Feb., 1670–1, and proved 28 March, 1671.

EDMUND BRIDGES. Was a blacksmith.. Sold out and moved to Ipswich in 1644. Had wife Alice. One child born here.

SEBASTIAN BRIGHAM. Was captain of the first military company. Had wife Mary. Returned to England about 1657. Four children born here.

WIDOW JANE BROCKLEBANK. Brought with her two sons. Buried 26 Dec., 1668.

JOHN BURBANK. Death not of record. Will dated 5 Apr., 1681, proved 10 Apr., 1681, mentions himself as being "aged & decreped." Had five children. Descendants in male line now residing here.

EDWARD CARLTON. Had wife Ellen and four children. Returned to England.

HUGH CHAPLIN. Had wife Elizabeth and four children. Buried 22 – 1 mo., 1653. Descendants in male line now residing here.

PETER COOPER. Had wife Emma (or Ame) and four children. Buried 15 Jan., 1667–8. Will dated 3 Jan., 1667–8, proved 31 March, 1668.

WIDOW CONSTANCE CROSBY. She was buried 25 Jan., 1683–4. Four children.

THOMAS DICKINSON. Had wife Jenet and six children. Buried 29 – 1 mo., 1662. Will dated 8 March, 1661–2, proved 17 Apr., 1662. Descendant in male line now residing here.

JOHN DRESSER. Had wife Mary and five children. Buried 19 April, 1672. Will dated 5 March, 1671–2. Descendants in male line now residing here.

THOMAS ELITHORP. Had wife Abigail and four children. Death not of record. His widow petitioned the General Court for probate of his will 14 May, 1654.

WIDOW JANE GRANT. Death not of record. In the settlement of the estate of her son an affidavit was filed in Essex Probate containing so much of history of the family, that it is copied in full as follows:

"I Sam^ll Stickney S^r of Bradford do testify and say That I came over from England to New England in the same ship wth Thomas Grant & Jane Grant his Wife, who brought over wth them Foure Children, by name John, Hannah, Frances, & Ann, whome I was well acquainted with, & next or near neighbours unto in Rowley. And ye said John being deceased, I do affirm that the Sisters of John Grant above named, now by marriage known by ye names of Hannah Browne, Frances Keyes, & Ann Emerson are ye same y^t came over wth their Father & Mother, & by them owned wth said John for their children." Sworn to 20 July, 1698.

JOHN HARRIS.   Brought with him wife Bridget. Had six children. Died "aged" 15 Feb., 1694–5. Will dated 8 Jan., 1691–2, proved 27 March, 1695.

THOMAS HARRIS.   Moved to Ipswich with his wife Martha, 1644.

WILLIAM HARRIS.   Had wife Edee or Edith. One child born here. Moved to Middletown, Conn., about 1652.

ROBERT HASELTINE.   Married 23 – 10 mo., 1639, Anna ——, being the first couple married here. One of the three first settlers of Bradford, where he died 27 Aug., 1674. Will dated 25 Oct., 1673; proved 29 Sept., 1674. Ten children.

JOHN HASELTINE.   Brother of Robert above. Had wife Jane and four children. One of the three first settlers of Bradford. Died in Haverhill, 23 Dec., 1690; aged about 70 years. Will dated 17 Aug., 1689; proved 31 March, 1691.

MICHAEL HOPKINSON.   Was admitted to the First Church in Boston 6 – 11 mo., 1638; dismissed to "ye gathering of a church at Rowley," 24 – 9 mo., 1639; Had wife Ann and five children. Buried 28 Feb., 1648–9.

ROBERT HUNTER.   Had wife Mary; no children. Buried 5 – 6 mo., 1647.

WILLIAM JACKSON.   Had wife Joan and four children. Buried 5 May, 1688.

JOHN JARRAT.   Had wife Susannah and one child. Buried 11 – 12 mo., 1647. Will dated 11 – 11 mo., 1647; proved 27 – 7 mo., 1648.

MAXIMILIAN JEWETT.   Son of Edward and Mary (Taylor) Jewett, of Bradford, England. Baptized in Bradford, England, 4 Oct., 1607. Very early a deacon of the church. Had wife Ann and nine children. Died 19 Oct., 1684. Will dated 17 – 8 mo., 1684; proved 25 – 9 mo., 1684. Is on file in office of Clerk of Courts, Salem, Vol. XLIII, page 46.

JOSEPH JEWETT. Brother of Maximilian above and baptized in Bradford, England, 31 Dec., 1609. Brought with him wife Mary Mallinson, whom he married in Bradford, England, 1 Oct., 1634. Had nine children. Buried 26 Feb., 1660-1. Will dated 15 Feb., 1660; proved 26 March, 1661, and on file in Essex Probate. Descendants in male line now residing here.

GEORGE KILBOURNE. Son of Thomas and baptized at Wood Ditton, County Cambridge, England, 12 Feb., 1612. Had wife Elizabeth and six children. Died 14 Oct., 1685.

FRANCIS LAMBERT. Had wife Jane and six children. Buried 23–7 mo., 1647. Will dated 20 Sept., 1647; proved 28 – 1 mo., 1648. Descendants in male line now residing here.

THOMAS LEAVER, "linen weaver." Married 1 Sept., 1643, Mary Bradley. Had four children. Died 26 Dec., and was buried 27 Dec., 1683.

THOMAS LILFORTH. Moved to Haverhill before 1649. On Haverhill records he is called "Linforth."

THOMAS MIGHILL. Was first of Roxbury, probably in 1637, thence to Rowley, where he was ordained deacon 3 Dec. 1639, of the church then formed. He brought with him wife Ellen, who was buried 12 July, 1640, and the first person buried here. He married second, Ann Parrat, sister of Francis Parrat. The date of his burial, of record, is 14 – 5 mo., 1654, but as the inventory of his estate was taken 24 June, 1654, doubtless the true date of burial is 14 – 4 mo., 1654. Will dated 11 June, 1654; proved 27 – 1 mo., 1655. Nine children. Descendants in 'male line now residing here.

JOHN MILLER. Was a minister and assistant to the Rev. Mr. Rogers, and first town clerk. Had wife Lydia and one child of record here. Moved to Yarmouth 1641, thence to Roxbury, thence to Groton, where he died 12 June, 1663.

THOMAS MILLER. Had wife Isabel, and was a carpenter. About 1652 he removed to Middletown, Conn., where he died 14 Aug. 1683, aged above 70 years

THOMAS NELSON. The wealthiest of Rogers' Company. He married here a second wife, Jane Dummer. Brought with him two children; second wife had two. Went to England on business and there died Aug. 6, 1648. Will dated 24 Dec., 1645; proved 21 – 10 mo., 1649. Descendant in male line now residing here

JOHN NEWMARCH. Was first of Ipswich, to which place he soon returned.

THOMAS PALMER. Had wife Ann and three children. Death not of record. Will dated 2 Aug., 1669 ; proved 28 Sept., 1669.

FRANCIS PARRAT. Had wife Elizabeth and seven children. Was town clerk and deacon of the church. Went to England on business and there died in 1656. His will, dated 18 Nov., 1655, proved 30 Sept., 1656, mentions himself as "intending to take a journey to England."

JOHN REMINGTON. He was first of Newbury. Lieut. of the military company. Brought his wife, Elizabeth ; had five children born here ; sold out and left town in June, 1659.

HUMPHREY REYNER. Was "Ruling Elder" of the church from its formation and the only Elder of record. He was born at Gildersome, in West Riding of Yorkshire, near Leeds. Brought with him wife Mary and three daughters. Buried 14 Sept., 1660. Will dated 10 Sept., 1660.

REV. EZEKIEL ROGERS. Was the founder and first minister of Rowley. Died 23 Jan., buried 26 Jan., 1660-1, in his 70th year.

HENRY SANDYS, (called Sands in town record). Was dismissed from the first church in Boston "to ye gathering of a church at Rowley" 24 – 9 mo., 1639; Brought with him wife Sybil ; had two children born here. Returned to Boston before 1647.

WILLIAM SCALES. Had wife, Ann, and two (perhaps three) children. Buried 10 July, 1682.

WIDOW MARGERY SHOVE. She was the mother of the Rev. George Shove, who was ordained and settled at Taunton 16 Nov., 1665. She sold her lot to Elder Reyner before 1661. I have heard a traditional story that her husband was a minister and intended assistant to the Rev. Mr. Rogers ; that he died on the voyage from England, and Mr. John Miller was employed in his stead.

HUGH SMITH. Brought with him wife, Mary, and had six children. Death not of record. Will dated 19 – 9 mo., 1655, proved 20 – 1 mo., 1656.

JOHN SPOFFORD. Full genealogy in N. E. Historic Gen. Register, vol. viii., page 335.

MARGARET STANTON. No further mention of her found save this entry in the town record, "Anno 1646 Margaret Stanton, buryed the second month the fifteenth day."

WILLIAM STICKNEY. See "The Stickney Family, a Genealogical Memoir of the descendants of William and Elizabeth Stickney, from 1637 to 1869. By Matthew Adams Stickney, Salem, Mass., 1869."

THOMAS SUMNER. The only further mention of him found is a petition and inventory on file in the office of the clerk of courts for Essex as follows:

"Petition of Robert Coates, Sr., of Lynn, and Jane Coates, his wife and daughter of George Sumner, who died by Small-Pox some forty years since, in Rowley, for administration of estate of Thomas Sumner, her brother, who married and died without issue; his wife is also dead, she having married twice, and said Jane is only heir living, she being about ten years old when her father died. To the Court to be held 1st Tuesday November, 1691."

"Inventory of above estate amounting to £106, returned by Robert Coates, administrator, 3 November, 1691."

RICHARD SWAN. Was admitted to the first church in Boston, 6 – 11 mo., 1638; dismissed to yᵉ gathering of a church at Rowley, 24 - 9 mo., 1639; brought with him wife Ann, and here married Ann, widow of John Trumble; had eight children; buried 14 May, 1678; will dated 25 April, 1678, proved 23 May, 1678.

THOMAS TENNEY. Brought with him wife Ann; had six children; died in Bradford, 20 Feb., 1699 – 700. Descendants in male line now in Rowley.

RICHARD THORLEY (now Thurlow). Sold out, and in 1651 was of Newbury with wife Jane.

JOHN TRUMBLE. Brought with him wife Ellen; he married, 6 mo., 1650, Ann, widow of Michael Hopkinson; he had seven children, and was buried 18 – 5 mo., 1657.

RICHARD WICOM. Had wife Ann and three children; buried 27 Jan., 1663 – 4.

WILLIAM WILD. He was first of Ipswich, and again of Ipswich in 1661, and probably earlier.

In 1640 Mr. Thomas Nelson had erected a saw-mill where Glen Mills now are, and soon after, certainly as early as 1643, he added a grist-mill.

John Pearson came about this time with quite a company, and erected, near Mr. Nelson's grist-mill, a fulling-mill, the first in this country.

Many of the first settlers were weavers. Johnson, in his "Wonder-Working Providence" (London, 1654) says of the Rowley people:

"These people being industrious every way, soon built many houses, to the number of about three-score families, and were the first that set upon making Cloth in this Western World; for which end they built a fulling mill, and caused their little-ones to be very diligent in spinning cotton-wool, many of them having been clothiers in England."

Gov. Winthrop, under date of 12th of Fourth month, 1643, says:

"Our supplies from England failing much men began to look abou them, and fell to a manufacture of cotton; whereof, we had a store from Barbadoes, and of hemp and flax; wherein Rowley, to their great commendation, exceeded all other towns."

Before 1660 other families appear of record as residents—some had come with Mr. Rogers as minors, others to work about the mills.

The following are the new comers who appear to have resided in this village before 1660.

JAMES BAILEY. Had wife Lydia and eight children; was fifty-one years old 1663; buried 10 Aug., 1677; will dated 8 Aug., 1677, proved 25 Sept., 1677. Descendants in male line now residing here.

RICHARD BAILEY. Brother of James above. See "Historical and Genealogical Researches" by Alfred Poore, also "Reminiscences of a Nonagenarian" by Sarah A. Emery, page 139, and "Northend Family," Historical Collections of Essex Institute, Vol. XII.

SAMUEL BELLINGHAM. Son of Governor Richard Bellingham, of Boston, and nephew of William Bellingham (above). Had wife Lucy. Moved away 23 July, 1650.

REV. JOHN BROCK. Harvard College, 1646; was assistant to Mr. Rogers from 1648 to 1650. Tarried here no more.

CHARLES BROWNE. Had wife Mary, daughter of William Acy, and nine children. Buried 16 Dec., 1687. Will recorded with Essex Deeds, 5 Ipswich, 303.

THOMAS BURKBY (now Burpee). He married Martha, widow of Anthony Sadler of Salisbury; and second, Sarah, daughter of John Kelley of Newbury. Had six children. Died 1 June, 1701.

RICHARD CLARKE. Married here, 6 mo., 1643, Alice ———; the second couple married in town. Had five children. Death not of record. Will dated 7 Feb., 1673-4, proved 31 March, 1674.

TOBIA COLMAN. 1653, then a minor, was a son of Thomas Colman, of Newbury. Removed to Newbury and was there 1673.

ISAAC COUSSINS. 1644, blacksmith. He bought the rights of Edmund Bridges, and 30-1 mo., 1652, sold the same to John Pickard and removed to Haverhill.

THOMAS CROSBY. Had wife Jane. Came from Cambridge, Mass. He was buried 6 May, 1661.

MARGARET CROSSE. "A widdowe," admitted to the First Church in Boston 6 – 11 mo., 1638; mentioned 5 – 6 mo., 1647, in the will of Robert Hunter as of our church; also mentioned 1650 in the will of William Bellingham. No other mention of her is found. Perhaps she married John Palmer.

JEREMIAH ELLSWORTH. Had three children. Died 6 May, 1704. Descendants in male line now residing here.

LEONARD HARRIMAN. Had wife Margaret and five children. Died 6 May, 1691. Will proved 29 Sept., 1691.

DANIEL HARRIS. Weeelwright; had wife Mary. One child born here. Moved to Middletown, Conn., in 1652.

EDWARD HAZEN. See full genealogy in N. E. "Historic Gen. Register," Vol. 33, page 229.

ANDREW HIDDEN. Was about forty years old in 1662; had wife Sarah and twelve children. Died 18 Feb., 1702 (Town Record); 20 Feb., 1701–2, "an old man" (Church Record). Will dated 18 Feb., 1701–2; proved 1 April, 1702.

JOHN HILL. Remained but a short time, see page 70.

WILLIAM HOBSON. Was son of Henry and from Yorkshire, England; married 12 – 9 mo., 1652, Ann, daughter of Elder Humphrey Reyner. Had three children. Buried 17 July, 1659. Descendants in male line now residing here.

RICHARD HOLMES. Millwright. Was eighty-eight years old March, 1692. Had wife Alice and eight children. He died in Bradford at the house of his daughter Elizabeth Pearl. Will dated 15 July, 1695; proved 13 Jan., 1695–6.

NICHOLAS JACKSON. Had four children. Died 13 Feb., 1697–8. Descendants in male line now residing here.

ROBERT JOHNSON, JR. Son of Robert Johnson, who came with Mr. Rogers, but settled in New Haven, Conn. Death not of record. Will dated 13 – 7 mo., 1649; proved 26 – 1 mo., 1650. Legacy to poor in our church.

JOHN JOHNSON. Brother of Robert Johnson, Sr., mentioned above; Came with Rogers' company, but first sat down at New Haven. Had wife Hannah and five children; was captain of the military company. Died 29 Jan., 1685–6. Descendants in male line now residing here.

HENRY KINGSBURY. Was of Ipswich, 1648, of Rowley 1656 and '63, and of Haverhill, 1668.

ABEL LANGLEY. Had three children, all by his third wife. In a deed dated 7 Oct., 1693, beginning "Joseph Quilter of Ipswich....in behalfe of his cousin Abell Langley son of Abel Langley of Rowley, deceased." Quilter is called executor of the will of Abel Langley, deceased. I find no record of the will or death of Abel Langley.

WILLIAM LAW. Had eight children. Buried 30 March, 1668.

RICHARD LEIGHTON. Had wife Mary and five children; buried 2 June, 1682; will dated 27 May; proved 26 Sept., 1682.

RICHARD LONGHORNE. Was about forty-five years old, 1662; had wife Mary and nine children. He died in Haverhill while there on business 13 – 12 mo., 1668; will dated 10 Feb., 1668; proved 30 March, 1669.

JEREMIAH NORTHEND. Came from Yorkshire, England, with Mr. Rogers' company, then but twelve years old. He returned after a few years, and was buried in Rowley, England, 14 April, 1702.

EZEKIEL NORTHEND. (See full genealogy in Historical Collections of Essex Institute, Vol. XII).

JOHN PALMER. Married Ruth, daughter of William Acy; and for second wife married Margaret Northend, sister of Ezekiel above. Had six children; he was about seventy years old, 1693, and died "aged" 17 June, 1695; will dated 23 Aug., 1693; proved 1 July, 1695.

JOHN PEARSON. Had wife Dorcas and thirteen children; was ordained deacon of our church 24 Oct., 1686, and died 22 Dec. 1693. Descendant in male line now residing here.

REV. SAMUEL PHILLIPS. Harvard College 1650; settled colleague with the Rev. Mr. Rogers as second minister of Rowley June 1651; had wife Sarah and nine children; died 22 April, 1696; will on file in Essex Probate.

JOHN PICKARD. "Carpenter." His mother, widow Ann Lume, died here 19 March 1661–2. He had wife Jane and eight children; buried 24 Sept. 1683. An abstract of his will is printed in Historical Collections of Essex Institute, Vol. IV, page 20. Descendants in male line now residing here.

SAMUEL PLATTS. Had six children. I find no record of his death or settlement of his estate. His widow Philippa married 9 April, 1690.

JONATHAN PLATTS. Cousin of Samuel Platts above; had wife Elizabeth and eight children; buried 18 July, 1680; will proved 28 Sept., 1680.

MARK PRIME. Had wife Ann and two children; buried 21 Dec., 1683. Descendants in male line now residing here.

JACHIN REYNER. Nephew of Elder Humphrey and son of John, of Plymouth. Had wife Elizabeth and six children; died 8 July, 1708; will dated 1 July, 1708; proved 2 Aug., 1708.

HENRY RILEY. Was the village blacksmith; died 24 May 1710, "in yᵉ 82 year of his age" (gravestone); "not in full communion" (church record); no children; will in Essex Probate, Book 10, leaf 123.

DANIEL ROUSE. Had in 1650 an estate valued for taxation £19 – 10 – 00. He soon left town.

EDWARD SAWYER. Had wife Mary and four children. Buried 9 March, 1673–4. His nuncupative will was sworn to 31 March, 1674.

JOHN SCALES. Had wife Susannah and one child; buried 12 Jan., 1683–4; will dated 9 Jan., 1683–4; proved 27 March, 1684.

BENJAMIN SCOTT. Brought with him his wife Margaret. She was the Widow Margaret Scott who was executed in Salem 22 Sept. 1692, as guilty of "certain detestable arts called Witchcraft and Sorceries." He had nine children; death not of record; will dated 6 June, 1671; proved 26 Sept., 1671; inventory taken 14 July, 1671.

HENRY SEWALL. A very early settler; the ancestor of three chief justices of our highest court; he was buried here the "First Month, 1656."

JOHN SMITH. Married Faith Parrat, sister of Francis Parrat; had three children, and was buried 19 – 5 mo., 1661; will dated 13 July, 1661; proved 14 Nov., 1661.

HENRY SMITH. Was taxed here 1650, when his estate was valued £15 – 03 – 04. I find no other mention of him except the inventory of his estate taken 16 – 1 mo., 1655; personal property amounted to £14 – 03 – 00; no real estate.

WILLIAM TENNEY. Ordained deacon of our church 3 Feb. 1667–8; had wife Katherine and six children; died 5 Aug. 1685; will dated 3 Aug., 1685.

JOHN TILLISON. Had removed to Newbury, before 1651.

JOHN TODD. Had wife Susannah and ten children; he kept the "Ordinary:" died 14 Feb., 1689–90; will dated 13 Feb. 1689–90; proved 25 March, 1690. Descendants in male line now residing here.

THOMAS WOOD. Had wife Ann and eleven children; buried 12 Sept., 1687.

Joseph Wormwell. 1642; lived a short time on a parcel of ground belonging to Thomas Nelson; not identified with our people and soon removed; had wife Miriam; one child born here; he died in Scituate.

In Great Britain from the 14th century till 1752, the legal and ecclesiastical year began at March 25 (Annunciation Day), though it was not uncommon to reckon it from January 1.

The change from the reckoning of Julius Cæsar to that of Pope Gregory XIII was made by act of the British parliament in September, 1752, the 3[d] of the month being called the 14th, and from that time the legal year began January 1.

The former reckoning is called "old style" and the latter "new style."

Hence the double dating. Thus the revolution of 1688 occurred in February of that legal year, or, as we should now say, in February, 1689; and the date will often be found written Feb., 1688-9.

In this Volume of Records the original has been carefully followed in words, in letters, in punctuation, and in blank spaces, so that the reader has all the advantages that can be gained from the original, save in handwriting alone.

These marks   +   +   +   indicate words illegible.

If errors are found they may aid in recalling the words of Marcus Antoninus:

"Our understandings are always liable to error; nature and certainty are very hard to come at, and infallibility is mere vanity and pretence."

Geo. B. Blodgette.

ROWLEY RECORDS.

The suruey of the Towne of Rowley taken the tenth of the eleauenth Anno Dñi 1643. by Mr: Thomas Nelson, Mr: Edward Carlton, Humphrey Reyner, ffrancis Parrat, appointed for that purpose by the fremen of the said Towne who also are to Regester the seuerall lotts of all the Inhabitants granted and laid out, and to leaue theirof a Coppy with the Recorder of the Shire accordinge to the order of the Generall Court.

A regester of all the house Lotts in such seuerall streets, as are formerly mentioned in the booke.

Bradford streete

Imp to Thomas Ellethrop one Lott containinge one Acree and an halfe, bounded on the South side by the Comõns; part of it lyinge on the west side, and part of it on the East side of the street

To John Dresser one lott containinge one Acree and an halfe, bounded on the South side by Thomas Ellethrops house Lott: part of it lyinge on the west side, and part of it on the East side of the streete.

To Hugh Chaplin one Lott Containinge an Acree and an halfe, bounded on the South side, by John Dressers house lott: part of it lyinge on the west side, and part of it on the East side of the streete.

To Peter Cooper one Lott containinge an Acree and an halfe bounded on the South side, by Thomas Millers house lott: part of it lyinge on the west side, and part of it on the East side of the streete.

To Thomas Sumner one Lott Containinge an Acree and an halfe bounded on the south side by Peter Coopers house Lott: part of it lyinge on the west side, and part of it on the East side of the streete.

To John Burbanke one Lott containinge an Acree and an halfe bounded on the South side by Thomas Sumners house Lott : part of it lyinge on the West side, and part of it on the East side of the streete.

To Thomas Palmer one Lott Containinge an Acree and an halfe, bounded on the South side by John Burbankes house Lott : part of it lyinge on the West side, and part of it on the East side of the streete

To William Wild one Lott containinge an Acree and an halfe bounded on the South side by Thomas Palmers house Lott : part of it lyinge on the West side, and part of it on the East side of the streete.

To William Jackson one Lott Containinge an Acree and an halfe bounded on the South side by William Wilds house Lott : part of it lyinge on the west side, and part of it on the East side of the streete

To Hugh Smith one Lott Containinge an Acree and an halfe bounded on the South side by William Jacksons house Lott : part of it lyinge on the west side, and part of it on the East side of the streete

To Michaell Hopkinson one Lott Containinge an Acree and an halfe bounded on the South side by Hugh Smiths house Lott : part of it lying on the west side, and part of it lyinge on the East side of the streete.

To John Bointon one Lott Containinge an Acree and an halfe bounded on the South side by Michaell Hopkinsons house Lott : part of it lyinge on the west side, and part of it on the East side of the streete

To William Bointon one Lott Containinge an Acree and an halfe bounded on the South side by John Bointons house Lott : part of it lyinge on west side, and part of it on the East side of the streete.

To Thomas Dickinson one Lott Containinge an Acree and an halfe bounded on the South side by William Bointons house Lott : part of it lyinge on the west side, and part of it on the East side of the streete

To Joseph Jewet one Lott Containinge two Acrees bounded on the South side by Thomas Dickinsons house Lott : part of it lyinge on the west side, and part of it on the East side of the streete.

To Maximilian Jewet one Lott Containinge two Acres and

bounded on the South side by Joseph Jewets house Lott: part of it lyinge on the west side, part of it on the East side of the streete.

To Jane Grant one Lott Containinge one Acree and an halfe bounded on the South side by Maximiliam Jewets house Lott: part of it lyinge on the west side, part of it on the East side of the streete

To John Spofford one Lott Containinge an Acree and an halfe bounded on the South side by an high way: part of it lyinge on the west side, and part of it on the East side of the streete.

To George Kilborne one Lott Containinge an Acree and an halfe bounded on the South side by John Spoffords house Lott: part of it lyinge on the west side, and part of it on the East side of the streete

To Margaret Stanton one Acree, bounded on the South side by George Kilbornes house lott: part of it lyinge on the west side, and part of it on the East side of the streete

Wethersfield streete

Imp to John Remington two Acrees bounded on the west side by the Com̄ons: part of it lyinge vpon the North side of the streete, and part of it on the South side.

To James Barkar one lott Containinge one Acree and an halfe bounded on the west side by John Remingtons house Lott part of it lyinge on the north side of the streete and part of it on the south side

To William Stickney one Lott Containinge one Acree and an halfe bounded on the west side by James Barkars house lott, and the high way: part of it lyinge on the North side of the streete and part of it on the south side

To William Scales one Lott Containinge an Acree and an halfe, bounded on the west side by William Stickneys house lott part of it lyinge on the Northside of the streete and part of it on the South side:

To Mathew Boyes one lott Containinge two Acrees, bounded on the west side, by William Scales his house Lott: part of it lyinge on the North side of the streete and part of it on the south side.

To Jane Brockelbanke one lott Containinge two Acrees, bounded on the west side by Mathew Boyes: part of it lyinge on the North side of the streete, and part of it on the South side.

To Thomas Mighill one Lott Containinge Three Acrees, bounded on the West side, by the high way, and by a small parcell lyinge in Com̄on : part of it lyinge on the north side of the streete and part of it on the south side.

To M^rs : Margery Shoue one Lott Containinge two Acres, bounded on the west side by Thomas Mighills house lott : part of it lyinge on the north side of the streete, and part of it on the South side.

To Humphrey Reyner one Lott Containinge three Acrees, bounded on west side by Mrs Margery Shoues house Lott : part of it lyinge on the north side of the streete, and part of it on the South side.

To M^r : Ezekiell Rogers six Acres, bounded on the West side, by a small parcell of Com̄ons : part of his Lott lyinge on the North side of the streete, and part of it on the south side.

To Mr John Miller one Lott Containinge two Acres, bounded on the South side by Nicholas Jacksons house lott, the west end vpon the Streete

To John Jarrat one lott Containinge two Acres, bounded on the south side by Mr John Millers Lott, the west end lyinge vpon the streete.

To ffrancis Parrat two Acres, bounded on the south side by John Jarrats house Lott, the West End and the North side by the streete

To Mr Edward Carlton one Lott Containinge three Acrees, bounded on the South end by the streete on the west side by the Com̄on and by Mr Henry Sands house lott

To M^r : Henry Sands one Lott Containinge two Acres, bounded on the South side by the Com̄on and the West end by the streete.

To Thomas Leauer one Lott Containinge an Acree and a halfe bounded on the South side by the Com̄on and the East end by the streete

To John Trumble one Lot Containinge an Acree and a halfe, bounded on the South side by Thomas Leauers house Lott, and the East end by the street

To John Haseltine one Lott Containinge two Acres bounded on the South side by John Trumble and the East end by the streete.

To Thomas Tenny one Lott Containinge an Acree and an halfe, bounded on the south side, by John Haseltines house lott, and the East end by the streete

To Robert Haseltine one Lott Containinge two Acrees bounded

on the South side, by Thomas Tennyes house Lott, and the East
end by the streete.

To Richard Swan one Lott Containinge two Acres bounded
on the South side, by Robert Haseltines house Lott, and the East
end by the streete

To Thomas Lilforth one Lott Containinge one Acree and an a
halfe, bounded on the South side by Richard Swans house lott and
the East end by the streete

To Richard Thorlay one house Lott, Containinge two Acres,
bounded on the West side by M^r: Edward Carltons house lott, and
the South end by the streete.

To ffrancis Lambert one house Lott, Containinge two Acres
the North side lyinge vpon the Northeast field, the West end vpon
the streete.

To Robert Hunter one house Lott, Containinge two Acres,
bounded on the North side by ffrancis Lamberts house lott, the
West end by the streete

To William Acy one house Lott, Containinge two Acres,
bounded on the North side, and East end by the streete

To Thomas Miller one house Lott, Containinge one Acree and
an halfe, bounded on the North side by William Tennyes house
Lott, the East end by the streete

To William Harris one house Lott, Containinge two Acres,
bounded on the South side by the Comon, the East end by the
streete.

To John Harris one house Lott, Containinge two Acres,
bounded on the South side by William Harris his house Lott, the
East end by the streete.

To Thomas Harris one house Lott, Containinge two Acres,
bounded on the South side by John Harris his house lott, the East
end by the streete.

To John Newmarch one house Lott, Containinge two Acres,
bounded on the South side by Thomas Harris his house lott the
East end by the streete

To M^r: William Bellingam one house Lott, Containinge ffoure
Acres, bounded on the North side by a peece of Comon, part of it
lyinge on the East side of the streete, and part of it on the West
side

To M^r: Thomas Nelson one house Lott Containinge six Acres,
bounded on the North side by a peece of Comon; part of it lyinge
on the East side of the streete and part of it on the West side.

To Thomas Barkar one house Lott, Containinge foure Acres, bounded on the North side by a peece of Comon; part of it lyinge on the East side of the streete, and part of it on the West side.

To Sebastiam Briggam one house Lott, Containinge foure Acres bounded on the North side by Thomas Barkars house lott: part of it lyinge on the East side of the streete and part of it on the West side

To George Abbat one house Lott, Containinge two Acres, bounded on the North side by Sebastiam Briggams house lott, the East end by the streete

To Edward Bridges one house Lott, Containinge An acree and an halfe bounded on the North side by the Crosse streete the East end by the high streete

To Custins Crosby one house Lott, Containinge one Acree and an halfe bounded on the North side by a peece of ground vnlaid out, and the East end by the streete

To Richard Wakam one house Lott, Containinge one Acree and an halfe bounded on the North side by Custins Crosbyes house lott the East end by the streete.

A Regester of the first diuision of plantinge Lotts, in the seuerall fields knowne by their seuerall names aboue mentioned in the booke:

Imp^s Bradford streete field

To Thomas Ellethrop foure Acres and a halfe of vpland lyinge next vnto the South fence the East end buttinge vpon his house lott.

To John Dresser foure Acres and a halfe of vpland, lyinge vpon the North side of Thomas Ellethrops planting lott, the East end of it buttinge vpon his house lott

To Peter Cooper foure Acres and a halfe of vpland, lyinge vpon the North side of John Dressers plantinge lott: the East end butinge vpon his owne house lott.

To Thomas Sumner foure Acres and an. halfe of vpland, lying vpon the North side of Peter Coopers planting lott: the East end buttinge vpon his owne house lott.

To John Burbanke foure Acres and an halfe of vpland, lying vpon The North side of Thomas Sumners plantinge lott: the East end butting vpon his owne house lott.

To Thomas Palmar foure Acres and an halfe of vpland, lying vpon the North side of John Burbankes plantinge lott: the East end buttinge vpon his owne house lott.

To William Wild foure Acres and an halfe of vpland, lying vpon the North side of Thomas Palmars plantinge lott: the East end butting vpon his owne house lott.

To William Jackson foure Acres and an halfe of vpland lying vpon the North side of William Wilds planting lott: the East end butting vpon his owne house lott.

To Hugh Smith foure Acres and an halfe of vpland, lying vpon the North side of William Jacksons planting lott: the East end butting vpon his owne house lott.

To Michaell Hopkinson foure Acres and an halfe of vpland, lying vpon the North side of Hugh Smiths planting lott: the East end butting vpon his owne house lott.

To John Bointon foure Acres and an halfe of vpland, lyinge vpon the North side of Michaell Hopkinsons planting lott: the East end butting vpon his owne house lott.

To William Bointon foure Acres and an halfe of vpland, lying vpon the North side of John Bointons planting lott the East end butting vpon his owne house lott.

To Thomas Dickinson foure Acres and an Halfe of vpland, lying vpon the North side of William Bointons planting lott: the East end butting vpon his owne house lott.

To Joseph Jewet foure Acres and an halfe ofvpland, lying vpon the North side of Thomas Dickinsons planting lott: the East end butting vpon his owne house lott.

To Maximilian Jewet foure Acres and an halfe of vpland lying vpon the North side of Joseph Jewets planting lott: the East end butting vpon his owne house lott.

To Jane Grant foure Acres and an halfe of vpland, lying vpon the North side of Maximilian Jewets planting lott: the East end buttinge vpon her owne house lott.

To John spofford foure Acres and an halfe of vpland, lying vpon the North side of Jane Grants planting lott: the East end buttinge vpon his house lott.

To George Kilborne foure Acres and an halfe of vpland, lyinge vpon the North side of John Spoffords plantinge lott: the East end buttinge vpon his house lott.

To Custins Crosby foure Acres and an halfe of vpland, lying vpon the North side of George Kilbornes planting lott: the East end vpon John Remingtons house lott.

To Richard Wakam foure Acres and an halfe of vpland, lying vpon the North side of Custins Crosby: the East end butting vpon John Remingtons house lott.

To Jane Brockelbanke foure Acres and an halfe, lying vpon the North side of Richard Wakams planting lott: the East end butting vpon John Remingtons house lott.

To Mathew Boyes foure Acres and an halfe of vpland, lying vpon the North side of Jane Brockelbankes planting lott: the East end butting vpon John Remingtons house lott.

To William Scales foure Acres and an halfe of vpland, lying vpon the North side of Mathew Boyes his planting lott: the East end of it butting vpon the East fence of the said Bradford streete field.

To William Stickney foure Acres, of vpland, lying vpon the North side of William Scales his planting lott: the East end of it butting vpon the aboue said fence.

To James Barkar foure Acres and an halfe of vpland, lying part of it vpon the North side of William stickney his planting lott: and part of it vpon his owne house lott: both parcells within the said Bradford streete ffield.

To John Remington foure Acres of vpland, lying vpon the North side of James Barkars planting lott.

The Northeast ffield

To Sebastiam Briggam fourteene Acres of vpland, lying next to the Warehouse fence, the one end butting vpon the path leading to Newberry, the other vpon the salt marsh.

To Thomas Barkar fifteene Acres of vpland, lying vpon the North side of Sebastiam Briggam: butting vpon the aboue said places.

To Mr: Thomas Nelson twenty foure Acres of vpland, lying vpon the North side of Thomas Barkars lott: butting vpon the abouesaid places

To Mr: William Bellingam thirteene Acres of vpland, lying vpon the North side of Mr: Thomas Nelsons lott: butting vpon the abouesaid places.

To William Harris eight Acres of vpland, lying vpon the North of Mr: William Belllngam butting vpon the aboue said places

To Thomas Harris eight Acres of vpland, lying vpon the North side of William Harris: butting vpon the aboue said places

To John Harris eight Acres of vpland, lying vpon the North side of Thomas Harris: butting vpon the aboue said places.

To John Newmarch eight Acres, the South side butting to John Harris lott: the other side bounded with meadow.

To George Abbatt eight Acres of vpland, lying vpon the East side of Newberry path, on the one side, and a peece of ffresh marsh on the other..

To Mr: Ezekiell Rogers twenty one Acres of land, lying on the West side of the way that leadeth to Newberry, the Northend of it butting vpon the head of Humphrey Reyners lott and some others.

To ffrancis Parrat eleauen Acres of vpland, one end of it butting vpon the Cart path on the North side of Satchels meadow the other end vpon a small peece of rough Marsh

To Mr: Edward Carlton twelue Acres of vpland, lying on the West side of ffrancis Parrats lott: butting vpon the abouesaid places.

To Robert Hunter eight Acres of vpland, lying vpon the West side of Mr: Edward Carltons lott: butting vpon the abouesaid places.

To William Acy eight Acres of vpland, vpon the West side of Robert Hunters lott: butting vpon the abouesaid places.

To ffrancis Lambert eight Acres of vpland. lying vpon the west side of William Acy his lott: butting vpon the abouesaid places.

To Richard Thurlay eight Acres of vpland, lying vpon the West side of ffrancis Lamberts lott: butting vpon the aboue said places.

To Mr: Henry Sands eight Acres of vpland, lying vpon the west side of Richard Thurlay his lott: butting vpon the aforesaid places.

To Robert Haseltine eight Acres of vpland, lying vpon the west side of Mr: Henry Sands: butting vpon the aforesaid places.

To John Haseltine eight Acres of vpland, lying vpon the West side of Robert Haseltine: butting vpon the aboue said places

To John Jarrat eight Acres of vpland, lying vpon the West side of John Haseltines lott: butting vpon the aboue said places.

To Thomas Tenny ffoure Acres and an halfe of vpland, lying

next vnto the west fence of the Northeast ffield ; one end of it
butting vpon the abouesaid Cart path on the North side of Satchels
med'ow the other end vpon John Jarrats lott.

To Thomas Leauer ffoure Acres and an halfe of vpland lying
vpon the West side of the path that leadeth to newberry the South
end of it, butting vpon North end of M^r: Ezekiell Rogers his lott.

To John Trumble foure Acres and an halfe of vpland, lying
vpon the west side of Thomas Leauers lott : one end butting vpon the
North end of M^r: Ezekiell Rogers his lott.

To Humphrey Reyner thirteene Acres of vpland, lying on the
west side of John Trumbles lott : the South end lyinge, partly
vpon the North end of M^r: Ezekiell Rogers, partly vpon the North
end of ffrancis Parrats lott.

To Thomas Lilforth ffoure Acres and an halfe of vpland,
lying vpon the West side of Humphrey Reyners lott : the South
end butting vpon the North end of M^r: Edward Carltons lott.

To M^r: John Miller Eight Acres of vpland, the one end
butting vpon the ffence that leadeth to the Mill River, the other end
vpon Satchells Meadow.

To Richard Swan Eight Acres of vpland, lying vpon the
Northwest side M^r: John Millers lott : butting vpon the aforesaid
places

To Thomas Mighill Twelue Acres of vpland, part of it lying
vpon the Warehouse fence, another part of it Joyning vpon a peece
of land of M^r: Ezekiell Rogers.

To Mr Ezekiell Rogers six Acres of vpland Joyning vpon the
Southwest side of Thomas Mighills lott.

To Thomas Mighill one Acree and an halfe of vpland one part
of it Joyning vpon Mr Ezekiell Rogers lott : an other part of it
ioyning vpon Joseph Jewets lott.

To Edward Bridges six Acres of vpland ioyning vpon the East
side of Richard Thurlay his house lott : one end of it butting on a
meadow called Satchells meadow the other end vpon a Cart path.

To Mr William Bellingham three Acres of vpland ioyning
vpon the East side of Edward Bridges lott : one end of it lying
towards the aforesaid Satchells meadow the other end butting vpon
the afore Cart path.

To ffrancis Parrat ffoure Acres and a quarter of vpland, the
South end butting vpon the aforesaid high way the Northeast side
vpon the aboue said Satchells Meadow the other side vpon a
swampe.

A regester of the first diuision of fresh Meadows knowne by their seuerall names afore mentioned in the booke.

Imp Batchelours meadow

To Thomas Ellethrope halfe an Acree of Meadowes, lying vpon the West side of the brooke butting vpon the vpland and the brooke

To John Dresser halfe an Acre lying vpon the North side of Thomas Ellethrops meadow : butting as aforesaid.

.To Hugh Chaplin halfe an Acre of Meadow lying vpon the North side of John Dressers Meadow : butting as aforesaid.

To Peter Cooper halfe an Acree lying vpon the North side of Hugh Chaplins Meadow, butting as aforesaid

To Thomas Sumner halfe an Acree lying on the North side of Peter Coopers Meadow : one end of it butting vpon the brooke the other end vpon John Burbankes meadow.

To John Burbanke halfe an Acre of Meadow, the East end butting vpon the West end of Thomas Sumners Meadow : and the other end vpon the vpland.

To Thomas Palmar halfe an Acree lying vpon the South side of John Burbankes Meadow : both ends butting vpon the vpland

To William Wild one Acre of Meadow lying vpon the South side of Thomas Palmars Medow : butting as aforesaid.

To William Jackson halfe an Acre of Meadow, lying vpon the North side of Thomas Sumner and John Burbankes Meadow : the East end butting vpon the brooke, the West end vpon the vpland.

To Hugh Smith halfe an Acree, lying on the North side of William Jacksons Meadow : butting as aforesaid.

To Michaell Hopkinson halfe an Acre, lying vpon the North side of Hugh Smiths Meadow : butting as aforesaid.

To John Bointon halfe an Acree of Meadow, lying vpon the North side of Michaell Hopkinsons Meadow butting as aforesaid

To William Bointon halfe an Acre, lying vpon the North side of John Bointons Meadow : butting as aforesaid.

To Thomas Dickinson halfe an Acre, lying on the North side of William Bointons Meadow : butting as aforesaid.

To Joseph Jewet one Acre and a quarter, lying on the North side of Thomas Dickinsons Meadow : butting as aforesaid.

To Maximilian Jewet one Acre and a quarter, lying on the North side of Joseph Jewets Meadow butting as aforesaid

To John Spofford one Acre of Meadow lying on the North side of Maximilian Jewets Meadow : butting as aforesaid.

To George Kilborne one Acre of Meadow, lying on the North side of John Spoffords Meadow : butting as aforesaid.

To John Remington one Acre and a quarter of Meadow lying vpon the North side of George Kilbornes meadow : butting as aforesaid.

To James Barkar one Acre of Meadow lying on the North side of John Remingtons Meadow : butting as aforesaid.

To William Stickney one Acre, lying on the North side of James Barkars Meadow : butting as aforesaid.

To William Scales one Acre, lying on the North side of William Stickney : butting as aforesaid.

To Custins Crosby Vx : one Acre of Meadow, lying in the South corner of the said Meadow, on the East side of the brooke : the West end butting on said brooke the East end on the vpland

To Mathew Boyes one Acre and a quarter of Meadow lying on the North side of the said Custins Crosbyes Meadow butting as aforesaid.

To Jane Brockelbanke Vx : one Acre and a quarter lying vpon the North side of Mathew Boyes his Meadow butting as aforesaid.

To Edward Bridges one Acre of Meadow, lying on the North side of Jane Brockelbankes Meadow : butting as aforesaid

To George Abbatt one Acre and a quarter, lying vpon the North side of Edward Bridges : butting as aforesaid.

To Sebastiam Briggam thre Acres and a quarter, lying on the North side of George Abbatt : butting as aforesaid.

To Thomas Barkar thre Acres, lying on the North side of Sebastiam Briggam Butting as aforesaid.

To Richard Wakam on Acre of Meadow, lying on the North side of Thomas Barkars Meadow ; the West end butting vpon the aforesaid brooke : the Northeast side Joyning to the vpland.

Satchells Meadow

Imp to Mr : Ezekiell Rogers tenn Acres of Meadow, lying vpon the West side of the brooke of the said Satchells Meadow : the south end of it butting vpon Mr : Edward Carltons house lott the North end vpon Thomas Mighells Meadow.

To Thomas Mighell thre Acres of Meadow : lying on the West side of the aforesaid brooke ; Joyning to the Northend oı Mr : Ezekiell Rogers his Meadow.

To Mrs Margery Shoue Vx : one Acre and a quarter, lying on the North side of Thomas Mighills Meadow, on the west side of the said brooke.

To Mr John Miller one Acre and a quarter lying on the South side of Thomas Leauers Meadow : the other parts of it for the most part Joyning vpon the vpland.

To Thomas Leauer one Acre ; lying on the North side of Mr John Millers Meadow both ends butting vpon vpland.

To John Trumble one Acre, lying on the Northwest side of Mrs Margery Shoues Meadow one end butting on the brooke the other on Thomas Leauers part of it, and part of it on the vpland.

To John Haseltine one Acre and a quarter, lying on the Northwest side of John Trumbles meadow, the one end butting on the brooke, the other on Thomas Leauers Meadow.

To Thomas Tenny one Acre of Meadow lying, on the North West side of John Haseltines Meadow the North west side of it Joyning on a fence the on end on the aforesaid brooke.

To Robert Haseltine one Acre and a quarter of Meadow, lying on the East of the aforesaid brooke the North west side Joyning vpon the fence, the one end on the said brooke the other vpon the vpland

To Richard Swan one Acre and a quarter of Meadow, lying on the Southeast side of Robert Haseltine, butting as aforesaid.

To Thomas Lilforth one Acre of Meadow, lying vpon the South east side of Richard Swan : butting as aforesaid.

To M^r : Henry Sands one Acre and a quarter of Meadow, lying on the South East side of Thomas Lilforth : butting as aforesaid.

To M^r : Edward Carlton thre Acres of Meadow, lying vpon the Southeast side of Mr Henry Sands his Meadow : butting as aforesaid.

To ffrancis Parrat two Acres and a quarter of Meadow lying vpon the Southeast side of M^r : Edward Carltons Meadow butting as aforesaid.

To John Jarrat one Acre and a quarter, lying on the Southeast of ffrancis Parrats Meadow : butting as aforesaid

To Richard Thurlay one Acre and a quarter, lying on the Southeast side of John Jarrat : butting as aforesaid.

To ffrancis Lambert one Acre and a quarter of Meadow lying on the Southeast side of Richard Thurlay : butting as aforesaid.

To William Acy one Acre and a quarter, lying on the South-east side of ffrancis Lambert : butting as aforesaid

To Robert Hunter one Acre and a quarter, lying on the South-east side of William Acyes Meadow : butting as aforesaid.

To Humphrey Reyner thre Acres of Meadow lying on the Southeast side of Robert Hunter : butting as aforesaid.

To William Harris one Acre and a quarter of Meadow lying on the Southeast side o Humphrey Reyner : butting as aforesaid.

To John Harris one acre and a quarter, lying vpon the South-east side of William Harris : butting as aforesaid.

To Thomas Harris one Acre and a quarter, lying on the Southeast side of John Harris : butting as aforesaid.

To M^r : William Bellingham fiue Acres of Meadow, lying on the Southeast side of Thomas Harris : butting as aforesaid.

To John Newmarch one Acre and a quarter of Meadow, lying vpon the East side of the brooke, in the South east Corner of the Meadow : the other side lying close to the vpland.

To Mr Thomas Nelson ten Acres of Meadow lying on the Southeast side of of M^r : William Bellingams meadow : the West end butting, partly vpon John Newmarch his meadow, and partly vpon the vpland.

To Thomas Barkar two Acres of Meadow, lying on the South-east side of M^r : Thomas Nelsons Meadow : both ends butting vpon vpland.

To Sebastiam Briggam one Acre and thre quarters, lying on the Southeast side of Thomas Barkars Meadow : butting as afore-said.

The little Meadowes

Imp : to Custins Crosby halfe An Acre of Meadow, the East side ioyning on a swampe the rest of it for the most part compassed with vpland

To William Bointon halfe an Acre, the East side lying neare to Custins Crosbyes Meadow : both ends butting on the vpland.

To John Bointon halfe an Acre, lying on the Northwest side of William Bointons meadow : butting as aforesaid.

To Hugh Smith halfe an Acre, lying on the North west side of John Bointons Meadow : butting as aforesaid.

To William Jackson halfe an Acre, lying on the North west side of Hugh Smith his Meadow butting as aforesaid

To Thomas Palmar halfe an Acre, lying on the Northwest side of William Jacksons Meadow : butting as aforesaid.

To John Burbanke halfe an Acre, lying on the Northwest side of Thomas Palmars Meadow : butting as aforesaid.

To Peter Cooper halfe an Acre, lying on the Northwest side of John Burbankes Meadow : butting as aforesaid.

To Thomas Ellethrop halfe an Acre, lying on the North west side of Peter Coopers Meadow : butting as aforesaid.

To Thomas Sumner halfe an Acre of Meadow, lying neare to the Northwest part of Batchelours meadow : Joyning on the brooke that comes out of the said meadowe.

A regester of the first diuision of salt Marsh.

Imp : to Thomas Ellethrope one Acre neare the oister banke the west end butting neare the vpland : the East end vpon the Warehouse riuer.

To John Dresser an Acree lying on the North side of Thomas Ellethrops Marsh : butting as aforesaid.

To Hugh Chaplin an Acre, lying on the North side of John Dresser : butting as aforesaid.

To Peter Cooper an Acre of salt Marsh, lying on the North side of Hugh Chaplins Marsh : butting as aforsaid.

To Thomas Sumner one Acre of salt Marsh, lying on the North side of Peter Coopers Marsh : butting as aforesaid.

To John Burbanke an Acre, lying on the North side of Thomas Sumners Marsh : butting as aforesaid.

To Thomas Palmar an Acre, lying on the north side of John Burbankes Marsh : butting as aforesaid.

To William Wild an Acre, lying on the North side of Thomas Palmars Marsh : butting as aforesaid.

To William Jackson one Acree the North side Joyning vpon a Creeke the South side vpon the vpland both ends butting vpon Maximilian Jewets ffirst diuision of Rough marsh

To Hugh Smith an Acre, lying on the North side of William Wilds Marsh : butting as aforesaid.

To Michaell Hopkinson an Acre, lying on the North side of Hugh Smithes marsh : butting as aforesaid.

To John Bointon one Acre of salt Marsh, lying on the North side of Michaell Hopkinson : butting as aforesaid.

To William Bointon an Acre lying on the North side of John

Bointons Marsh : the East end butting on the Warehouse Riuei, the West end vpon the vpland.

To Thomas Dickinson one Acre of salt Marsh, the North end of it butting vpon a salt Crieke, lying on the West side of John Burbankes Rough Meadow.

To Joseph Jewet two Acres of salt Marsh, lying vpon the East side of Thomas Dickinsons Marsh : the North end butting vpon a salt Creeke, the Southend vpon the North side of William Bointons salt Marsh.

To Maximilian Jewet two Acres of salt Marsh, lying vpon the East side of Joseph Jewets Marsh : butting as aforesaid.

To John Spofford an Acre, lying vpon the East side of Maximilian Jewets Marsh : the North end butting vpon a great Creeke, the South end vpon a small Creeke.

To George Kilborne an Acre of Salt marsh, lying vpon the East side of John Spoffords Marsh : butting as aforesaid.

To Richard Wakam one Acre, lying on the East side of George Kilbornes Marsh : butting as aforesaid.

To Custins Crosby Vx : an Acre, lying vpon the East side of Richard Wakam : butting as aforesaid.

To Edward Bridges one Acre, lying vpon the East side of Custins Crosby Vx : butting as aforesaid.

To George Abbat two Acres of Salt marsh, lying on the East side of Edward Bridges : butting as aforesaid.

To Sebastiam Briggam ten Acres, part of it lying vpon the East side of George Abbatts salt Marsh, and the rest of it vpon the North side of a Creeke that issueth out of the Warehouse Riuer, the head whereof lyes towards George Abbatts planting lott.

To Thomas Barkar ten Acres of salt Marsh, lying vpon the North side of Sebastiam Briggams Marsh : the East end butting on a salt Creeke, the West end neare the vpland.

To Mr : Thomas Nelson twenty Acres of salt Marsh, lying vpon the North side of Thomas Barkars Marsh : butting as aforesaid.

To Mr William Bellingham ten Acres, lying vpon the North side of Mr Thomas Nelsons Marsh : the East end butting vpon a salt Creeke the West end vpon the vpland.

To Thomas Harris two Acres of salt Marsh, lying vpon the North side of Mr : William Bellinghams Marsh : the East end butting vpon a Creeke, the West end vpon a peece of Rough meadow

To John Harris two Acres of salt Marsh, lying vpon the North side of Thomas Harris his Marsh : butting as aforesaid.

To William Harris two Acres, lying on the North side of John Harris his Marsh the East end butting on a Creeke the west end on Robert Hunters marsh

To John Newmarch two Acres of salt marsh, the Northend of it butting vpon a salt Creeke, the South end vpon Thomas and John Harris Rough marsh.

To Robert Hunter two Acres, lying vpon the East side of John Newmarch his Marsh: the Northend butting vpon a salt Creeke, the South end vpon North side of   Harris his marsh.

To William Acy two Acres, lying vpon the East side of Robert Hunters Marsh: butting as aforesaid.

To ffrancis Lambert two Acres, lying upon the East side of William Acy butting as aforesaid.

To Richard Thorlay two Acres of salt marsh, lying on the East side of ffrancis Lambert: butting as aforesaid.

To John Remington two Acres of salt marsh, lying vpon the Northwest side of Humphrey Reyners Rough meadows, neare vnto the Cowbridge: part of it lying vpon the Cowbridge Creeke; the southwest side vpon some Rough meadow.

To James Barkar an Acre, lying vpon the Northwest side of John Remingtons Marsh: part of it lying vpon the aforesaid Creeke

To William Stickney one Acre of salt marsh, lying vpon the Northwest side of James Barkars Marsh: part of it lying vpon the aforesaid Creeke.

To William Scales an Acre of salt marsh, lying on the North west side of William Stickneys Marsh: the northeast end butting vpon the aforesaid Creeke.

To Mathew Boyes two Acres, lying on the Northwest side of William Scales his Marsh: butting as aforesaid.

To Jane Brockelbanke Vx: two Acres lying on the Northwest side of Mathew Boyes: butting as aforesaid.

To Thomas Mighill six Acres, lying on the Northwest side of Jane Brockelbankes Marsh: butting as aforesaid.

To Mrs Margery Shoue Vx: two Acres, lying on the Northwest side of Thomas Mighills Marsh: butting as aforesaid.

To Mr John Miller two Acres of salt Marsh, lying on the North west side of Mrs Margery Shoues Marsh: butting as aforesaid.

To John Jarrat two Acres, lying on the Northwest side of Mr: John Millers Marsh: butting as aforesaid.

To ffrances Parrat foure Acres of salt Marsh, lying on ye west side of the aforesaid Creeke at the turning of the Corner the North end butting vpon a Creeke the Southend on the vpland.

To Mr Edward Carlton six Acres of salt Marsh, lying on the West side of ffrancis Parrats Marsh : butting as aforesaid.

To Mr Henry Sands two Acres, lying on the West side of Mr Edward Carltons Marsh : the Northend butting vpon the aforesaid Creeke the Southend vpon some Rough Marsh.

To Thomas Lilforth one acre, lying on the West side of Mr Henry Sands : butting as aforesaid.

To Richard Swan two Acres, lying on the west side of Thomas Lilforth : the Northend butting vpon the aforesaid Creeke, the Southend on the vpland.

To Robert Haseltine two Acres lying on the West side of Richard Swans Marsh : butting as aforesaid.

To Thomas Tenny one Acre, lying on the West side of Robert Haseltines Marsh : butting as aforesaid.

To John Haseltine two Acres, lying on the West side of Thomas Tenny : butting as aforesaid.

To John Trumble one Acre, lying on the West side of John Haseltine : butting as aforesaid.

To Thomas Leauer one Acre lying on the West side of John Haseltines Marsh butting as aforesaid.

To Mr Ezekiell Rogers twenty Acres of salt Marsh, lying on the North side of the Cowbridge Creeke ; th South side ioyning to Mr Edward Carltons Rough Meadow, the East end vpon his owne, the West end vpon the Creeke.

To John Smith two Acres, lying on the Northwest side of Mr Ezekiell Rogers salt Marsh, the Southwest end lying on the said Creeke, the other end vpon William Tennyes Meadow.

The Regester of the second diuision of Salt Marsh.

Imp : to Mr Ezekiell Rogers twenty Acres, the West side of it lying along by the vpland, and also the North end : the South end vpon a salt Creeke.

To Humphrey Reyner eighteene Acres, lying on the East side of Mr Ezekiell Rogers Marsh the South end butting vpon the said Creeke, the North end on the vpland.

To Thomas Ellethrop one Acre, lying vpon the East side of a peece of salt Marsh that was reserued for such as were expected to come to sit downe with us, at the laying out of the diuision : the southend butting on a creeke, the other on the vpland.

To John Dresser one Acre, lying on the East side of Thomas Ellethrops Marsh : butting as aforesaid.

To Hugh Chaplin one Acre, lying on the East side of John Dressers Marsh : butting as aforesaid.

To Peter Cooper one Acre, lying on the East side of Hugh Chaplin : butting as aforesaid.

To Thomas Sumner one Acre, lying on the East side of Peter Coopers Marsh : butting as aforesaid.

To John Burbanke one Acre, lying on the East side of Thomas Sumner : butting as aforesaid.

To Thomas Palmar one Acre, lying vpon the East side of John Burbankes Marsh : butting as aforesaid.

To William Wild one Acre, lying on the East side of Thomas Palmars Marsh : butting as aforesaid.

To William Jackson on Acre, lying on the Northeast side of William Wild : the Southeast end butting on a Creeke the Northeast end vpon the vpland.

To Hugh Smith one Acre of Salt Marsh, lying on the Northeast side of William Jacksons Marsh the Southst, end lying towards a Creeke the Northwest end butting on the vpland.

To Michaell Hopkinson one Acre, lying on the North side of Hugh Smithes Marsh : the East end lying neare to a Creeke, the West end butting on the vpland.

To John Bointon one Acre, lying on the North side of Michaell Hopkinsons Marsh : the East end butting on a Creeke, the West end on the vpland.

To William Bointon one Acre, lying on the North side of John Bointons Marsh : butting as aforesaid.

To Thomas Dickinson one Acre, lying on the North side of William Bointons Marsh : butting as aforesaid.

To Joseph Jewet two Acres of salt Marsh, lying on the North side of Thomas Dickinsons Marsh : runing about 24 rod into the Marsh, the West end butting on the vpland.

To Maximilian Jewet two Acres, lying on the North side of Joseph Jewets Marsh : butting as aforesaid.

To John spofford one Acre, lying on the North side of Maximilian Jewets Marsh : butting as aforesaid.

To George Kilborne one Acre, lying vpon the North side of John Spoffords Marsh : butting as aforesaid.

To John Remington two Acres of salt Marsh ; lying vpon the North side of George Kilbornes Marsh : the East end butting vpon a Creeke, the West end vpon the vpland

To James Barkar one Acre, lying vpon the Northwest side of John Remingtons Marsh : the Northeast end butting about fourty rod wthin the Marsh, the Southwest vpon the vpland.

To William Stickney one Acre, lying on the Northwest side of James Barkars Marsh : butting as aforesaid.

To William Scales an Acre, lying on the Northwest side of William Stickneyes Marsh : butting as aforesaid.

To Mathew Boyes two Acres, lying on the Northwest side of William Scales his Marsh : butting as aforesaid.

To Jane Brockelbanke two Acres, lying, one part on the North side, another on the West end of Mathew Boyes Marsh the East end of it butting vpon the vpland, the west end runeing about fourty rod into the Medow.

To Thomas Mighill six Acres lying vpon the West side of Jane Brockelbanke ; the Northend butting vpon a Creeke the Southend, partly vpon the vpland, and partly on the Northend of Maximilian Jewets Marsh.

To Mrs Margery Shoue two Acres, lying on the west side of Thomas Mighill : the Northend butting vpon a Creeke, the Southend on the vpland.

To Mr John Miller two Acres, lying on the west side of Mrs Margery Shoues Marsh : butting as aforesaid.

To John Jarrat two Acres of salt Marsh, lying on the West side of Mr John Millers Marsh : the Northend butting on ffrancis Parrats Marsh the Southend vpon the vpland.

To ffrancis Parrat foure Acres, lying betwixt two Creeks the Southend butting vpon John Jarrats Marsh the North end vpon Mr Edward Carltons Marsh.

To Mr Edward Carlton six Acres, lying betwixt two Creeks the Southend butting vpon ffrancis Parrats Marsh the North end vpon some salt Marsh vnlaid out.

To Mr Henry Sands two Acres of salt Marsh, lying on the West side of John Jarrats Marsh : the Southend butting vpon the vpland, the Northend vpon a Creeke.

To Thomas Lilforth one Acre, lying on the West side of Mr Henry Sands : butting as aforesaid

To Richard Swan two Acres, lying on the Northwest side of Thomas Lilforth : the one end partly butting on the vpland and partly on a pond, the other end vpon a Creeke.

To Robert Haseltine two Acres, lying on the East side of Richard Swans Marsh : the North end butting on the vpland, the South end on a Creeke.

To Thomas Tenny one Acre, lying on the East side of Robert Haseltine : butting as aforesaid

To John Haseltine two Acres, lying on the East side of Thomas Tennyes Marsh butting as aforesaid.

To John Trumble one Acre, lying vpon the East side of John Haseltines Marsh : butting as aforesaid.

To Thomas Leauer one Acre, lying on the East side of John Trumbles Marsh : butting as aforesaid.

To Richard Wakam one Acre, lying on the East side of Thomas Leauers Marsh : butting as aforesaid.

To Custins Crosby Vx : one Acre of salt marsh, lying on the East side of Richard Wakams Marsh ; butting as aforesaid.

To Edward Bridges one Acre, lying on the East side of Custins Crosby Vx : butting as aforesaid.

To George Abbat two Acres, lying on the East side of Edward Bridges his Marsh : butting as aforesaid.

To Sebastiam Briggam ten Acres, the East side lying toward the Iland called the Sawyers Iland, the Southend butting on the vpland the North end on a Creeke.

To Thomas Barkar ten Acres, lying on the West side of Sebastiam Briggams Marsh : butting as aforesaid.

To Mr Thomas Nelson thirteene Acres, lying on the West side of Thomas Barkars Marsh : butting as aforesaid.

To Mr William Bellingham ten Acres, lying on the West side of Mr Thomas Nelsons Marsh : butting as aforesaid.

To William Harris two Acres, bounded vpon the North side wth a Creeke the East end butting on Mr William Bellinghams Marsh, the West end on an Iland.

To John Harris two Acres, lying vpon the South side of William Harris his Marsh : the East end butting on Mr William Bellinghams Marsh, the West end on an old Causey.

To Thomas Harris two Acres, lying on the South side of John Harris his Marsh : butting as aforesaid.

To John Newmarch two Acres, lying vpon the South side of Thomas Harris his marsh : butting as aforesaid.

To Robert Hunter two Acres, part of it lying on the East side, and part of it on the west side of the old Causey aforesaid. bounded on each side by a salt Creeke.

To William Acy two Acres lying vpon the southwest side of Robert Hunters Marsh : the South end butting on the vpland the North end on a Creeke.

To ffrancis Lambert two Acres lying on the West side of William Acyes Marsh the North side bounded by a small Creeke, the West end butting on a peece of Rough Meadow.

To Richard Thurlay two Acres, ioyning to his first diuision of salt Marsh: the East side bounded by a great Creeke, the west side by William Harris his salt Marsh.

A Regester of the second diuision of ffresh Marsh Comonly called the first diuision of Rough Meadows.

Imp: to John Burbanke one Acre, the Northeast end of it butting vpon an Iland, that lyes in the salt Marsh, the South west end vpon the vpland.

To William Jackson one Acre, lying on the west side of John Burbankes Meadow: butting as aforesaid.

To John Bointon one Acre lying on the West side of Willia Jacksons Meadow: butting as aforesaid.

To William Bointon one Acre, lying on the west side of John Bointons Meadow: butting as aforesaid

To Joseph Jewet one Acre, the Southend butting on the vpland, the North end on a Creeke.

To Maximilian Jewet one Acre, sixty rod wherof, lyes on the West side of Joseph Jewets Meadow: the North end butting on a Creeke, the Southend on some Rough Meadows vnlaid out: the other hundred rod, ioynes on the aforesaid Creeke, about fourty rod distant from his aforesaid sixty.

To John Spofford one Acre, lying on the south side of Maximilian Jewets hundred rod of Meadow: both end butting on vpland

To George Kilborne one Acre, lying on the Southwest side of John Spofford: butting as aforesaid.

To Richard Wakam one Acre, lying on the Northwest side of George Kilbornes Meadow the West end butting on the vpland, the East end vpon Custins Crosbyes Meadow.

To Custins Crosby Vx: one Acre, lying part of it betwixt Maximilian Jewet and Richard Wakams Rough Meadow; and part of it beyond a Creeke ouer against it: the North side bounded by the vpland.

To Edward Bridges one Acre of Rough Meadow, lying on the East side of George Abbats planting lott: and also neare vnto the head of the Creeke.

To George Abbat one Acre lying on the Northwest side of Edward Bridges Meadow: butting on his owne planting lott.

To Sebastiam Briggam fiue Acres, thre Acres and thirty rod whereof, lying at the West end of his salt Marsh, and pt of it at the North side of the same Marsh: the rest of it lying neare vnto a great pond and part of it ioyning vpon the west side of John Harris Rough Meadow.

To Thomas Barkar fiue Acres, thre wherof lying betwixt his owne salt Marsh and vpland, the other two lying neare to the fore-named pond.

To Mr Thomas Nelson eight Acres and one quarter, fiue Acres wanting twenty rod wherof, lying betwixt his owne salt Marsh and the vpland: the rest of it lying betwixt Thomas Barkars Rough Meadow and the way that leads to Newberry.

To John Harris one Acre of Rough Meadow, lying on the East side of Sebastiam Briggams Meadow: the North end butting vpon the vpland.

To William Harris one Acre, lying on the East side of John Harris his Meadow: butting as aforesaid.

To Thomas Harris one Acre, lying on the East side of Thomas Barkars Rough Meadow: the South end butting vpon the vpland the North end vpon John and William Harris Meadow.

To John Newmarch one Acre lying betwixt the vpland and his owne salt Marsh.

To Mr William Bellingham fiue Acres, the South end butting on William Tennyes planting lott, the North end ptly on a small Creeke, and partly on the vpland

To Robert Hunter one Acre, lying on the West side of some part of Mr William Bellinghams Meadow: part of the South end, butting on the vpland, and the North end on a Creeke.

To William Acy one Acre, lying vpon the West side of Robert Hunters Meadow; the South end butting on a swampe the North end on a Creeke.

To ffrancis Lambert one Acre, lying on the Northwest side of William Acyes Meadow: the Southwest end butting on a swampe, the Northeast end on a Creeke.

To Richard Thurlay one Acree lying on the Northwest side of ffrancis Lamberts Meadow: butting as aforesaid.

To Mr John Miller one Acre, lying on the Northwest side of Richard Thurlay: butting as aforesatd.

To John Jarrat one Acre, lying on the Northwest side of Mr

John Miller: the Southwest end butting on the vpland, the North-east on a Creeke.

To ffrancis Parrat two Acres of Rough Meadows, lying on the Northwest side of John Jarrats Meadow: butting as aforesaid.

To Mr Edward Carlton thre Acres, lying on the Northwest side of ffrancis Parrats Marsh: butting as aforesaid.

To Mr Henry Sands one Acre, lying on the Northwest side of Mr Edward Carltons Marsh: butting as aforesaid.

To Robert Haseltine one Acre, lying on the Northwest side of Mr Henry Sands: butting as aforesaid.

To John Haseltine one acre, lying on the Northwest side of Robert Haseltines Marsh: butting as aforesaid.

To Thomas Tenny one Acre, lying on the Northwest side of a Cart path leading to the Cowbridge: the Southwest end butting on the vpland the Northeast end vpon a Creeke

To John Trumble one Acre, lying on the North West side of Thomas Tennyes Marsh: butting as aforesaid.

To Thomas Leauer one Acre, lying on the Northwest side of John Trumbles Meadow: butting as aforesaid.

To Humphrey Reyner thre Acres, lying on the Northwest side of Thomas Leauers Meadow: the Southwest end butting vpon Mrs Margery Shoue Vx: her Meadow, the North east end vpon a Creeke.

To Mrs Margery Shoue Vx: one Acre, the Northeast end of it lying neare to Humphrey Reyners Rough Marsh

To John Remington one Acre, lying on the North West side of Humphrey Reyners Meadow the Southwest end butting vpon the vpland, the Northeast on his owne saltmarsh.

To James Barkar one Acre, lying vpon the West side of John Remingtons Marsh: the Southend butting vpon Rough Marsh not laid out the Northend

To William Stickney one Acre, lying vpon the West side of James Barkars Marsh: the Southend butting on the aforesaid Rough Meadow, the North end on his owne salt Marsh

To William Scales one Acre, lying on the West side of William Stickneys Meadow: butting as aforesaid.

To Mathew Boyes two Acres lying on the West side of William Scales Meadow: butting as aforesaid.

To Jane Brockelbanke two Acres, lying vpon the West side of Mathew Boyes Meadow: butting as aforesaid.

To Thomas Mighill thre Acres, lying upon the West side of Jane Brockelbankes Meadow: butting as aforesaid

To Richard Swan one Acre, butting vpon the South end of M[r] Henry Sands and Thomas Lilforths first diuision of salt Marsh : the other pts of it are Compassed with vpland.

To M[r] Ezekiell Rogers ten Acres of Rough Marsh the west of it ioyning vpon his first diuision of salt Marsh beyond the Cowbridge, the Northend butting on the vpland, the Southend vpon some Rough Marsh vnlaid out.

To Hugh Smith one Acre, lying in the West end of the Meadow called the Long Meadow : both ends bounded by the vpland

To William Wild one Acre, lying on the East side of Hugh Smithes Meadow : butting as aforesaid.

To Thomas Palmar one Acre, lying on the East side of William Wild : butting as aforesaid.

To Thomas Ellethrop one Acre, lying on the East side of Thomas Palmar : butting as aforesaid.

To Peter Cooper one Acre lying on the East side of Thomas Ellethrops meadow : butting as aforesaid.

To Hugh Chaplin one Acre and an halfe of Meadow, lying on the East side of Peter Coopers Meadow butting as aforesaid

To John Dresser one Acre, lying on the East side Hugh Chaplins Meadow : butting as aforesaid.

To Richard Clarke one Acre, lying on the East side of John Dresser : butting as aforesaid.

The third diuision of ffresh Marsh Comonly called the second diuision of Rough Meadows.

Imp To Michaell Hopkinson one Acre of Rough Meadow, neare vnto the Cowbridge : the North side lying along by the vpland the West end butting vpon the high way.

To Thomas Dickinson one Acre, lying on the East side of Michaell Hopkinsons Meadow : the East end butting on the vpland.

To Joseph Jewet one Acre, lying neare to Thomas Dickinsons Meadow : the North end butting vpon the vpland, the South end also, and West side bounded by a Creeke.

To Maximilian Jewet one Acre, lying on the East side of Joseph Jewets Meadow : the North end butting on the vpland the south end on a Creeke.

To Mathew Boyes one Acre, lying on the East side of Maximilian Jewets Meadow butting as aforesaid.

To Jane Brockelbanke Vx : one Acre lying on the East side of Mathew Boyes Meadow : the North end butting on the vpland the South end vpon some Rough Meadow vnlaid out.

26   ROWLEY TOWN RECORDS.

To John Remington one Acre of Rough Meadow, the North
end butting on his ffirst diuision of Rough Marsh, the South end on
the vpland.

To Thomas Mighill thre Acres, Joyning to his first diuision of
Rough Meadows the South side of it Joyning to the oxe pasture
ffence.

To Mr Ezekiell Rogers ten Acres, lying on the East side of his first
diuision of Rough Meadow beyond the Cowbridge : the Northend
butting on vpland, the South end on Mr Edward Carltons Meadow,
the East side on some Rough Meadow not laid out.

To Custins Crosby one Acre of Rough Meadow, the west side
bounding vpon vpland : the South and North end also butting vpon
vpland.

To George Abbat one Acre, lying on the East side of Custins
Crosbyes Meadow : butting as aforesaid.

To Sebastiam Briggam fiue Acres, lying on the East side of
George Abbats Meadow : butting as aforesaid.

To Thomas Barkar fiue Acres, lying on the East side of Sebastiam Briggams Meadow : butting as aforesaid.

To Humphrey Reyner thre Acres, the West side bounded by
vpland, and part of the East also : the North end butting on a pond.

To Mrs Margery Shoue Vx : one Acre Joyning vpon her owne
and Mr John Millers first diuision of salt marsh

To Thomas Crosby one Acre, ioyning to his second diuison of
salt Marsh : the South side of it bounded with the vpland.

To Richard Swan one Acre, pt of the South end buttting vpon
Thomas Crosbyes Rough Meadow the Northend of it on a Cart path
that leadeth towards the Sawyers Iland : the East side bounded
partly by his owne Salt Marsh the west side by a great pond.

To Robert Haseltine one Acre, the East side bounded by the
vpland : the north end butting vpon the abouesaid Cart path the South
end vpon his owne salt Marsh.

To William Harris one Acre, lying on the west side of M^r
William Bellinghams second diuision of salt Marsh : the Southend
butting on the vpland, the North end vpon John Newmarch his salt
Marsh.

To John Harris, one Acre lying on the West side of William
Harris : butting as aforesaid

To Thomas Harris one Acre, lying on the West side of John
Harris Meadow : butting as aforesaid.

To John Newmarch one Acre, lying on the West side of
Thomas Harris Meadow : butting as aforesaid.

To Robert Hunter halfe an Acre, lying on the East side of an old Causey leading to Newberry: the South end butting on the vpland

To ffrancis Lambert one Acre, Joining wth the East side vpon his second diuision of salt Marsh: the Northend butting vpon Newberry bounds, the South end on the vpland

To Mr Thomas Nelson Eleauen Acres, and thre quarters ten wherof being his second diuision of Rough Meadow, the other Acre and thre quarters being part of his first diuision of Rough Meadow; which eleauen Acres and thre quarters lyes on the West side of ffrancis Lamberts Meadow: butting as afqresaid.

To Mr William Bellingham fiue Acres lying on the West side of Mr Thomas Nelsons Meadow: butting as aforesaid.

To Mr John Miller one Acre of Rough Meadow, the North side lying neare to Newbery bounds: the East end butting vpon the vpland, the West end on some Rough Meadow vnlaid out.

To John Jarrat one Acre, lying on the South side of an Acre (vnlaid out) ioyning to Mr John Millers Acre butting as aforesaid.

To ffrancis Parrat two Acres Joyning to the North end of his vpland in the Marshffield: both ends butting on the vpland.

To Richard Thurlay one Acre part of the East side bounded by vpland: the South end also butting partly vpon vpland, the Northend vpon some Rough Meadow vnlaid out.

To M^r: Edward Carlton thre Acres: the North side bounded by Mr Ezekiell Rogers Marsh, the South side by the vpland, part of the East end butting vpon Richard Thurlay his meadow, another part by the Cart way that goes ffrom the Cowbridge to the vpland, the West part bounded by a Creeke.

To John Haseltine one Acre

A Regester of the second diuision of vpland, laid out in the ffield called the Marsh ffield.

Imp: To Richard Clarke one hundred and seauen Rod of vpland, thirty wherof ioynes to his second diuision of Salt marsh. the rest of it lying on the West side of the high way that leadeth vnto newberry: the East end butting on the said high, way the West end on some vpland.

To John Dresser one hundred and seauen Rod, part wherof ioynes to his second diuision of salt Marsh; the rest of it lying on ye West side of the aforesaid, way on the North side of Richard Clarkes vpland: butting as aforesaid.

To Hugh Chaplin one hundred and seauen rodd, part wherof ioynes to his owne salt Marsh, the rest of it lying on the west side of the aforesaid highway, on the North side of John Dressers vpland : butting as aforesaid.

To Peter Cooper one hundred and seauen Rod ; part wherof ioynes to his second diuision of salt Marsh ; the rest of it lying on the West side of the aforesaid high way, on the North side of Hugh Chaplins vpland : the East end butting on the aforesaid high way the West end on a swamp

To Thomas Ellethrop one hundred and seauen rod part wherof Joynes to his owne salt Marsh, the rest wherof lyeth on the west side of the aforesaid high way, on the North side of Peter Coopers vpland: both end butting as aforesaid.

To John Burbanke one hundred and seauen Rod part wherof ioynes to his owne salt Marsh, the rest of it lying on the North side of Thomas Ellethrops vpland : butting as aforesaid

To Thomas Palmar a hundred and seauen rod, lying on the west side of Newberry path on the North side of John Burbanke butting as aforesaid.

To William Wild one hundred and seauen Rod of vpland lying on the North side of Thomas Palmars land : butting as aforesaid.

To William Jackson one hundred and seauen Rod of vpland, ioyning vpon his second diuision of salt Marsh.

To Hugh Smith one hundred and seauen Rod, part wherof ioynes to his owne salt Marsh : the rest of it lyes on the West side of a Cart path : the north side of it bounded by Humphrey Reyners vpland.

To Michaell Hopkinson one hundred and seauen Rod part wherof Joynes to his owne salt Marsh : the rest of it lyeth on the west side of Newberry high way, on the North side of William Wild his vpland : the East end butting on the said path the west end on a swamp

To John Bointon one hundred and seauen Rod : part wherof ioyns to his owne salt Marsh, the rest of it on West side of the aforesaid high way, lying on the North side of Michaell Hopkinsons land butting as aforesaid.

To William Bointon one hundred and seauen Rod of land part whereof ioynes vpon his owne salt Marsh ; the rest of it lyes on the West side of the aforesaid high way : on the North side of John Bointons vpland butting as aforesaid.

To Thomas Dickinson one Acre part wherof ioynes to his owne salt Marsh ; the rest of it lyeth on the west side of the aforesaid high way on the North side of William Bointons vpland : butting as aforesaid.

To Joseph Jewet two Acres, part wherof ioynes to his owne salt Marsh ; the rest of it lyeth on the North side of Thomas Dickinsons vpland : butting as aforesaid.

To Maximilian Jewet two Acres part wherof ioynes to his owne salt Marsh, the rest of it lyeth on the West side of the aforesaid high way on the North side of Joseph Jewets vpland : butting as aboue.

To John Spofford one hundred and seauen Rod part wherof ioyns to his own salt Marsh, the rest of it lyeth on the West side of the aforesaid high way, on the North side of Maximilian Jewets vpland : butting as aforesaid.

To George Kilborne one hundred and seauen Rod, lying on the North side of John Spoffords vpland : butting as aforesaid.

To Richard Wakam one hundred and seauen Rod, lying on the North side of George Kilbornes vpland : butting as aforesaid.

To Edward Bridges one hundred and seauen Rod, lying on the North side of Richard Wakams vpland : butting as aforesaid.

To John Remington two Acres, lying on the East side of the high way leading vnto Newberry, the South end butting on a Cart path the North end vpon another Cart path.

To William Stickney

To Mathew Boyes two Acres of vpland, lying on the East side of William Scales vpland : butting as aforesaid.

To Jane Brockelbanke two Acres, lying on the East side of Mathew Boyes his vpland : butting as aforesaid.

To Thomas Mighill six Acres, thre Acres and sixty Rod wherof ioynes to his second diuision of salt marsh, the rest of it lyeth on the East side of Jane Brockelbanks vpland : butting as aforesaid

To Mr Thomas Nelson twenty Acres, twelue wherof lyeth on the East side of Newberry high way : the Northend butting vpon the rough Marsh the Southend on a Cart path : thre Acres of it Joynes to his second diuision of salt marsh : the Southeast end butting on a Cart path : the other fiue Acres, lying on the East side of Thomas Mighills vpland : either end butting on a Cart path.

To Mr William Bellingham ten Acres of vpland, six Acres and twenty rod of it ioyning vpon his second diuision of salt marsh the Southeast end of it butting on a Cart path the rest of it lying on the East side of Mr Thomas Nelsons fiue Acres : the south end butting vpon the Cart path the North end vpon a swampe.

To William Harris two Acres, bounded on the East side by a Cart path : the Northend butting on the Rough Marsh, the South end on a swampe.

To John Harris two Acres, lying on the west side of William Harris his vpland : butting as aforesaid.

To Thomas Harris two Acres, lying on the west side of John Harris his vpland : butting as aforesaid.

To John Newmarch two Acres, lying on the West side of Thomas Harris his vpland : butting as aforesaid.

To Robert Hunter two Acres lying on the West side of John Newmarch vpland : the North end butting vpon the Marshes, the South end neare to a swampe.

To William Acy two Acres, lying on the west side of Robert Hunters vpland : the North end butting on the Marshes, the south end on a Cart path.

To ffrancis Lambert two Acres lying on the West side of William Acyes vpland : butting as aforesaid.

To Custins Crosby Vx : two Acres, part of it ioyning to the South side, and part of it to the North side of her second diuision of Rough Meadow : the North end butting on one Cart way, the South end on another.

To George Abbat two Acres of vpland part of it lying on the North side, and part of it on the South side of his second diuision of Rough Meadow : butting as aforesaid.

To Sebastiam Briggam ten Acres of vpland, seauen wherof and thirty rod, lyeth part of it on the South side and part of it on the North side of his second diuision of Rough Marsh butting as aforesaid : the rest of it ioyning on his second diuision of salt Marsh.

To Thomas Barkar ten Acres of vpland, three wherof and one quarter, lyeth partly on the South side, and partly on the North of his second diuision of Rough Meadow. the rest of it ioyning to the Southend of his second diuisiō of Salt marsh.

To Humphrey Reyner six Acres, part of it lying at the North end of his salt Marsh. the rest of it ioyning, partly to the East side and partly to the West side of his second diuision of Rough Meadow.

To Mrs Margery Shoue Vx : two Acres, ioyning to her second diuision of salt Marsh.

To Mr John Miller two Acres, one wherof ioynes vpon his second diuision of salt marsh, the other lyeth on the East side of Mr William Bellinghams vpland : the South end butting on a Cart path, the North end on a swampe.

To John Haseltine two Acres, lying on the East side of Mr: John Millers Acre of vpland : butting as aforesaid.

To Thomas Tenny one hundred and seauen rod, lying on the East side of John Haseltines land : butting as aforesaid.

To John Jarrat two Acres, lying on the East side of Thomas Tennyes vpland : butting as aforesaid.

To Robert Haseltine two Acres, lying on the East side of John Jarrats vpland : butting as aforesaid.

To Richard Swan two Acres, lying on the East side of Robert Haseltines vpland : butting as aforesaid.

To Mr Ezekiell Rogers twenty Acres, lying on the Southeast side of the high way leading to Newberry : part of it ioyning on his second diuision of salt Marsh.

To Thomas Lilforth one hundred and seauen Rod, lying on the South side of a Cart way ; the East side ioyning on the West end of Richard Wakams vpland : the south end butting on a swamp

To Thomas Crosby two Acres, lying on the West side of Thomas Lilforthes vpland : the North end butting on a Cart part, the South end on a swampe.

To Mr Edward Carlton six Acres, lying on the West side of Thomas Crosbyes vpland : butting as aforesaid.

To ffrancis Parat ffoure Acres, lying on the West side of the high way leading to Newberry : the North end butting vpon the Marsh, the South end vpon a Cart path.

To Richard Thurlay two Acres lying on the West side of ffrancis Parrats vpland : butting as aforesaid.

A Regester of the third diuision of Salt Marsh.

Imp : to Thomas Dickinson one Acre of salt marsh : the West end butting against his second diuision of salt Marsh, the East end on a Creeke.

To Joseph Jewet two Acres lying on the North side of Thomas Dickinsons Marsh : butting vpon the East end of his second diuision of salt Marsh.

To Maximilian Jewet two Acres, one wherof ioyning to the East side of Humphrey Reyners salt Marsh : the North end butting vpon the vpland. The other Acre, lying on the North side of Joseph Jewets third diuision of salt Marsh : the West end butting on his owne second diuision of salt Marsh.

To Custins Crosby Vx : foure Acres, two wherof butting vpon a Creeke at the East end of John Remingtons second diuision of salt Marsh the North and South sides both bounded with Creekes. The other two Acres on the North side of Maximilian Jewets. The West end butting against George Kilborne and John Spoffords second diuision of salt marsh.

To John Remington two Acres, lying on the West end of the Iland called the Long Iland : part of the South side bounding on a Creeke : the East end butting on the Iland.

To Mathew Boyes one Acre lying on the South side of John Remingtons marsh butting on the said Iland.

To Jane Brockelbanke Vx : one lying on the South side of Mathew Boyes his Marsh butting as aforesaid.

To Thomas Mighill six Acres lying on the North side of John Remingtons Marsh the East end butting on the Iland the West end on a Creeke.

To Mrs: Margery Shoue two Acres lying on the North side of Thomas Mighills Marsh the East end butting on the Iland

To George Abbatt two Acres, lying on the North side of Mrs Margery Shoues Marsh : butting as aforesaid

To Thomas Barkar two Acres lying on the north side of Mr Thomas Nelsons marsh butting as aforesd

To Mr Thomas Nelson twenty Acres lying on the East side of Thomas Barkars Marsh : the South end butting on the Iland

To Mr Samuell Bellingham ten Acres lying on the south side of Mr Thomas Nelsons Marsh : the West end butting on the Iland

To Thomas Harris two Acres lying on the South side of Mr Samuell Bellinghams Marsh : butting as aforesaid.

To John Newmarch two Acres lying on the south side of Thomas Harris his Marsh. butting as aforesaid.

To Robert Hunter two Acres, lying on the South side of John Newmarch his marsh : butting as aforesaid.

To William Acy two Acres, lying on the South side of Robert Hunters Marsh : butting as aforesaid.

To ffrancis Lambert two Acres, lying on the South side of William Acyes Marsh : butting as aforesaid.

To Mr Edward Carlton, six Acres, Joyning to his second diuision of salt Marsh Compassed wth Creekes.

To Mr John Miller two Acres, Joyning to the East side of George Abbatts second diuision of salt Marsh : the Northend butting on the Iland called Sawyers Iland : the other end on a Creeke

To John Jarrat two Acres lying on the East side of Mr John Millers Marsh : butting as aforesaid.

To ffrancis Parrat ffoure Acres lying on the East side of John Jarrats marsh : one end abutting on the vpland the other on a Creeke.

To Thomas Crosby two Acres, lying on the North side of ffrancis Parrats Marsh the West end abutting on the vpland the East end on a Creeke.

To Richard Swan two Acres of Salt meadow pt of it lying on the West side of Thomas Crosbyes meadow aforesaid : the South end abutting on the vpland the North end on the Creeke: The rest of it Joynes on his first diuision of Rough Marsh.

To Sebastiam Briggam ten Acres of Salt Marsh. Joyning to pt of his first diuision of Salt Marsh. bounded on the Warehouse Riuer on the one side, & on a Creeke on the other.

To William Harris two Acres of Salt Marsh Joyning to pt of Sebastiam Briggams third diuision of salt marsh bounded by the Warehouse Riuer on the one side and a Creeke on the other.

To John Harris two Acres of Salt Marsh. Joyning on the North end of William Harris his marsh bounded by a Creeke.

To Thomas Miller two Acres of Salt Marsh lying on the South side Humphrey Reyners Salt Marsh ; in the Marsh ffield the South-west end abutting on an Iland. The Northeast end on John Scales his Salt marsh.

To Robert Haseltine two Acres of Salt Marsh lying on the Southeast side of Thomas Millers Marsh abutting as aforesaid

To John Haseltine two Acres of Salt Marsh lying on the South Side of Robert Haseltines marsh one Corner of it comeing to an Iland : The rest of it bounded by a Creeke called the Shadd Creeke on the one side the other side by a little Creeke

To Daniell Harris two Acres of Salt Marsh lying on the East side John Haseltines marsh bounded wth Creekes saue only on the North Corner wch Joynes on Isaac Cousins Saltmarsh.

To Isaac Cousins two Acres the Southend abutting on Daniell Harris his Marsh the North end on Charles Brownes. the West side bounded ptly on a Creek & ptly on the Comons.

To Charles Browne two Acres of salt Marsh lying on ye North side Isaac Cousins Meadow the East end abutting on a great Creeke the West end on the Comon.

To John Scales two Acres lying on the North side of Charles Brownes Meadow the East end abutting on a Creeke the West end on humphrey Reyners & Thomas Millers Salt Marsh.

To Thomas Dickinson two Acres lying on the South side Maximilian Jewetts marsh the East abutting vpon a Great Creeke vpon Humphrey Reyners marsh.

Vplands laid out to Certaine persons in the ffield Called the Rye ffield as ffolloweth.

Imp^r To Custins Crosby Vx: two Acres of vpland Joyning vpon the streete ffence the East & West end abutting each vpon a swampe.

To John Remington two Acres of vpland lying on the South side of Custins Crosbyes land, the West end abutting on a swampe the East end on Jane Brockelbanks ground.

To Mathew Boyes two Acres of vpland lying on the South side of John Remingtons vpland. the West end abutting vpon a swampe, the East end abutting partly on Jane Brockelbanks land & ptly on the fence.

To Jane Brockelbanke Vx: two Acres of vpland lying on the Northeast Corner of the abouesaid ffield. the North end abutting vpon the streete fence the East side Joyning vpon another ffence.

To Thomas Mighill foure Acres and an halfe of vpland on the South side of Mathew Boyes vpland. the West end abutting vpon a swampe the East end vpon a fence

To Humphrey Reyner foure Acres and an halfe of vpland lying on the South side of Thomas Mighills vpland abutting as aforesaid.

To Thomas Barkar fiue Acres of vpland lying on the South side of Humphrey Reyners vpland abutting as aforesaid

To Sebastiam Briggam fiue Acres of vpland lying on the South side of Thomas Barkars vpland abutting as aforsaid.

Certaine Parcells of vpland laid out more in seuerall ffields vnder mentioned to Certaine psons as ffolloweth.

Imp^r to Mr Thomas Nelson thirty six Acres of vpland in the ffield called the Mill ffield twenty six wherof was laid out to him as pt of his first diuision of vpland the other tenn was giuen him for incouragement towards building the Mill.

To the said Mr Thomas Nelson two Acres and three quarters of vpland Joyning to his Satchells Meadow in the Northeast ffield.

To the said Mr Thomas Nelson two Acres of vpland Joyning to the South side of pt of his ffirst diuision of Rough Marsh neare to Newberry high way.

To Thomas Barkar thre quarters of an Acree of vpland Joyning to his Satchells Meadow.

To the said Thomas Barkar one Acree and a quarter of vpland Joyning to the South side of his ffirst diuision of Rough Marsh

To Sebastiam Briggam fiue Acres of vpland Joyning to the East end of Satchells Meadow.

To Mr Edward Carlton three Acres and a quarter of vpland lying on the West side of Satchells Meadow

To Thomas Miller foure Acres and an halfe of vpland Joyning to the Rodd of ground laid out on the East side of ffrancis Parratts Planting lott in the Northeast ffield the South end abutting vpon a Cart neare Satchells meadow the North end on some ground vnlaid out

To the said Thomas about three quarters of an Acre of vpland Joyning to his abouesaid planting lott on the north end of it being an odd pcell of ground in Consideration of the Honynes of his said lott

To Mr Samuell Bellingham eight Acres of vpland the East side ioyning vpon a fence the north end abutting vpon a Cart Way leading to the 'Warehouse, the South end vpon a swampe.

To Mr Edward Carlton six Acres of vpland the East end abutting vpon Mr Samuell Bellinghams vpland the South side ioyning to a swampe to the Country way.

To Mr Samuell Bellingham eleauen Acres of vpland Joyning to his house Lott.

To ffrancis Parrat thre Acres of vpland lying on the South side of Mr Samuel Bellinghams vpland the West end abutting on the streete.

To Mr Ezekiell Rogers six Acres of vpland lying on the South side of ffrancis Parrats vpland abutting as aforesaid

To Mr Thomas Nelson twenty two Acres of vpland part of it ioyning vpon the South side, & part of it vpon the East end of his house Lott.

To Thomas Barkar seauenteene Acres of vpland lying vpon the South side of Mr Thomas Nelsons vpland the West end abutting vpon the streete

To Sebastiam Briggam sixteene Acres of vpland lying on the South side of Thomas Barkars vpland, pt of the East end abutting vpon pt of Thomas Barkars vpland the west end abutting on the streete.

To Mathew Boyes, three Acres thre quarters of vpland ioyning to the North side of Bradford streete ffield the west end abutting vpon one swampe the East end vpon another

To John Remington thre Acres & a quarter of vpland part of it Joyning to the West side & pt of it to the North end of his house Lott.

To James Barkar one Acre of vpland lying on the East side of John Remingtons vpland the one end abutting vpon the Northend of his house lott the other end vpon a ffence

To William Stickney two Acres of vpland lying on the East side of James Barkars land abutting as aforesaid

To William Scales one Acree of vpland lying on the East side of William Stickneyes vpland abutting as aforesaid

To Mathew Boyes two Acres of vpland lying on the East side of William Scales his vpland abutting as aforesaid.

To Jane Brockelbanke Vx : two Acres of vpland lying on the East side of a pcell of ground giuen to Mathew Boyes abutting as aforesaid.

To Thomas Mighill foure Acres of vpland lying on the East side of Jane Brockelbankes house lott, pt of it abutting on the streete pt of it lying at the northend of his house Lott.

To Mrs Margery Shoue Vx : one Acree & a quarter of vpland lying on the East side of Thomas Mighills vpland one end abutting on the North end of her owne house lott the other end on Mr Eze-kiell Rogers fence

To Humphrey Reyner two Acres of vpland lying on the East side of Mrs Margery Shoues vpland abutting as aforesaid

To Mr Ezekiell Rogers six Acres of vpland lying on the East side of Humphrey Reyners house lott, one end of it abutting vpon the streete the rest of it Joyning vpon the north end of his owne house lott.

To John Haseltine one Acree & an halfe of vpland neare to his house lott in Cousideration of the badnes of his Planting lott in the North east ffield the East end abutting vpon a swampe

To Thomas Tenny two Acres of vpland lying on the North side of John Haseltines vpland, vpon the aforesaid like Consideratiō abutting as aforesaid.

To Robert Haseltine two Acres of vpland lying vpon the North side of Thomas Tennyes vpland one wherof was giuen him vpon the Cousideratiō as aforesaid the other vpon another Consideration abutting as aforesaid.

To Richard Swan one Acree of vpland lying on the north side of Robert Haseltines vpland vpon Consideration of the badnes of his planting lott abutting as aforesaid.

Certaine vplands laid out in the ffield Called Pollipod ffield.

To John Remington thre Acres lying along by the South ffence the West end abutting vpon the Cart way w^{th}in the ffence the other end

To John Scales five Acres lying on the North side of John Remingtons, the West end abutting as aforesaid the East end

To Jane Brockelbanke Vx : two Acres & twenty Rod lying along by a swampe side the South end abutting vpon a swampe by the side of John Scales lott the North end vpon the head ffence.

To Mathew Boyes two Acres & three quarters lying on the East side of Jane Brockelbankes abutting as aforesaid

To William Skales two Acres & an halfe lying on the East side of Mathew Boyes abutting as aforesaid.

To William Stickney two acres & an halfe lying on the East side of William Scales abutting as aforesaid

To James Barkar thre Acres lying on the East side of William Stickney, abutting as aforesaid.

To John Jarrat   Acres lying on the East side of James Barkar abutting as aforesaid.

Vplands laid out in the ffield Called the Mor-land ffield

To Humphrey Reyner six Acres of vpland lying on the South side a swampe, the one end abutting on the West ffence the other end on the East ffence

To Thomas Mighill three Acres lying on the south Side Humphrey Reyners abutting as aforesaid.

To John Pickard two Acres three quarters lying on the South side Thomas Mighills abutting as aforesaid

To Isaac Cousins three Acres & a quarter lying on the South side of John Pickards vpland abutting as aforesaid

Vplands laid out in the ffield Called Batchelours Plaine

To Richard Clarke two Acres of vpland lying along by the West ffence one end abutting against the North fence the other against the South ffence

To John Dresser one Acree and an halfe lying on the East side Richard Clarkes vpland abutting as aforesaid.

To Hugh Chaplin one Acre lying on the East side John Dressers land abutting as aforesaid

To Peter Cooper one Acree lying on the East side of Hugh Chaplins land abutting as aforesaid

To Thomas Ellethrope one Acree lying on the east side of Peter Coopers land abutting as aforesaid.

To Michaell Hopkinson one Acree & an halfe on the East side of Peter Coopers land abutting as aforesaid.

To John Bointon one Acree lying on the East side of Michaell Hopkinsons land abutting as aforesaid.

To William Bointon one Acre lying on the East of John Bointons land abutting as aforesaid.

To Joseph Jewet eight lying on the East side of William Bointon

To Maximilian Jewet seauen Acres lying on the East side of Joseph Jewets land abutting as aforesaid

To Jane Grant three Acres lying on the east side of Maximilian Jewets land abutting as aforesaid.

To John Spofford thre Acres & a quarter lying on the East side of Jane Grants land abutting as aforesaid

To George Kilborne thre Acres & a quarter lying on the East side of John Spoffords land abutting as aforesaid

To Richard Wikam three Acres lying on the East side of George Kilbornes land abutting as aforesaid.

To Custins Crosby Vx: three Acres lying on the East side of Richard Wikams land abutting as aforesaid.

To William Jackson an hundred Rod of ground lying at the East end of William Wilds house lott.

To Hugh Smith halfe an Acre of land lying at the East end of his house lott.

To Michaell Hopkinson halfe an Acre of land Joyning to the East end of his house lott.

To John Smith one Acree and an halfe for an house lott ioyning to the Southeast side of Thomàs Leauers house lott the East end abutting on the streete

To the said John Smith foure Acres of vpland in the ffield Called Pollipod ffield lying on the West side of a Swampe neare to his house lott the Northend lying neare to a pcell of ground Granted to John Haseltine, the west side of it ioyning to a swampe.

To the said John Smith two Acres and an halfe of Salt Marsh ioyning to the North side of the first diuision of Mr Ezekiell Rogers

Salt Marsh beyond the Cow bridge the west end abutting vpon a Creeke the East end vpon William Tennyes Marsh

To the aforesaid John Smith one acre & an halfe of fresh marsh the North Corner of it Abutting on a Creeke the East side abutting on Mrs Margery Shoues first diuision of Salt Marsh the west and south pts of it bounded by the vpland.

To William Tenny one house lott Containing an Acre and an halfe Joyning to the South side of Marke Primes house lott.

To the said William Tenny ffoure Acres of Meadow Joyning with the west end to John Smiths Salt Marsh beyond the Cowbridge the East end abutting on Newberry line each side bounded by vpland.

To William Tenny two Acres & an halfe of vpland on the South side of James Baley his lott the East end abutting on the Country high way the west end on a swampe.

To the said William Tenny two Acres of vpland lying south east side of James Baley his other lott the East & West end abutting on rough meadows.

To James Baley one house lott Containing an Acree & an halfe lying on the North side of Edward Sawers house lott

To James Baley two Acres of Salt marsh lying beyond the Cow-bridge the North side bounded by a River the South side by Edward Hassens marsh the East end abutting on an Iland the West on a Creeke.

To James Baley one Acre of Rough Marsh lying on the East side of Mr Samuell Bellinghams ffirst diuision of Rough marsh lying round about an Iland.

To James Baley two Acres of vpland lying on the South east side of Edward Sawers lott the West end abutting on a swampe the East end on the Rough marshes.

To the said James Baley two Acres and an halfe of vpland ly-ing on the South side Abell Langley his lott the East end abutting on the Country high way the west end on a swampe

To Abell Langley two Acres of vpland lying on the South side of William Acyes lott the East end abutting on the Country high way the West end on a swampe. This land is granted to him in Consideratiõ of the badnes of his planting lott.

To William Acy two Acres of vpland lying on the South side of ffrancis Lamberts lott the West end abutting vpon a swampe the East end vpon Comõn ground. this Land is granted vpon the afore said Consideration.

To John Lambert two Acres of vpland lying on the south side of Richard Thurlay his lott. the west end abutting on a Cart way the East end on Com̄on ground granted on the aforesaid Consideration

To Richard Thurlay two Acres of vpland the West end abutting on a Cart way the East end on Com̄on grounds. Granted to him vpon the aforesaid Consideration.

To Joseph Jewet six Acres of vpland being pt of that Land Called Satchells Ground bounded by a swampe on the northeast side wch is now in the possession of Joseph Jewet aforesaid & John Tod the Southeast end abutting on Thomas Mighills Lott. the South West side bounded by Mr Ezekiell Rogers his Lott the north west end by a Cart way

To John Johnson one Acre of vpland bounded on the Northeast side by Thomas Mighills land and on the Southeast end by Mr Ezekiell Rogers lott.

To Marke Prime one house lott Containeing an Acre & an halfe Lying on the South side of William Acyes house lott.

To the said Marke Prime two Acres & an halfe of vpland in the Northeast ffield bounded on the Southwest side by a Cart way and another on the east the North west end bounded by Thomas Millers lott.

To Richard Lighton one house lott Containing an Acre & an halfe lying on the South side of Nicholas Jacksons house lott.

To the said Richard Lighton two Acres & an halfe of vpland in the Northeast ffield the West side bounded by Com̄on lands the East side by a Cart way leading to the meadows the South end abutting on a Cart way leading to the Cowbridge the North end on a swampe.

To John Pearson one house lott Containeing an Acree & an halfe lying on the South side of Richard Lighton.

To the said John Pearson one Acre of vpland in the North east ffield the North west end of it Abutting vpon the Country way pt of it Joyning to George Abbatts rough marsh.

To the said John Pearson an Acre & an halfe of vpland lying on the northwest side of the Cart way leading to the Cowbridge.

To Nicholas Jackson an Acre and an halfe for an house lott lying on the South side of Mr John Millers lott.

To the said Nicholas Jackson two Acres and an halfe of vpland, bounded by the Cart way leading to the meadows the South end abutting on the Cowbridge Cart path.

To Edward Sawer one house lott Containeing by estimatiō an Acre & an halfe lying on the South side of James Baley his house lott.

To Edward Sawer two Acres & an halfe of vpland in the North-east ffield bounded on the South side by John Haseltines Rough Marsh.

To Richard Holmes one house lott Containeing an Acree Joyning vpon Edward Sawers house lott.

To Daniell Harris one house lott Containeing an Acre lying on the west side of William Law his house lott.

To Thomas Sawer one house lott Containing an Acree & an halfe bounded on the South west by John Newmarch his house lott on the north west by Thomas Mighill planting lott.

To Thomas Burkby one house lott Containeing by estimatiō an Acree and an halfe lying on the South side of Mr Samuell Bellinghams house lott.

To John Tillison one house lott Containeing an acree & an halfe lying on the South side of Thomas Burkbyes lott

To John Hill a house lott Containing an Acree & an halfe lying on the South side of John Tillisons house lott.

To Sebastiam Briggam an Acree of Salt Marsh lying att the South east end of his Planting lott in the North east field rounded by the Warehouse Riuer.

To John Haseltine one Acree of rough marsh in Consideration of an Acree laid downe by him neare to Newberry gate bounded on the North side by a swampe. the East end abutting on Abell Langley his first Diuision of Rough Marsh.

To Thomas Dickinson six Acres of vpland lying on the North side of prospect hill ioyning to the South side of Richard Clarkes house lott.

Certaine Parcells of Meadow laid out to these men vnder recorded in Consideration of Meadowes laid down by them in the little Meadow being pt of their first Diuision of fresh Marsh

To Richard Clarke halfe an Acre of Meadow lying in on the West side the bridge called Sandy bridge in Consideration of halfe an Acre of Meadow laid downe by him in a Meadow called the little Meadow: the South end abutting vpon the vpland the North end vpon a fence.

To Peter Cooper halfe an Acree vpon the aforesaid Consideration, lying on the West side of Richard Clarkes Meadow abutting as aforesaid

To John Burbanke halfe an Acree lying on the East side of Mr Edward Carltons Meadow beyond the Cowbridge vpon the same Consideration as aforesaid, the South end abutting vpon the vpland the North end vpon Mr Ezekiell Rogers his rough marsh.

To Thomas Palmar halfe an Acre of Meadow lying on the East side of John Burbankes meadow vpon the aboue mentioned Consideration abutting as aforesaid.

To Isaac Cousins two Acres lying on the East side of Thomas Palmars Meadow both ends abutting vpon the vpland.

To John Bointon one Acre lying on the East of Isaac Cousins his Meadow, in Consideration of halfe an Acree laid downe in the little meadow & in Consideration of the badnes of his diuision of Rough marsh

To John Burbanke one acre lying on the East side of John Bointons Meadow in Consideration of an Acre of rough Marsh laid downe by him abutting as aforesaid

To William Tenny three quarters of an Acree lying on ye East side of John Burbankes Meadow in lieu of his vpland at the ffarme abutting as aforesaid.

To James Baley thre quarters of an Acre lying on the east side William Tennyes Meadow vpon the aforesaid Consideratio abutting as abouesaid

To John Pickard an Acre & an halfe in Lieu of halfe an Acree laid downe in a little meadow neare bradford streete end and for an Acre due to Robert Swan bought by the said John lying on the East side of James Baley his meadow abutting as aforesaid.

To Hugh Smith one Acre lying at the East end of John Harris his Planting lott in the North east ffield. Joyning on the west end of Joseph Jewets ffirst Diuision of Rough marsh in Consideration of an Acre of meadow laid downe by him in the little Meadow

To Maximilian Jewet an Acre & an halfe of salt Marsh lying at the Southeast end of his third Diuision of Salt Marsh in Consideratio of his diuision of fresh meadows laid downe in Pollepod Meadow and of a way that lyes through his Meadow to hogge Iland

To Peter Cooper a little peece of salt Marsh lying at The South ends of his owne and Richard Clarkes second diuision of Salt Marsh compassed about with Creeks

To Hugh Chaplin an Acree of Salt marsh lying at the South end of his second diuision of Salt marsh in Consideration of the badnes theirof bounded by a Creeke at the South end.

To Thomas Miller an Acre of Rough Marsh in the ffield Called the Marsh field the West end abutting on vpland, of Humphrey Reyners the South side lying along by a Cart path.

To the said Thomas Miller an Acre of Rough marsh lying on West side the Country high way in the marsh ffield bounded on thre sides by the vpland:

To James Baley one Acre lying on the west side of Thomas Millers Marsh each end abutting on the vpland

To Michaell Hopkinson thre Acres lying on the west side of James Marsh abutting as aforesaid.

To John Pearson two Acres lying on the West side of Michaell Hopkinsons Marsh abutting as aforesaid.

To Richard Swan to Acres lying on the west side of John Pearsons marsh abutting as aforesaid

To Charles Browne   Acres of Rough Marsh lying on the West side of Richard Swans marsh the North end abutting on the vpland the South end on Richard Thorlay his Meadow

To Daniell Harris one Acre lying on the west side of Charles Brownes Meadow the North end abutting on the vpland the South end on a fence.

To John Scales an Acre & an halfe lying on the West side of Daniell Harris his Marsh abutting as aforesaid.

To Thomas Dickinson an Acre & an halfe lying on the West side of John Scales his Marsh abutting as aforeside

To Michaell Hopkinson two Acres & an halfe of meadow lying at the South end of Batchelours Meadow wthout ye fence.

To Mr Samuell Bellingham two Acres & an halfe of Meadow lying on the West side of the Brooke called Symons Brooke begining at the Bridge and so lyes Northward Compassed by the brooke & the vpland.

To William Jackson one Acree of Salt Marsh the North side bounded by a Creeke the South side by the vpland both ends abutting vpon Maximilian Jewets first diuision of rough marsh

To Joseph Jewet seauen Acres of vpland and a halfe the south side ioyning vpon Ipswish line the East end abutting vpon the Country way towards Ipswish the North west side bounded be the Coīmon.

To John Tod a Swampe in the Northeast ffield vpon these Conditions ffollowing Vid: that he shall haue the vse of it for nothing so long as he keepes the Ordinary: but when he layes downe the said ordinary he is to pay three pounds to the Towne for the said Swampe and then it his owne for euer. Prouided that the Towne reserue liberty to fall and Cary away the Wood growing in the said swampe for theirs or any of their vse. This swampe is bounded as followeth namely by Thomas Mighill planting lott on the South West and by Humphrey Reyners lott pt of it on the South side & pt of it on the East side and on the North side by seuerall small Lotts.

To Mr Edward Carlton three Acres of vpland lying on the South side of John Pearsons house lott, the East end abutting vpon a swampe the West end on the streete

To Mr Samuell Phillips fourteene Acres of vpland lying on the South side of Mr Edward Carltons land abutting as aforesaid

To Mr Thomas Nelson six Acres of land at the ffarme Called Mannings ffarme bounded on the Northeast side by John Crosses ffarme the Northwest end by the land left for a high way ioyning vpon Rowleyes bounds

To Ezekiell Northend & Richard Holmes an acre and an halfe bounded on the northeast side by John Crosses ffarme the North west end by the aforesaid land of Mr Thomas Nelson.

To Ezekiell Northend one Acre of land. in a swampe Joyning vpon the aforesaid land of Ezekiell Northend and Richard Holmes

To Ezekiell Northend and John Harris halfe an Acre of land Joyning vpon the Northwest end of Mr Thomas Nelsons land.

To ffrancis Lambert one Acree & an halfe Joyning to the north side of his house lott.

To Richard Swan three quarters of an Acree of vpland Joyning to the North side of Thomas Lilforths house lott.

To Mr Thomas Nelson two Acres of vpland Joyning vpon Richard Swans Planting lott at the oxe pasture gate

Sold to John Palmar a certaine pcell of Salt Marsh to the Value of one pound Joyning to his third diuision of Salt Marsh.

To ffrancis Parrat thre quarters of an Acree of rough Marsh Joyning on the north side of his second diuision of Rough Marsh.

To the said ffrancis Parrat two Acres of Salt marsh lying betwixt his owne third diuision of Salt marsh and a great Creeke that branches it selfe out into two armes the one wherof being the bounds betwixt vs and Newberry

To him the said ffrancis Parrat two Acres of vpland Joyning to his Third diuision of Salt marsh.

To John Trumble two Acres of Salt Marsh one wherof in Consideration of an Acree laid downe in Batchelours Meadow the

North end bounding vpon the South end of his owne and John Bointons second diuision of Salt Marsh the South end bounded vpon the maine River & a Creeke.

To John Remington two Acres & thre quarters of Salt Marsh the North West end abutting on the Cart Way leading to Mr Nelsons Iland the South West side bounded by Vx : Crosbyes Saltmarsh the South East side by Mathew Boyes his Marsh.

To Mathew Boyes two Acres & thre quarters of Salt marsh lying on the South east side of John Remingtons marsh. the other sides of it Compassed by a Creeke

To Samuell Brocklebanke two Acres & thre quarters of Salt Marsh lying on the North west side of Ezekiell Northends marsh the other sides of it compassed by a great Creeke.

To Ezekiell Northend one Acre of Salt Marsh lying on the South east side of Samuell Brocklebankes meadow. both ends abutting vpon two Creekes.

To Thomas Dickinson one Acre lying on the South west side of Vx : Crosbyes Meadow Compassed by a great Creeke

To Joseph Jewet   Acres of Salt Marsh at the East end of his third diuision of Salt Marsh. the North east side of it bounded by Maximilian Jewets Saltmarsh

To Maximilian Jewet   Acres of Salt marsh pt of it in Consideration of an high way laid out through his lott to hogg Iland. bounded on the West side by Joseph Jewetts marsh the North & North east sides of it Thomas Dickinsons Marsh and the South end by a great Creeke.

To Thomas Dickinson two Acres & thre quarters lying on both sides the Way to hogg Iland. the West side of it bounded by Maximilian Jewets Meadow the North and South ends of it bounded by two great Creekes.

To John Pickard foure Acres of Salt Marsh lying on the Southeast side of Thomas Dickinsons Marsh Compassed about With Creekes.

       Certaine Diuisions of Meadow laid out in the Meadow Called Crane Meadow

To Mr Thomas Nelson fifty Acres of Meadow pt of it lying on South East side of the Crane Meadow brooke, the South east end of it abutting vpon the vpland the South West side bounded by Mr Ezekiell Rogers his Meadow the North east side vpon vpland the the North West end vpon the brooke the rest of it lying vpon the

North west side of the said Brooke the North east end of it bounded by a great swampe the south east side vpon the brooke the North-west side vpon the vpland. the West end vpon Ezekiell Northends Meadow. there is also allowed measure in this fifty Acres for and high through this diuision to the lotts lying beyond it.

To M⁺ Ezekiell Rogers twenty fiue Acres of Meadow lying on the South east side of the aforesaid brooke and on the South west side of M⁺ Thomas Nelsons Meadow. the South east end abutting vpon the vpland. the North west end vpon a brooke. the South west end vpon a great pond and vpland

To Ezekiell Northend seauen Acres of Meadow lying on the West side of M⁺ Thomas Nelsons meadow the North end abutting vpon the vpland. the South end vpon the brooke.

To Richard Holmes 2 Acres of Meadow lying on the west side of Ezekiell Northends meadow abutting as aforesaid.

To Richard Longhorne & William Law six Acres lying on the West side of Richard Holmes his Meadow abutting as aforesaid saue onely that an Iland lyes in the middle of it

To Abell Langley six Acres of Meadow lying on the West side of Richard Longhornes & William Law his meadow abutting as aforesaid.

To William Acy six Acres of Meadow. lying on the West side of Abell Langleyes meadow abutting as aforesaid.

To John Lambert six Acres of Meadow lying on the West side of William Acyes Meadow the South west end runing ouer a swampe & abutting vpon vpland.

To John Tod for Meadow bought of Richard Thurlay & for his owne diuision fiue Acres the East end abutting on John Lamberts Meadow the North side bounded by a swampe the South side by the vpland.

To Marke Prime fiue Acres of Meadows part of it bought of Richard Thurlay. the rest of it bought of M⁺ Edward Carlton lying at the west end of John Tods meadow both sides bounded as abouesaid.

To Thomas Crosby six Acres of Meadow lying at the West end of Marke Primes Meadow the west end abuttting vpon vpland both sides bounded as aforesaid.

To Abell Langley one Acre of meadow lying on the east side of John Lamberts Meadow abutting on a great swampe and vpland.

To John Smith six Acres of Meadow lying on the East side of Abell Langley his Meadow abutting as aforesaid.

To Edward Hassen three Acres of meadow lying on the South

east side of John Smithes Meadow the Northeast end abutting vpon a pond the South west end vpon the vpland

To Leonard Harriman seauen Acres of Meadow lying on the Southeast side of Edward Hassens Meadow pt of it bought of William Hobson and pt on John Harris the East end abutting vpon a brooke the west end vpon the vpland

To Thomas Abbatt three Acres & an halfe of Meadow lying on the South side of Leonard Harrimans Meadow abutting as aforesaid.

To Mr Ezekiell Rogers twenty-fiue Acres of Meadow belonging to his farme he had by his Wife lying on the South side of Thomas Abbatts Meadow. the North West end abutting vpon vpland, the South east end vpon a swampe ouer the brooke.

To Samuell Brockelbanke nine Acres of Meadow lying on the South West side of Mr Ezekiell Rogers his meadow the North West end and south west side bounded by vpland the South east end abutting vpon the brooke

To Mr Ezekiell Rogers eleauen Acres of Meadow lying aboue the pond neare the way to Hauarell

To Samuell Brockelbanke eleauen Acres of meadow lying beyond the Pen brooke bounded wth swampe & vpland

To ffrancis Parrat twelue Acre & an halfe of meadow pt of it lying beyond the brooke Called Crane Meadow brooke the South west end bounded by the vplands towards Hauarell path. the North east by a marked tree growing by the vpland the one side bounded by the brooke the other by the vpland the rest of it lying on the hither side the brooke the southeast end abutting vpon Richard Swans Meadow the North West end vpon the vpland. one side bounded by the vpland the other by the brooke aforesaid. this meadow on the hither side the brooke lyes in two places the vpland comeing betweene.

To Richard Swan fiue Acres & thre quarters of meadow the Southwest end abutting vpon ffrancis Parratts Meadow the Northeast end vpon the vpland by a marked tree the South east side by Comon meadows vnlaid out, the North West side by the brooke a little pcell of this meadow lyes beyond the brooke.

Vplands laid out at the plaine Called the Great plaine.

Imp to Edward Hassen foure Acres & an halfe of vpland at the plaine Called the great plaine lying next the south ffence by the

Country way the East end abutting towards the fence the west end towards other.

To John Smith 5 Acres of vpland lying on the north side of Edward Hassens land abutting as aforesaid.

To Thomas Tenny two Acres & an halfe of land lying on the north side of John Smithes land abutting as aforesaid.

To William Tenny two Acres of land lying on the north side of Thomas Tennyes land abutting as aforesaid

To John Trumble two Acres of land, lying on the north side of William Tennyes land abutting as aforesaid.

To Thomas Leauer two Acres of land lying on the north side of John Trumbles Land abutting as aforesaid.

To John Scales eight Acres & an halfe of land lying on the north side of Thomas Leauers land abutting as aforesaid

To James Baley two Acres of land lying on the north side of John Scales his land abutting as aforesaid

To Thomas Miller two Acres of land lying on the north side of James Baley his land abutting as aforesaid.

To Charles Browne two Acres & an halfe of land lying on the north side of Thomas Millers land abutting as aforesaid

To Robert Swan two Acres of land lying on the north side of Charles Brownes land abutting as aforesaid.

To Richard Swan eight acre of land lying on the north side of Robert Swans land abutting as aforesaid.

To John Harris foure Acres & a quarter lying on the north side of Richard Swans vpland abutting as aforesaid

To John Palmar foure Acres and a quarter of land lying on the north side of John Harris his land abutting as aforesaid

To ffrancis Parrat thirteene Acres & an halfe of land lying on the north side of John Palmars land abutting as aforesaid.

To Richard Thurlay eight Acres & an halfe of land lying on the north side of ffrancis Parrats land abutting as aforesaid.

To William Acy eight Acres & an halfe lying on the north side of Richard Thurlay his land the east end abutting as aforesaid the west end on a swampe.

To John Lambert eight Acres & an halfe lying on the north side of William Acyes land the East end abutting as aforesaid the west end mostly on the aforesaid swampe

To Abell Langley eight Acres & an halfe of land lying on the north side of John Lamberts Land the east & west end abutting towards the ffence.

To Richard holmes foure Acres & a quarter of land lying on the north side of Abell Langley his lott abutting as aforesaid.

To Ezekiell Northend eight Acres & an halfe of land lying on the north side of Richard Holmes his land abutting as aforesaid

To Richard Longhorne foure Acres & a quarter of vpland lying on the north side of Ezekiell Northend his land abutting as aforesaid.

To William Law floure Acres & a quarter of vpland lying on the north side of Richard Longhornes land abutting as aforesaid.

To John Tod foure Acres & a quarter of vpland lying on the north side of William Law his vpland abutting as aforesaid.

Vplands laid out at the ffield called Bradford streete plaine

To Leonard Harriman one Acree & an halfe of vpland in Bradford streete plaine the north end abutting on John Bointons lott the South end on the ffence

To Maximilian Jewet six Acres lying on the West side of Leonard Harrimans vpland the North end abutting ptly on John Bointons lott and ptly on a swampe the South end on a Swampe

To Thomas Dickinson six Acres of vpland lying on the west side of Maximilian Jewetts Lott the north end abutting on a swampe the south end on the ffence.

To John Bointon an Acree & an halfe of vpland lying at the head of Maximilian Jewets & Leonard Harrimans lotts the west end abutting on   the East end on

To John Trumble foure Acres & an halfe of vpland lying on the north side of John Bointons vpland abutting as aforesaid.

To Hugh Smith two Acres of vpland & one quarter lying on the north side of John Trumbles lott abutting as aforesaid

To William Jacksen an Acree & an halfe of vpland lying on the north side of Hugh Smithes lott abutting as aforesaid

To Thomas Palmar two Acres & an halfe of vpland lying on the north side of William Jacksons lott abutting as aforesaid

To John Burbanke two Acres & an halfe of vpland lying on the north side of Thomas Palmars Lott abutting as aforesaid

To Peter Cooper an Acre & an halfe lying on the north side of John Burbankes lott abutting on the fence at both ends

To Hugh Chaplin an Acree & an halfe of vpland lying on the north side of Peter Coopers lott abutting as aforesaid.

To John Pickard eight Acres & an halfe of vpland lying on the north side of Hugh Chaplins lott abutting as aforesaid

To Robert Haseltine seauen Acres of vpland lying on the north side of John Pickards lott abutting as aforesaid

To Richard Wikam an Acre & an halfe lying on the north side of Robert Haseltines lott abutting as aforesaid

To James Barkar an Acre & an halfe of vpland lying on the north side of Richard Wikams lott abutting as aforesaid

To William Stickney one Acre & an halfe of vpland lying on the north side of James Barkars lott abutting as aforesaid

To William Scales one Acre & an halfe of vpland lying on the north side of William Stickney his lott abutting as aforesaid

To Maximilian Jewett one Acre & an halfe of vpland lying on the north side of William Scales his Lott abutting as aforesaid

To Thomas Dickinson one Acre of vpland lying on the north side of Maximilian Jewets lott abutting as aforesaid

To Hugh Chaplin one Acree of vpland lying on the north side of Thomas Dickinsons lott abutting as aforesaid.

To Thomas Palmar one Acre of Rough Marsh lying on the left hand the Country way leading to newberry next to newberry Gate

To ffrancis Parrat one Acree & an halfe of vpland Joyning to his fence at Sawyers Iland bounded by the salt marsh on each side.

To Jeremiah Elsworth seauen Akers laide out in the feild caled Bradford street Plaine butting on the North vpon John Pickard lott and on the Southside of Richard Wicam lott. purchased of Robert Hesseltine

Acording to Agreement of the towne for the despose by way of Salle of a percell of land that laid in Common Neere vnto and adjoyning the warehouse. the abouesaid land was purchased By Thomas Barker according to the prise Agreed of Betweene Him and the towne and the aboue said land by these p'sents is Confirmed by the towne vnto the said Thomas and his heires According as it lieth Bounded on the East by the warehouse Riuer on the North by the planting lott of Sebastin Brigham on the west by land laid out to Mr Bellingham on the south adjoyning to the farme of Humpray Brodstreete

Item laid out to Ezeakell Northen two Acres of meadow which he purchased of Mr Nelson which meadow was due to him Mr Nelson for part of his Crane meadow that was laid out within Newbery bounds and it lieth to Ezeakell Northen in three small persells at the South end of the pine plaine Called Andeuer plaine on the south side of the high way neare vnto the path one part of it the other part lieth more Sutherly downe a Glade of Swampey meadow the other

part lyeth a longe by the Small Brooke side that Runes easterly into
the falls Riuer lieing a litell more westerly than the Glade that Runes
through the other two parts falls into the Brooke

———————•———————

Young Cattell :
Rich Swan.

Maxy Jewitt	o – 2 – 6
John Tod	o – 1 – 8
Rich Balie	o – 1 – 3
Will Boynton	o – 3 – 4
Mˢᵗ Rogers	o – 16– 8
Robt Hesletine	o – 6 – 8
Tho Dickingson	o – 1 – 6
Humfry Rayner	o – 3 – 4
Will : Sales	o – o – 9
Ed. Carlton	o – 10– o
John Hesletin	o – 5 – o
John Smith	o – 3 – 8
John Remington	o – 3 – 4
Will Stickney	o – 1 – 2
Rich Swan	o – 6 – 8
Hugh Smith	o – 3 – 4
Will Wild	o – 5 – o
John Pickard	o – 5 – o
Tho Barker	o – 4 – 6
Will Asye	o – 5 – o
Charles Browne	o – 1 – 8
Vxor Lambert	o – 5 – o
Will Law	o – 3 – 4
Tho Barker	o – 7 – 6
Tho Mihill	o – 5 – o
Tho Abott	o – 5 – o
Will Tenny	o – 3 – 4
Vxor Hunter	o – 3 – 4

Calves :
John + + and Tho Dickinson

Tho dickson in Corn..	o – o +
Will Harris	o – 1– +
Tho Dickinson	o – 1– +
John Pickard	o + +
Ed Sawyer	o + +
Tho Mihill	o + +
Vxor Lambert	o – 3 +
Dan: Harris	o – o +
Vxor Brockelbank	o – + +
Tho Dickinson	o – 3 +
	o –17 +
owing to him	o – 5– +
Mark prime	o – 1 +
John Hill	+ + +
Joh Scals	o – o– +
Will Jackson	o – o– +
Hugh Smith	o – o– +
John Spoford	o – 1– +
Zek Northend	o – o– +
Rich Swan	o – 3– +
Ed Carlton	o – 2– +
Tho Lilforth	o + +
Sebast Brigham	o + . +

+ + Baly for keping cows
+ + Will Teney 26 weks and
+ days........... 10 – 6 – o
+ day burning..... o – 1 – o
+ . day more...... o – 1 – 4
+ + +............ 5 – 5 – 4
Every Cow is to pay for this
halfe year. ....o – 1 – 5

Rich Thurell........ o – 15– 9
of John Jarratt..... o – 1 – 8
Vxor Brockelbank.. o – 3 – 4
petter Cooper...... o – 5 – o
Mrs Shoue......... o – 4 – 2
of Ez Northend.... o – 1 – 7

A Towne meeting the 20th of the 11th 48.

Thomas Barker, Humfrey Reyner, Mathew Boys, Williā Acee, Thomas Leuer, were chosen to order the affaires of the Towne this yeare

Thomas Dickinson was Chosen to be Cunstable this yeare

Mr Richard Swan William Law Williā Jackson and John Scales were to be ouerseers of the Hy wayes and Comōn Gates and ffences and to see to the execution of all such orders as shall be made this yeare

John Pickard is Chosen Marshill for Gathering all the ffines and fforfettures this yeare

Ed Carleton ffrancis parrat are chosen to assist the fiue men in Laying the ministry rate this yeare

Ed Carleton Capt: Briggā Thomas Mighell ffrancis Parrat Mathew Boys Joseph Jewett and Mr Rogers were Chosen to Judge and determine euery mans proportion of Land + + +
+ + + + + + + + + +

Jeremiah + + +
Math + + +
Rich Swane
To thomas mill + +

Maxe Jewit & brother Dickinson
for bringen 4 Catell   o – 2 – o
for Andrew goeing to
Newbury   o – 1 – 6

this to be laid one 10 + but 4 lost & they + +
Some 15 – 12 – 4d Cowes at both ends 2s – 6d a head
Young Catle come to 3s 1d a beast

paster Catle Charges fenceing broth Rich Swane........ o – 5 – o
Thomas Teny for same worke .... o – 7 – o
Robt heseltine .... 1 – 12– o
Thomas Dickenson and deacon Mighell .... o – 5 – o
Same Stickney 3 days & seeken..................... o – 6 – 6
litle John burbanke 2 days .... o – 2 – o
Thomas Dickinson for bringen home Catell ....   1 – o

Robt heseltynie for Gatherin paster Catèll.............. 2 – 0

3 – 0 – 6

Number of them 62

Eder Rainer 2 y^t but half pay
leauetenent & Same brocklbanke calus
paster Catle 1 – 4 ther Charges 3 – 12 which dus come to every
beast 1 – + + a head

+ + + +	+ + + +	Pete Cooper 1	3 one laken
+ + + +	+ + + +	Hew Chaplin 1	2
+ + Smith...	–2	John Dreser...1	2
John Picard....	–2 one lacke	Rich Wicā....1	1 wants one
Wid Crosby....	–1	Rich Loughor.	2
Thom Dicinsō.2	–2	John Spofa 2	3
Rich Swā.....1	–2 and one	Dan Harr.....	2
Will Asie.....1	–2	Will Law.....1	2
John Scales....1	–3	John Tood....	1
Mr Carletō....1	–5	Jo Hares	
Edw Hasen....2	–2	Jo Parme	
Abell Langlay.2	–2	Rich Homes...	1
Sam Broke....4	–3 one lack	Wid Crose....	1
Math Boy.....2	–2	Mar Crose.....	1
Will Scale....1	–2	Ez Norend....1	4
Will Sticney...	–2	Th Miller	
John Remtō...5	–4 & one bull +	Edw. Sayer....	1
Leonard Har 0	–2	+ + Balie...1	
Willi Boyn....0	01	Will Tenie	2
John Boynto...	–1	+rke Prime	2
Widow Hobki 0	–1	+ + burkby	1
Hew Smith ...	2	+ + + +	
Tho Parm.....1	2	+ + + +	1

+ 13 – 50 – ther is to be Reserued for the heard att pentuckett
7 – 8 – 0 for which euery beast is to pay one shilling fouer pence
(1 – 5 laid)

What is in the pastur		What is with the hird	
Mr Rog	3	.... 4 one lake	
Eld Rane	4	.... 2 & one bull	
Jerm Ellwo		.... 2 one lacke	
Josef Jewet		 1	
Tho Abatt		 1	
Jam Balis		... 1	

It is ordered and Agreed that the Commans which belong To the Towne of Rowley : shall rune fiue Mills from Towne euery way wher we haue propriatie if they be not laid out to any particular person :

It to the end euery man may haue an equall sharre in the Commons According to purchase it is agreed that euery Acre and halfe Lot shall haue one gate and halfe a gate

Also euery half Two Acre lott shall haue two gates and a quarter

It Euery tow Acre lott shall haue foure Gates and one halfe gate :

It euery Thre Acre lott shall haue thirteen Gates and one half:

It euery four Acre Lott shall haue twentie tow gattes [and one half] and the six acre lots shall haue forty fiue Gates

It is ordered that all house Lotts That are or shall bee Laid out shall fence against all Common Pastiers and Inclosures which are not laid out for house lotts the ouerseers shall vew all such fences.

It is ordered that ther shall bee Eight Good and suficient Bulls provided by the towne According to thes Devisions now made Viz. from Richard Clarks to and with John Boyntons : from Will Boyntons to and with Leften^t John Remington : from James Barkers to And with Elder Rainers : with Richard Wicome one from John Pickerd to and with Thomas Barker from Mr Rogers to and with Thomas Crossbes : from Mr Nellson house to and with Richard holmes : from Ezekiel Northend To and with vxor Lambert : from Charles brown to and with John Smith which bulls are to be provided before the sixteenth of march next insueing the publication theroff by all and euery seuerall Companyes abouesaid and soe to be kept from Time to time vnles the select men see caus and doe alter the same which Bulls are not to be young^r than two year old nor kept till aboue fiue yere old in case any Company fail in the due observation of thes order they shall pay for euery moneth neglect nineteen shillings six pence provided that all those bulls be suficient in the Judgment of the ouerseers

Orders made 11 month 1649

it is ordered that all the Towne Streets shall be made and manteined 4 Rod wide at the least and in Case any be found defectiue after fouerteene days warninge he shall be liable to pay for euery Rod of fence so defectiue twelue pence

Concerning Catle

It is ordered and agreed that all comon Gates and perticuler mens ffences ioyning vpon any Corne feild shall be manteined against Great Catle at all times and if they be not sufently made to turne Great Catle at any time when Catle may doe hurte vpon Corne,

It is ordered that all perticuler mens ffences shall be made and repaired against all maner of Catle and hogs of or aboue ten shillings prise between the 20th of the first month and the first of the 9 month

It is ordered that euery man that hath any Catle to pay for in any of the Herds that they shall bring in theyr full payments both for quality time and place therof according as they shall be appoynted by the fiue men, and for euery defect the delinquent shall p ay six pence the shilling

Memorandū that the 3d & 4 Orders in this page in case of deffect the 4 men who are Chosen for to see to the execution of the orders this yeare shall haue recourse vnto the order of Court prouided herin for the same penalty and theyr direction therabout. in the 8 page of the Booke of Orders an order for swine

It is ordered that the ffence betweene vs and Nubery shall be made Sufficient with 3 Rales according to the order agreed by the towne and such diuisions as shall be made therof to euery street by Mr Carleton and Joseph Jewet and according vnto theyr direction and if any be defective in theyr proportiō of fence they shall be liable to pay for euery defect of a rodd of ffence not so made as aforesaide vpon the 20 of the 3d month to pay 6d a rodd

It is ordered that all the ffences about the ox pasture shall be made and manteyned sufficient $+$ $+$ $+$ Catle before the first of the $+$ $+$ $+$ $+$ $+$ $+$ any defect the delinquent $+$ $+$ $+$ $+$ $+$ $+$

the fourth order is dated to be done betweene the 10th & the 3d month vpon the fyne aforesaid

Towne Orders made this last $+$ $+$

It is ordered and agreed that the Prudential men dureing the time of theyr being shall haue ffull power to order and transact all the Comon affaires of the Towne of Rowley as to make Orders impose ffines for the better manageing the affaires of the said Towne provided that they doe nothing Contrary to the orders of the Generall Court, provided also that they dispose noe land for Inheritance without the consent of the Towne provided allso thay let noe Towne land but for ther present year

provided that they make noe adission to the minestry Rate aboue 60 pounds for one minister w^thout the consent of the towne

Covenanted with our Bretheren that went to sit downe at Pentuckit this yeare 1649

Imp that they shall take Care of and keep all that Hearde of Catle which we may put within the ffence which is now made or shall be made this yeare the towne paying them wages as is agreed and this they promise to doe 7 yeares

Ite it is further agreed betweene the town and the said Bretheren that they shall be ffreed of all Charges for the ministry or Constable rates for such a proportion of Landes as is now giuen them and for such Catle as they may keep vpon the same accomodations that is to say 4 oxen 6 Cows 4 Calues prouided if they haue any addition of Lande or Catle then they shall be liable to pay Charges for the same

5 men Chosen for this yeare ensuing,

Capt: Briggam, Thomas Mighel, Maximilia Jewet, Thomas Barker, Thomas Leuer.

Thomas Dickinson chosen Constable this yeare 1649

ouerseers for the execution of towne orders and Hy wayes this 1649

> Hu Smith   Samuell Brokelbanke
> John Smith   John Person

Brother Joseph Jewitt and Deacon Mighell to view the bounding of midows by the 4 of 3^d month

John Person John Pickard and Will Boynton are chosen to warne towne meetings this 7th of febuary 49.

febuary 7th 49.

Tho; Mighell, Math: Boyes and Joseph Jewett were chosen to determyne any difference that may arise betwene any aboute ther fence and allsoe bounds of midows

febuary 7th – 49.

It is granted to Tho Mighell that, that strete which is betwene his house and his mault Kilne shall Remayne as it is now (provyded that when the fence is Repayred againe it shall be mayde thre Rod wide ; notwithstanding the order to the Contrary.

the 14 day of febuary 1649.

delved vnto the marshall by the select men divers fynes amounting to the soome of 2 – + + +

December the 18 deliverd to the marshall of rowley in fyns 1 – 10 +

+ + + + + + + + + +
+ + + tie sixt of febuary 1649

It is ordered that thre men shall be apoynted to warne towne meetings each one in ther severall Circuits, he which warns from John Persons to Mr Nelsons shall have 4 pence a tyme he which warnes the midle of the towne shall have 2 pence a tyme and he which warnes Bradford strete shall have 2 pence a tyme, and in Case any pson or famyly that is att home be vnwarned he that warnes in that quarter shall pay for every defecte herein six pence

It is ordered that the Clarke who is to Call towne meetings shall attend as other men and shall Call the houre apoynted if the day be Cleare otherways att the discretion of the selectmen or a maior pt of them and shall give in att that tyme a list of the names of those who are absent vnto those who are apoynted to heare the Case of such as are delinquent hearin for which worke the Clarke shall have fouer pence a meting provyded that he Call when the meeting is ended if he be desyred and in Case the Clarke fayle in any pt of his office he shall be lyable to pay twelve pence a time

It is ordered that if any man who is warned to Come to towne mettings be not ther when he is Called he shall be lyable to pay six pence and if he Come not att all twelue pence neather shall he departe without leave vpon the penalty of one 1^d

It is ordered that those who are apoynted to heare the Case of such as are delinquent in not Coming to towne meetings, shall giue notis in generall at that meeting of the tyme when such shall come to make ther defence, and in Case they Come not att the tyme apoynted ther neclect shall make them lyable to be fyned, and in Case such as are apoynted to Judge in this Case be defective not giueing notice to them or attending to hear them it shall be lawfull for the select men to fyne them for every default herein tow

shillings six pence : for which worke of Judgeing they shall receue
of euery shilling in fynes — 2 pence

It is ordered that all the Catle in the Towne that are Capable
of hearding shall be sent to the heards neyther shall any dispose of
his Cattle to be kept or hearded in any other place : vpon paine of
paying for euery Beast desposed Contrary to this order : soe much
as any man shall pay for hearding of his beast : of the same year
and age : provided that if when the Catle is giuen in : it Appear
that ther is more Catle than well can be kept in the heards. Then
by the Consent of the selectmen any man may haue Libertie to
dispose of his cattle : where he pleaseth : provided allso that if any
can make provission for his Cattle out of his owne land soe as he
keep them of the Commons he shall haue libertie soe to doe :

It is ordered that no man shall Refuse to keep the Cattle or
Cowes vpon the saboth Day : Being lawfully warned ther vnto that
is two Dayes before vpon the penalltie of 5 shillings : half theroff
to the Towne and half to him that shall keep in his place : and in
case any neglect to keepe the yonge cattell beinge warned as aboue
saide he shall pay doubell to the foresaide fine.

It is ordered that such as shall be appoynted to any Common
Day worke by any of the ouerseers such persons shall be ready for
ther worke at 7 a'clock in The morning : provided the worke be in
the towne and in case any man fail heareing he shall pay three pence
an houre for euery houre he falls short of his time soe appoynted :
allso in case the worke be out of the Towne euery man shall be
ready at the fore appoynted time at what place the ouerseer shall
appoynt in the Towne that they shall meet togeyther at : vpon the
the like penaltie

Estats for the Counstable +   +. +   +   +

Joseph Jewet...................................268 – 01 – 8
Ezeakell Northen..............................182 – 16 – 8
will law.. 44 – 15 – 00
James Bayley .... 64 – 10 – 00
John Harris...................................... 71 – 05 – 00
marke prime .... 59 – 10 – 00
Richard liton.................................... 25 – 18 – 04
John Tod.. 67 – 13 – 04
Charles Browne................................. 52 – 09 – 02

Edward Sawer .... 39 – 18 – 4
Abell langley................................. 41 – 05 – 00
Thomas Burkeby.............................. 43 – 05 – 00
Henry Reyley................................. 4 – 00 – 00
Richard holmes............................... 82 – 02 – 06
John Lambert.................................151 – 07 – 08
Henry Smith................................... 15 – 03 – 04
Daniell Rouse................................. 19 – 10 – 00
John Pallmer...........................ː...... 78 – 08 – 04
Richard longhorne for Mr Nelsons to the mill 50......245 – 00 – 00
      his owen........................ 74 – 10 – 00
Will tenney................................... 66 – 17 – 8
+   +   +   +   +   +   +   +   +   +

The names of those that has Calues & the number of them 1650

Rich Clar	– 2	Jo Scales	– 1
John Drese	– 2	Ed Hasen	– 1
Hew Chap	– 2	Tho Leauer	+
Peter Coupe	– 2	Tho Crosby	– 1
John Burban	– 1	T Tenne	– 1
Thom Pallme	– 1	Ri Swan	– 2
Will Jackson	+	Will Asie	+
Hew Smi	– 2	Fra Parat	+
Wd Hobkison	– 1	Wd Lamber	– 2
+ + + +	– 1	Ab Langla	– 2
+ + + +	– 1	Chs Broune	– 1
+ + + +	– 2	Mar Prime	+
+ + + +	– 2	Will Tenne	+
+ + + +	10	Jam Balie	2
+ + Grant	2	Ed Sayer	2
+ + d Harima	3	Rich Homes	5
+ + Killb	2	Wd Crose	1
+ + Reminton	4	Ezecl Nored	6
+ + Barker	1	W Law	4
Will Stickne	2	Jo Tood	2
Math Boys	4	Rich Longhor	+
Brokelb	2	Tho Barker	2
Tho Mighe	3	Cap	2
Eld Rainer	2	J Elsewo	2
Mr Roges	4	Jo Picard	2
J Person	1	Wd Crosby	1

Rich Litan   I   Rich Wicom   +

Jo Smith   2

Charges for Calues

for burning by hugh Smith.......................... 0 – 2 – 0

for him and thomas dickinson....................... 0 – 4 – 0

for making trough................................. 0 – 3 – 3

for boys labor.................................... 0 – 2 – 4

for John boynton for dryuing...................... 0 – 1 – 8

for one pole...................................... 0 – 1 – 8

ther is in the towne

of tow aker lots—twenty– + +

of thre aker lots—thre

of fouer aker lots —fouer

of Six aker lots—one

of tow tow aker lots—one

of Aker and halfe lots twenty-eight

the medow of the lots in the towne

for a six aker lott 100 - akers

for a fouer aker lott 050 - akers

for a thre aker lott 030 - akers

for a two aker lott 010 - akers

for a aker and halfe lott 4 akers

for a two two aker lott 20 akers

ther is to pay to the Country Rate for : 665 ak + + + + +

ther is att Mst Dumers farme of vnbrokon vpland + + + +

August 1650
paid to mst Carlton by the Constable
Oxen

Will asie	+ 4	daniel haris	+ 2
francis parrat	+ 5	John palmer	– 2
richard Swan	+ 4	John tod	+ 2
thomas tenny	+ 6	richard longhō	– 4
John Scales	+ 2	M^r rodgers	+10
John Smith	– 2	John pickard	+ 4
Edward hasen	+ 2	deackon mighell	+ 4
John pearson	+ 2	leiftenant	+ 6
John lambert	+ 4	Mathew boys	+ 4

mark prym	+ 1	William Scales	— 2
abell langly	+ 2	William Stickney	— 6
thomas burkbe	+ 2	huge Chaplin	+ 2
James balise	+ 2	John trumbl	2
richard holmes	— 2	William Jacksō	— 4
ezāk northen	+ 2	peter Cooper	— 2
John Spoford	+ 2		

oxen

Richard Swan paid by fransis paret   1 – 4
Jon Spofford paid — butter...........................   8d
tho burckbe paid by bro paret for himselfe and abell and Jo tod 1 – 6
and 2 pence warneing, to paid Eze : nor : paid by brother
parret for him selfe and Will law and dan harris........... 1 +
Will Acce paid by brother paret........................ 1 +
will Jacsō paid — butter for an ox.......................   +
Tho mighill paid in corne.............................+ +
and a pene by bro parrat consent .... 0 – 1
James balis paid — butter   + +
Vxor bo——bnk paid Worke........................... 1 +
hugh Chaplin paid butter
rich longhorne — paid — apart......................... + +
Jo pickard paid — butter............................. 1 +
Jo person — paid — butter........................... + 1
Jon Skales paid by brother parret   + +
Ed : hassen paid butter   + +
tho tene paid by bro parret   2 – 0
Will Stick paid by bro parret   1 +
bro boyes paid by bro parret   3 +
bro remienton paid by bro parr—   2 +
mast rog paid to sister lamb   3 +
and to bro + +   + +

According to the order made in the year 1650 That the fences
in all Comon feilds about or belongin to the towne of Rowley
shold be devided acording to proportion of land and midows and
the quanitety with marks of seuerall numbers to deserne euery mans
owne fence by : Accordingly the northeast feild fences with some
others : wer proportioned and devided by Decon Mighell Joseph
Jewit Richard Swane and John Smith : endin at number one and
soe vpward   The markes are as foloweth
Number I to Mr Carlton : thirty rail Lengths
        II To Mr Ezekil Rogers fifty one rail Lenghts
        III John Scales seuenteen raile Lenghts

IIII Richard Swane fifteen rail Lenghts
　V Thomas Crosbee fourteen Lenghts
　VI Thomas Teney twelue rail Lengths
　VII John Smith fifteenth Rale Lengths
VIII John Trumbl nine rale length
VIIII Thomas Leauer nine rail Lengths
　X John Smith fifteen rale lengths
　XI Mr Shewell eight rale Length
　XII frances Parrat Twentie rale Length
XIII Thomas Crosebe fiftene rale Length
XIIII Robert Swane eight rale Length
　XV Thomas Crosbee fifteene rale Length
XVI William Asee thirty and one rale Length
XVII Abell Langley seuenteene rale Length
XVIII James Baley eight rale Length
XVIIII Marke Pryme six rale Length
　XX Thomas Miller six rale Length
　XXI William Law and Richard Langhorne both haue fifteen
　　　rale Lengths
XXII Thomas Abot fifteene rale Length
XXIII John Johnson sixteene rale Length
XXIIII Widdow Lambart fourteene rale Length
XXV Thomas Mighel seuen rale Length
XXVI Mistres Margry Shoue : sixteene rale Length
XXVII Elder Rainer twenty six rale Length
XXVIII Wiliam Teney eight rale Length
XXVIIII John Pearson　Two rale Length
XXX Edward Sawier foure rale Length
XXXI Thomas Miller　Ten rale Length

those that are aboue writon beginne at Mr Carltons ground at the Bridge at the towne end and goes to the hundred and fortie rod of the feild fence which is to be made and maintained by the ox paster propriators

the hundred and forty Rod of the feild fence which they who have gats in the ox pastur are to make and mainetaine its thus numbred as foloweth

the seuerall markes which is set at end of euey mans proportion the first I to Mr William Belingam Thirty one rail Length
　II Abell Langley six rale Lengths
　III John Lambart twelue rale Length
　IIII John Johnson six rale Length

V John Scals six rale Lenths
VI frances Parrat six rale Length
VII Mr Shewell Twelue rale Length
VIII William Asee six Rale Lengths
VIIII Mr Carlton six Rale Lengths
X Thomas Teney six rale Length
XI Thomas Crosbee six rale Length
XII John Smith six rale Length
XIII Richard Swane nine rale Length
XIIII Edward hasen three Rale Length
XV Mr Ezekiell Rogers nineteene rale Lengths
XVI Mr Thomas Nellson Thirty one rale Length
XVII Thomas Crosbee thirteene rale Length
XVIII Ezekiell Northend six rale Length
XVIIII Richard Holmes Three rale Length
XX Richard Langhorne Three rale Length
XXI William Law Three rale Length
XXII John Todd Three rale Length
XXIII John Pallmer Three rale Length
XXIIII John harris Three rale Length

heare ends that which belonges to the ox pasture Now foloweth that part of the feild fence which goes into the midow euery mans marke is at the end of his fence, number

one I to Thomas Barker eightteene rale Lengths
II Captaine Brigam ninteene rale Lengths
III Thomas Mighell twenty rale Lengths
IIII Mr William Bellingam twenty three rale Lengths
V Mr Thomas Nellson thirtie rale Lengths
VI John Pallmer three rale Lengths
VII John Todd Three rale Lengths
VIII John Harris foure rale Lengths
VIIII Richard Holmes Three rale Lengths
X Ezekiell Northend seuen rale Lengths
XI Thomas Crosbee seuen rale Lengths
XII Thomas Teney three rale Lengths
XIII John Scals Three rale Lengths
XIIII William Asee Three rale Lengths
XV Widdow Lambart two rail Lengths
XVI Abell Langley two rail Lengths
XVII Nicolas Jackson nine rale Lengths

XVIII Richard Lighton seauen rale Lengths

XVIIII from Leu Joh Rementons to widow broklbank all thos
    lots nine lenths is the streett Cald bradforth street

The fence betweene the ox pasture and the midow which is a two Rale fence at further sid of the ox pasture to yᵉ mill ward thos are the seuerall preportions as foloweth euery ox gate Two rale lengths and euer aker of midow foure and a half —— the seuerall marks is at the end of euery mans part of fence as Mʳ Seawells ends at Mark one and soe the rest folow in seuerall numbers

the first I Mʳ Seawell eight rale Lengths

    II frances Parrat foure rale Lengths

    III John Johnson foure rale Lengths

    IIII William Asee foure rale Lengths

    V widdow Lambart eight rale Lengths

    VI Abell Langley foure rale Lengths

    VII Richard Holmes Two rale Lengths

    VIII Ezekiell Northend foure rale Length

    VIIII Richard Langhorne Two rale Length

    X William Law Two rale Lengths

    XI John Todd Two rale Lengths

    XII John Pallmer Two rale Lengths

    XIII John Harris Two rale Lengths

    XIIII Mʳ Thomas Nellson Twenty rale Length

    XV Mʳ Bellingam Twentie rale Length

    XVI Mʳ Ezekiell Rogers twelue rail Length

    XVII Edward Hasen Two rale Lengths

    XVIII John Smith foure rale Lengths

XVIIII John Pearson eighteene rale Lengths

    XX Mʳ Edward Carlton Thirty rale Lengths

    XXI Robert Swane foure rale Length & halfe and Richard
    Swane seuentenee and half of length

    XXII William Boynton nine rale Lengths

    XXIII Will Teny and Thomas Teny nine Lengths

    XXIIII John Scals Thirteene rale Lengths

    XXV John Trumble and Thomas Leauer nine rale Lengths
    betwne them

XXVII Thomas Crosbee Thirty one lengths to ther riuer

The seuerall parts or devisions of fence that beelongs to a feild Comanly Called Polleepod feild acording to ther seuerall marks with the number of rales belongin to euery man which marks is sett at the end of euery devision this fiue rale fence they end at these markes

at mark I forty seuen rayle Lengths belongin to Edward hasen
       Thomas Teney Thomas Crosebee and Robart heseltyne
       not yet devided
    II Leuft John Reminton forty eight ral Length
   III John Scals seuenty three rale Length
  IIII Jaine Brocklbank Vx: thirty eight Length
     V William Stickney Thirty two Length
    VI Mathew Boyes fortie eight rale Length
   VII William Scalls Thirtie two rale Length
  VIII John Scals Ninty nine rale Lengths
 VIIII Thomas Crosbee Eighteene Lengths
     X Thomas Teny twenty foure rale Length
   XI Robart Heseltine Twenty four Length
  XII Richard Swane Twentie four rale length
heare foloweth the seuerall Devision or parts of fence that Comes
from Leauetenant Remintons Corner and Joynes vpon the aboue
writen fences belongen to polypod feild   at the Corner against
Leauᵗ Remintons house fourtene Length belonging to him ending
at number one in leter marked on the posts   I
Mathew Boyes nine raile Lengths ending at Mark of   II
William Scals thirteene rale Lengths ending at   III
James Barker Eleauen rale Lengths ending at   IIII
William Stickney Thirteene rale Lengths ending at   V
Leauᵗ John Reminton Thirty two rale Lengths ending   VI
James Barker Eleuen rale Lengths ending at Marke   VII
Williā Stickney Eightteene rale Lengths ending   VIII
at the Corner post of the head fence Leaᵗ John Rementon
     sixteene Lengths ending at   I
James Barker seuen rale lenths ending at or with numb II
William Stickney Thirteene raile Lengths ending   III
William Scals Ten rale Lengths ending at number   IIII
Mathew Boyes Twenty four rale Lenths ends   V
Samuell Brockelbanke six rale Lenths ending at   VI
    The seuerall Devisions of fence belongin to that field Called
Batchelers plaine with number of ther rale lengths and how they
ar marked geuen in by Joseph Jewit
                        End marks
George Kilburne begines at the East side Thirty eight rails at I
Joseph Jewit one the south sixty six raile Length from
    one to mark   II
John Grant Thirty six rale Lengths frome two to marke   III

Maximilian Jewit one the south sid eightene rale Length
   ending   IIII
Hugh Smith sixtie six rale Lengths from four to mark   V
William Boynton twelue rale Lengths from fiue to   VI
John Trumble Thirty rale Lengths from six to marke   VII
Petter Cowper Twelue rale Lengths from seauen to mar^k   VIII
Hugh Chapline Twelue rale Length from eight to   VIIII
John Dresser eighteene rale Length from nine to   X
Richard Clarke seauentene rale Lengths from ten to   XI
Joseph Jewit fifty two rale Lengths from eleuen to   XII
Maxemilian Jewit fifty six rale Lengths from twelue to   XIII
Joseph Jewit seuenty tow rale Lengths ending at marke   XIIII

   The Devisions in the streett fence of Bradforth streett are as foloweth   after ther seuerall marks frō number one & vpward this is that sid of the street fence which belongs to ther planting lots not the other sid

Richard Clarke begines at south Corner. ends at   I
John Dresser from the marke one and ends at   II
Hugh Chapline end at Number   III
Peter Cowper ends at Number   IIII
John Burbanke ends at Number   V
Thomas Pallmer ends at Number   VI
James Barker ends : at Number   VII
William Jackson ends : at Number   VIII
Hugh Smyth ends at Number   VIIII
John Trumble ends at Number   X
John Boynton ends at Number   XI
William Boynton ends at Number   XII
Thomas Dickinson ends at Number   XIII
Joseph Jewit ends at Number   XIIII
Maximillian Jewit ends at Number   XV
John Grant ends at Number   XVI
Lennerd Harryman ends at Number   XVII
George Kilburne ends at Number   XVIII

   The Record of the seuerall Devisions of fence belongen to that feild Cald Comanly Bradforth street planting Lots Giuen in by John Trumble the marke is at end of each part of fence
Richard Clarke begines at the Corner twelue rail Length   I
John Dresser Thirteene rail Lengths ends at   II
Hugh Chapline Thirteene rale Lengths ends at   III
Petter Cowper Twenty six rale Lengths ends at   IIII
   he hath ye lot of Thomas Elethorp

John Burbauke Thirteene rale Lengths ends at   V
Thomas Pallmer Thirteene rale Lengths at   VI
James Barker Thirteene rale Lengths ends at   VII
William Jackson Twelue rale Lengths ends at   VIII
Hugh Smith Twelue rale Lengths ends at   VIIII
John Trumble Thirteene rale Lengths at   X
John Boynton Thirteene rale Lengths at   XI
William Boynton Ten rale Lengths ends at Corner   post
The fence aboue roiten is the south sid now foloweth
The head fence
Richard Clarke begines at the Corner of the head fence
    and hath eleuen rale lengths ending at ....number I
John Dresser Nine rale Lengths ends at number   II
Hugh Chapline Nine rale Lengths ends at............   III
Petter Cowper Twenty rale Lengths ends at..........   IIII
John Burbanke Nine rale Lengths ends at............   V
Thomas Pallmer Ten rale Lengths ends at............   VI
James Barker Nine rale Lengths ends at..............   VII
William Jackson Nine rale Lengths ends at...........   VIII
Hugh Smith Eleuen rale Lengths ends at..   VIIII
John Trumble Nine rale Lengths end at..............   X
John Boynton Nine rale Lengths ends at..............   XI
William Boynton Nine rale Lengths ends at...........   XII
Thomas Dickinson Nine rale Lengths end at..........   XIII
Joseph Jewit Nine rale Lengths ends at..............   XIIII
Maximilian Jewit Nine rale Lengths ends at..........   XV
at the North Corner of the fence toward the oxe pastur
Thomas Dickinson begines at Cornerpost Twelue
    Lengths ends at...............................   XVI
Joseph Jewit Twelue rale Lengths ends at............   XVII
Mamimillian Jewit Twelue rale Lengths ends at.......   XVIII
John Grant   ends at.............   XVIIII
Lennard Harryman   ends at.............   XX
George Kilburne end at the end of the fence

    The Devisions of fence in the feild Cald Ipswich lots are as
foloweth

    1 Captaine Brigam fence begines at a white oake tree
marke at the roott with the mark one : eighty five lenths
next to hugh smith and mighill hopkinson land laid out
for them one the south east sid of the swampe below
ther houses
    I

2   Widow Barker Turnes the corner by Ipswich high ⎫ II
way from the marke II seuentie three rale lengths   ⎭

3   Elder Rainer beegines at the marke............   III
And hath sixty rale Lengths the fence Comes homeward

4   Deacon Mighell begines at marke..............   IIII
and goees about the Corner Towards Isaack Cousens
fifty six lenths

5   Widow Brocklbanke begines at the mark.......   V
Twentie foure lenth and Turnes the Corner by Isaac
Cousens goeing to mark six

6   Mathew Boyes begines at marke   VI
and soe alonge to Braddforth street Twentie Three Length

7   Leauetenant Reminton begines at the post marke.   VII
and soe to the post marked eight Twenty four rale Lengths

8   John Pickard begines at the marke.............   VIII
and soe alonge to the home lot of sister grant Twenty
four lenth and ends at the marke ner the bridg by
Richard Wickam house   VIIII

It is ordered that he or they who are appoynted to be
Marshalls to gather fynes and forfetures : they shall bee all by him
or them fathfully gathered vp (after he them or they haue
reseiued a warrant frō The select men) with in the space of fourteen dayes And shall pay them into the Constable withing the fore
said tyme and shall haue thre pence the shilling for his labour.
and incase the Marshall bee Defectiue in any part of his office he
shall bee lyable to pay for euery neglect two shilling :

It is ordered that for thee better obseruation of the orders of
the towne : the ouerseers who are yearly Chosen by the towne to
looke to high wayes shall see to the performance of all the orders of
the towne. or any other that shall bee made by the select men and
shall faithfully performe the said office and wher any two of them
shall find the breach of any towne order. They shall giue it in
vnder ther hands vnto some one or more of the Select men. and
thes they shall doe the same day or the day following and allsoe to
giue notice to the offender withing the same time and in case the
ouerseers be defectiue in any part of ther ofice they shall pay for
euery defect three shillings :

Publik Charges for the year past 1650

brother Paratt 2 day goen to Salem & to Ipsich		4^s . 6	
Jury brother Parrat one day	o	1 . o	
broth Maxe Jewitt 3 dayes	o	3 . o	
brother langhorne 4 days......................	o	4 . o	
Will Jackson 4 days	o	4 . o	
John Pearson 4 days..........................	o	4 . o	
grand Jury deacon Mighell 2 day & half	o	2 . 6	
Leautent Reminton the same..................	o	2 . 6	
Will Asee the same tyme.....................	o	2 . 6	
Hugh Smith the same........................	o	2 . 6	

Richard Swane Captaine Brigam and Sameull Brocklbanke each of them 5 shillings for Runng lyne twixt } 0—15 . 0
Ipsich & betwixt newbury

half day newbury fence Rich Swane...................	o	– o – 9	
for laying out fence ——half fence laying..............	1	2	
Decon Mighell——2 day...........................	o	3 . 4	
the Charges of the 5 men			
the Captaine	o	13 . 4	
Thomas Barker.............................	o	13 . 4	
the other 3 of them........................	3	o . o	
Thomas Abate 2 wolves...........................	2	o . o	
5 fockes.....................................	o	12	6
Hew Smith & Samvell Brokell.......................	o . 3 . o		
Joseph Jewit for lay out fence......................	3 . o		
John Smith the same............................	3 . o		
John Smith and John pearson ten dayes..............	o	15 . o	
John pearson for warning meetins and such publike service.	o	10 +	
Will Boynton for warneing meetings & goein to andifer..	o	9 +	
Item for focses John Brokellbanke the number 18.......	2	05 +	
Samvell Brokellbanke one wolfe.....................	1 – o +		
Thomas Miller.................................	2 – 6		
for goen to Ipswich Decon Mighell...................	o	1 – 2	
for maintainance of Mill dame men..................	o	10 – o	
To Thomas Miller for fenceing hors paster & ten pound			
lent ....15 – o –oo			
to Math Boyes for 5 weeks at Court..................	1–10 – o		
Captaine Brigame for the same service...............	1–10 – o		
for horses hir thre tymes to court to Bro Boyes	0–12 – o		
to Ipswich	0–1 – 9		
to brother Boyes for carage of towne about Powder......	0–13 – o		

all comes to 34 Pounds........ 18 – 05

the Rait laid this year for the towens vse.............. 35 – 4 –3

Contrey Rait this year is......·.....................23 – 4 –11
    Sinc : to alow   to John Reminton..... 0 – 2 – 0
                    to John Spoford ...... 0 –13 – 0
                    to Will Tenne........ 0 – 3 – 4
                    to John Scales···.... 0 – 1 – 0

Janevary the third 50 at a Towne meeting the Select then Chose for this yeare folowing
    Mathew Boyes John Trumble Thomas Leauer
    Constabl the same that was
    Ouerseers Joh Smith Edward hasen hugh Chaplin Samcull Brocklbank
    Marshall Will Law
    for warning Towne Meeting Thomas Teny who is allsoe to call towne meetings William Stickney William Boynton
    pinder John pallmer

At a towne [meeting] held the 12 day of the 2ᵈ moneth 1651
    It was Agreed and Voated that wheras ther was some vpland to the value of 359 acres lacking to make vp all the two acree lotts and the Greater lotts equall to the lotts called the acre and half lotts :
    That the fore said land should bee laid out vnto the seuerall lotts aboue mentioned in these places folowing Imprimes that the two acre lotts at the lower end of the towne shall lie at the plaine next beyond Mr Dumers on the Cowecomons and are to haue an acre and halfe for euery acre wanting at home to make them equall to the acre & half lots 2ly That ther shall bee laid out a plaine about a mile and halfe beyond that : Containeing about two hundred acres and it is agreed that those who ly ther shall haue two acres for one
3ᵈly it is agreed

At a Towne meeting held the 23ᵗʰ of the 2ᵈ moneth 1651
    It was granted by the towne that that parcell of ground which once was giuen vnto John Hill vpon Condition of his abyding in the Towne and doing seruice to the Towne he being now remoued from the Towne should be henceforth Thomas Burbies he satisfying John Hill for the Cost of fence and agreeing with the 3 men for the ground

At a towne meeting held the 12 of the 3ᵈ moneth 1651 it was agreed That the acre and half lotts shold haue each of them freely giuen two acres of vpland and this to be laid out as convenently for each of them as the layers out appoynted for the towne shall Judge fitt to doe the men apoynted thervnto are Thomas mighel frances parrat Joseph Jew,it mathew boyes & Richard Swan or any 4 of them

At a Towne meeting held the 19 day of the tenth moneth 1651 it was agreed vnto by the Towne that Mathew Boys should lay downe 4 acres of meadow which is att Cow Bridge : for and in Consideration of the same it was graunted to him to haue a peace of salt marsh which lyeth at the end of his owne at Mᵗ dumers farme or the farme soe Called and to haue the rest of his meadow in the Contry to make vp that peace equall to the aforesayd meadow layd downe and it was granted that the layers out of this meadow should determine how much he should haue for his meadow soe layd downe allsoe it was graunted that what meadow is due to him to make his lot equal in proportion vnto the acre and half lotts should be layed out with the other forenamed meadow Prouyded that this Meadow be not layed out of that meadow about the Pen or neere the playne :

December the 19ᵗʰ

Chosen for prudentiall men

Francis Parratt William asie Hugh Smith William Boynton Samuell Brocklebank

Ouerseers Edward Hasen William Teny Hugh Chaplin John Boynton

Marshall William Law

Constable John Pickard

+ + + + + + + + +

+ + + + + + +

Whereas there is an order + + + + + +
1648 for the bounding of + + + + + +
with holes stakes and stones and also + + + +
in november 1650 for the bounding of + + + +
in like manner neither of which hauing been prosecuted to full efect it is therefor further agreed and ordered : that euery man shall bound all his said lands meadows and fences at the Corners before the last of the first moneth next ensueing as followeth to wit with

a hole of one foot wide at least and a stake about the thicknes of the small of a mans legg or a hart of some oaken bolt which shall be driuen downe into the said hole : and lay also a stone in the hole at the foot of the stake and if any man shall faile soe to bound the same he shall forfeit the sum of fiue shillings for euery peec of fence meadow and vpland not soe bounded :

Wee the inhabitants of the Town of rowley having Chosen francis Parrat Richard Swan and Joseph Jewet to determine the bounds betwixt man and man where the stakes are falne and the bounds lost doe hereby giue power to them soe to doe. and what shall be by them so determined according to the aforesaid premises we doe hereby bynd our selues to stand to it as a finall determination of any such bounds :

It is ordered that Thomas Mighell Joseph Jewet Richard Swan and John Smith shall haue power to proportion to euery man that hath laid $+$ $+$ their Comon fence where and what quantity shall be laid vpon their lands lying within the northeast field Proportionable to other mens lands lying in the same field as also to lay fence to John Palmers six Acres he bought of Mr Carlton and to some land granted to Joseph Jewet Joining or near to John Palmers in Case they have none or not proportionable to their acres of land as other men haue :

An order to be made Conserning the wages of the towne Mowers to have 20d a day Labering men to have 18d a day in Summer : in tow months in winter to have 14d a day that is october and nouember, 3 months that is in december January and febuary : to have 12d a day. Reapers and other tradsmen, excepting Taylors, to have the same wages

At a Towne meeting held the 26th of the 11th moneth 1651 it was graunted vnto John Harris by the Towne that he should haue a peece of ground a rod wyde that lyes vpon the 2 acres of land which he bought of Capt Briggam at the Ware house lots next the old fence and it is to run the lenth of the 2 acres and noe further :

At the fore named meeting also vnto Charles Browne was graunted by the towne a peece of salt marsh about an acre in the roome of some planting ground that was due to him which marsh lyeth by some he had before at the shadd Creek

At that Town meeting held about nouember last 1651 When Charels browne had the graunt of his planting ground to be layd out at the place wher [Asps] doe grow befor the lot of richard Swan and John Scaels: ther was graunted vnto John Trumble a peece of Meadow which lyes at the Corner of his owne Marsh and at the end of James Balley beyond the Sandy Bridge

Towne Charges for the year past 1651

```
    +     +     +     +   for vewing fences
 +   +   +   +   +   +   ............... 0 – 5 – 3
 +   +   +   +   Brockellbanke............... 0 – 5 – 3
 +   +   +   ning the lyne...................... 0 – 5 – 0
```

Warning 20 tymes of town meeting................... 0 –13 – 4
Thomas teny alsoe for Caling .... 0 – 3 – 8
       Alsoe for a foxe .... 0 – 2 – 0
for the seruice of the 3 men.......................... 4 – 4 – 0
for Joseph Jewet.................................... 2 – 5 – 6
for William boynton................................ 0 – 9 –10
       allsoe to William boynton...................... 0 – 1 – 0
for Samuell Stickney............................... 0 – 6 – 6
for Mathew Boys................................... 0 – 9 – 3
for Edward Hasen and John Smith.................... 0 –16 – 6
for John Smith for going to Court.................... 0 – 4 – 6
       alsoe for Edward Hasen the lyke worke .... 0 – 3 – 6
for John Tod being on the Jurye..................... 0 – 4 – 0
for William Law 4 days .... 0 – 4 – 0
for Daniell Harris 4 days one half.................... 0 – 4 – 6
for Richard Swan................................... 0 – 4 – 6
for William Asie................................... 0 – 2 – 0
for John Spoferd for a horse......................... 0 – 2 – 0
for Francis Parrat.................................. 0 –10 – 0
       alsoe for tyme about Plum Iland .... 0 – 1 – 6
       alsoe for one day in laying the rate............. 0 – 1 – 6
for antony Crosby and John trumble goiing with hoggs
       to the neck..................................... 0 – 1 – 4
for John Trumble measuring the measures............. 0 – 2 – 0
for Thomas Miller about the mill .... 0 –10 – 0
for John Trumble his Keeping the booke.............. 0 – 6 – 8
       alsoe for wryting the Court order............... 0 – 1 – 0
for Thomas Leauer.................................. 0 – 1 – 6

memorandum disburst by Joseph Jewet about damadge
done to goodman Symons by the calues......... 0 –10 – 0
for Deacken Jewet going to Court.,.................... 2 – 6 – 8
for 14 foxes thomas Abbot.......................... 1 –15 – 0
for 3 Sumer days at court to John Pickard .... 0 – 3 – 0
for John Pickard on day about the lyne................ 0 – 2 – 0
for warning to bring in wayghts and measurs by Thomas
dickinson .... 0 –01 – 0
alsoe for takeing in contry rate 2 dayes........... 0 –03 – 0
alsoe for + + prosecutiõ ad a warrant seruice. 0 – 4 – 6
alsoe for going about newberye way............. 0 – 2 – 0
alsoe for a foxe that thomas thirill got .... 0 – 2 – 6
for Deackon myghell 2 dayes of the grand Jury......... 0 – 2 – 0
+ + about the towns brooke on day................ 0 – 1 – 6
+ + about the diuision of lands half a day.......... 0 – 0 – 9
+ + for one day into the Contry
+ + + + Mr Payn and for a horse .... 0 – 4 – 0
+ + + Hugh Smith and Samuell Brocklbank going
to Pentucket .... 0 – 6 – 0

16th of 12— 1651

Wheras their is hurt done yearly by Cattell eating and treading
on mens Rye in the northeast field in winter time vpon sudden
thaughes and at breaking vp of frosts at spring it is therrfore ordered
that if any Cattle be found within the said fild after the Publishing
hereof that it shall be lawfull for the Pinder to put them in the Pen
and to be paid for poundage as for Cattle in other places as also the
owners are hearby lyable to all damages done by any such Cattle
on mens Corne It is also ordered that no herds man or other shall
breake the aforesaid field after Indian hath + + + +
without liberty from the Selectmen
+ + + + + for any such + + +
+ + + + hereby declared that if any + +
oxen on the night or pt of it they shall be looked vpon as breakers
of this order and bee lyable to the aforesaid penalty

It is ordered Concerning the said field that all Cattle shall be
againe restrained from going into the same after the 20th of the
9th moneth and if any shall put his Cattle into it such Cattle shall
be lyable to be impounded and to pay damage as aforesaid.

The fifth of the first moneth 1652

It was graunted by the Towne that Edward Sauer Nickolas Jackson Richard Lighton and Jane Grant should haue each of them giuen one Cow gate : also that Richard Holmes should haue giuen vnto him on fourth part of a Cow gate :

At a towne meeting helld march the eight 1652 it was agreed that ffrancis Parrat thomas Dickinson and John trumble should apoint and layout High wayes to mens meadowes that had or haue none as yet laid out to them and giue vnto such men as haue ther meadowes Impaired by the lieing out of these wayes vpland in the Roome of vpland and meadow in the roome of meadow

At a meeteing held the 11th of March 1652 that the 3 men Chosen for laying out of High ways on the 8 of march shall also haue poure to lay out to those that haue meadow in long meadow and also John trumble for his bachieler meadow that in Concideration of that claus that these meadows will lie in fence in as much as they shall in ther judgment think fit for Recompence and to lay it out at the end of ther deuisions of salt marsh at the farme called Mr Dumers farme

At the forenamed meeting the 11th of March 1652 it was granted vnto Mr Samuell phillips 18 acers of marsh bought of Mr Woodman of newbery liing beyond Eastons Riuer

The 15th of first moneth 1652

Whereas there is hurt done yearly towards the spring time on Mens meadows by horses puting or being in the farme beyond the northeast field : and that we did intend the restraining of them as well as other Cattell in that order Concerning the field It is therefore ordered and this day declared that all mares horses and Colts shall be restrained from the aforesaid farm after this time vntill the select men giue leaue and if any mans mare horse or Colt be found thereon it shall be lawfull for any man to impound them and the owners shall pay for their poundadge three times soe much as for other Cattell that are found any where Contrary to order :

+   +   +   +   +   +

Hugh Chaplin

Cowes ——1	4 –10 – 0
heifer 3 yer old	3 –15 – 0
one ster of 3 yer old	4 –00 – 0
of 2 yer old ——2	5 – 0 – 0
yearing——1	1 –10 – 0
oxen——2	12 – 0 – 0
Swyne of one yer——2	1 –10 – 0
land 4 acres at home	12 – 0 – 0
at bactelors plain——1	2 – 0 – 0
vnbrok vp——Batc'es	1 – 0 – 0
Meadow 4 acres	2 –13 – 4
gates——2	1 – 0 – 0
	50 – 8 – 4

Thomas dickinson

Cowes——6	27– 0 – 0
heifer of 3 yer old 1	3–15 – 0
of 2 year old——3	7– 0 – 0
one yearing	1–10 – 0
oxen——2	12– 0 – 0
one hors of 2 year	10– 0 – 0
one half of 3 year	7– 0 – 0
land at home 5 acres	15– 0 – 0
at prospect hill——3	7–10 – 0
meadow· 10 acres	6–13 – 4
gates——4 one halfe	12– 0 – 0
	109– 8 – 4

William Jackson

Cowes——3	13–10 – 0
heifer 3 yers——1	3–15 – 0
one of 2 yer old	2–10 – 0
one yering	1–10 – 0
Swyne of a yeare——2	1–10 – 0
gates——2	1– 0 – 0
land at home 4 acrs	12– 0 – 0
vnbroak vp 2 acres	0–13 – 4

meadow——6 acres	4- 0 - 0
house	12- 0 - 0
	52- 8 - 4

Richard Clarke

Cowes——2	9- 0 - 0
of 2 year——2	5- 0 - 0
of yearings——2	3- 0 - 0
land at home 3 acres	9- 0 - 0
at plane ac an halfe	3- 0 - 0
meadow——4 acres	2-13 - 4
gates one an half	0-15 - 0
swine of a yer——2	1-10 - 0
house	4- 0 - 0
	37-18 - 4

John burbank

Cowes——2	9- 0 - 0
heifer of 3 yer	3-15 - 0
one stere of 2 year old	2-10 - 0
yearing——2	3- 0 - 0
Swine of a year——2	1-10 - 0
land——3 acr brok	9- 0 - 0
of vnbroken——3 acr	1- 0 - 0
+ + + + + +	4-13 - 0
house	4- 0 - 0
	38- 8 - 0

Peter Cooper

Cowes——4	18- 0 - 0
oxen——2	12- 0 - 0
of 2 year——2	5- 0 - 0
of yearings——3	4-10 - 0
Swine of a yer——2	1-10 - 0
land at home——5	17- 0 - 0
and at bachelors one acre	2- 6 - 8
and unbroak——7 acrs	
meadow——5	3- 6 - 8
gates——2	1- 0 - 0
house	8- 0 - 0
	72-13 - 4

Thomas Palmer

Cowes——4	13–10 – 0
one of 3 year	3–15 – 0
one of 2 yeare	2–10 – 0
one yearing	1–10 – 0
swine of a yeare——2	1–10 – 0
land at home 3 acres	9– 0 – 0
vntild——3 acres	1– 0 – 0
meadow 4 acres	2–13 – 4
gates——2	1– 0 – 0
house	7– 0 – 0
	43– 8 – 4

William Boynton

Cowes——4	18– 0 – 0
one of 2 yeare	
yearings——2	3– 0 – 0
one sow	1– 6 – 8
3 of one year	2– 5 – 0
meadow 6 acres	4– 0 – 0
2 acres at home	7– 0 – 0
broadforth lots 3 acres	11– 5 – 0
——3 quarters	
at plaine——one acre	2– 0 – 0
vntild one acre one quarter	0– 8 – 4
gates——2	1– 0 – 0
hous barne	6–10 – 0
	56–15 – 0

Deackon Jewet

Cowes——6	27– 0 – 0
one 3 yearing	3–15 – 0
of 2 yearings——2	5– 0 – 0
yearings——4	6– 0 – 0
3 swine of a yere	2– 5 – 0
half of a 3 yer old hors	7– 0 – 0
one of 2 yer old	10– 0 – 0
Ass——one	4– 0 – 0
land at home 3 acrs an hal	10–10 – 0

at plaine——4 acres hal.............................. 9– 0 – 0
meadow——10 acres..,............................... 6–13 – 4
gates——4 one half................................. 2– 5 – 0
housing ....,............12– 0 – 0

                                                105– 8 – 4

      John boynton
Cowes——3...13–10 – 0
heifer of 3 years..................................... 3–15 – 0
one steer of 2 years.................................. 2–10 – 0
one yearing swine.................................... 0–15 – 0
land at home 2 acre one h........................... 6–15 – 0
vntild——3 acres.....................................· 1– 0 – 0
meadow 4 acres....................................·.............. 2–13 – 4
gates——2.. 1– 6 – 8
house.. 5–10 – 0

                                                37–15 – 0

At a Towne meeting held the 8th day of the 8th moneth 1652 it was graunted by the Towne that the ten pounds which formerly was promised by them should be payd vnto the Deackons within a moneths warning by them giuen whether they shall need it to build or to purchase a house for the vse of Mrs shov

At the afore named meeting it was alsoe agreed vnto by the Towne that Mr Rodgers should haue for his labour in the minestry three score pounds in the yeare.

Accounts receiued from the Constable   +   +   +   + day of the tenth moneth 1652 and due from him to the Towne 37–1 t–9

Memorandom at a towne meeting held the 29 of 10th mounth 1652

Agreed by the towne that the 5 Select men then in being with ffrancis Parret and Matthew Boyes ar to draw vp the towne Grant and agreement with all the prtickullers therof wth the men that set downe at Pentuckit and also to Confirme and conclud the same acording to the abouesaid agreement

Wheras the Couenant made betwixt Robert Haseltine, William Wild, & John Haseltine on their pt and the Towne of Rowley on the other pt in the yeare one thousand six hundred forty nine at their goeing to sit downe at Merrimack was too Implicitely drawne vp both in regard of what vplands meadowes & other accomodations they were to haue of the Towne; wherin they were to be limited by the Towne, as also what they were to be tyed to doe for the said Towne of Rowley in Consideration of the aforesaid land meadow & other their accomodations by Couenant wᵗʰ the aforesaid Towne granted to them. It was therfore ordered by the Towne aforesaid at the request of the said Robert William & John at a lawfull Towne meeting held the third day of the ffourth moneth 1651 that the Select men then in being to witt Mathew Boyes, John Trumble, and Thomas Leauer should be desired to treate with the said Robert William and John about that aforenamed Couenant in the Townes behalfe, & so to draw up in writeing both what the said Towne of Rowley had granted to them and what in Consideratiō of that their said grant they were to expect from yᵐ wᶜʰ was by them pformed according to their presant light. It being yet vpon further Consideratiō found out that the true intent of the Townes grant to them was not Clearly & fully kⁿ it was therfore ordered by the said Towne of Rowley at a lawfull Towne meeting held the 29 day of the 10ᵗʰ moneth 1652 vpon debate with the aforesaid Robert, William & John. That Mathew Boyes & ffrancis Parrat with the Select men then in being Viz: Richard Swan William Stickney William Hobson Samuell Brockelbanke & William Tenny should againe draw up the Couenant & agrement wᶜʰ was formerly made betwixt the said Towne of Rowley. & the said Robert William & John in all the pticulars of it, according to what was at that meeting acknowledged both by the Towne and the said ptyes to be the true intent and meaning of that originall Compact and Couenant made betwixt the said Towne of Rowley and the said Robert William & John in the yeare 1649. And that a ffinall issue might be put to the said busines power was then given by the Towne to the aforesaid Comitte of Select men wᵗ Mathew Boyes and ffrancis Parrat to determine and Conclude on their behalfe wᵗ was the true grant of the Towne to them as also what was their Ingagement to the Towne and it is agreed to be as ffolloweth

Impˢ that the Towne of Rowley hath Granted to the said Robert Haseltine William Wilde and John Haseltine each of them ffourty Acres of vpland to be laid out to them as Conueniently as may be wᵗʰout the great preiudice & damage of the Towne

2^{ly} the said Towne of Rowley hath granted to the aforesaid ptyes each of them to haue Com̄ons for twenty head of Cattle wch said Com̄ons they haue liberty to ffence wholly or in p^t as they see cause. Prouided that the said Towne of Rowley doth declare that they did restraine them from liberty to erect any more then thre Tenements vpon any p^t of the aforesaid vpland or Com̄ons.

3^{ly} the Towne hath Granted to each of them twenty Acres of meadow and this meadow and Vpland to be laid out to them when they shall desire it, vnlesse some prouidence of God shall hinder.

4^{ly} they haue liberty Granted to gett each of them a thousand of pipestaues yearely dureing the space of seauen years which said time was to begin in the yeare 1649.

5^{ly} they are to haue liberty on the Com̄ons to Cutt fire wood for three familyes as also to Cutt timber for building and so for ffenceing for the takeing in of their said ground prouided that they are. not to ffall any ffenceing stuffe wthin a quarter of a mile of the Pasture ffence

6^{ly} they are to be ffreed from all Charges belonging to the Town for their Lands and houses and each of them ffoure oxen six Cowes and ffoure Calues dureing the space of seauen yeares wch yeares were to begin in the yeare 1649.

lastly they are to haue liberty to keepe swine on the Com̄ons.

In Consideratiō of all the aforesaid pticulars granted by the aboue said Towne of Rowley to the aforesaid Robert, William and John their heirs and assigns they haue Couenanted with the said Towne for them selues their heirs and assignes suffeciently to looke to the hird of Cattle that the Towne of Rowley shall put into the pasture dureing the time of seauen yeares which said time was to begin in the yeare 1649. Prouided that the Cattle be two yeares old and vpward that the Towne shall put into the said pasture Prouided also that the Towne shall giue them 2^s a day for so much time as they shall spend alooking to the said pasture

2^{ly} the said Robert William and John doe Couenant with the Towne to prouide Conuenient Dyet and lodging at indifferent tearmes to any that the Towne shall send to keepe any hird their.

In witnes that this present writeing is vnanimously assented vnto on both ptyes namely the aboue said Select men wth Mathew Boyes & ffrancis Parrat on the Townes behalfe, and Robert Haseltine William Wilde and John Haseltine on their p^t to be a true draught of the mutuall Couenant betwixt the said Robert John and William and the Towne of Rowley concerning their settleing at Merrimack in the yeare 1649 we the aforesaid Comittee of the Towne wᵗʰ the said Robert William and John haue Joyntly subscribed our hands this present 30ᵗʰ day of the tenth moneth 1652

ffrancis Parrat

Robert Haseltine   Mathew Boyes
William Wild   Richard Swan

his marke   William Hobson
John + Heseltine
                         his marke
                         William | Stickney
                         Samuell Brockelbanke
                         William Tenny

At a towne meeting Held the 14ᵗʰ of the 12ᵗʰ 1652 it was granted by the towne that William Scalles Will Stickney and James Barker should Haue that peece of Rough medow that lieth at the end of ther acres of Rough marsh at that deuision by the cowbridg to be vnto them for a hie way to come into ther meadow soe as they may not prejudice any others mans meadow but keepe vbon ther owen and that to be vnto each of them vpon a line acording vnto the lines of ther acres prouided it preiudice none that was laid out before this grant

At the affore named meetting it was also by the towne granted that John dreser should Inioy the grase growing on the hieway that Runes along by his acre of salte marsh to the oyster point: vntill the towne thinke good to dispose of it other ways

At a towne meeting held the 25 of 1 Mounth 1653 It was agreed vpon and votted that ffrancis Parret Joseph Jewett and Hugh Smith from the towne and in the name therof should Haue full poure to agre with those whom Ipswich or topsfeild shall apoint to that purpose and with them to determine and also to sett the bounds of the line that is betwixt our towne and them and ther determination to be the finall determination

At the Same meeting it was also agreed and votted that Richard Swan John Pickard and Samuell Brockelbanke should haue full poure in the name of towne to determine the line Betwene Nubery and vs and to fixe the ffinall Bounds with those that they shall apoint to that purpose in the name of ther towne

Defectiue fence giuen in by vs ouerseers at the south side of bradforth street feild

Inpˢ Richard Clarke 2 lenth

Hugh Chaplin 2 lenth
Peter Couper 2 lenth
at the head fence Richard Clarke 1 lenth
Hugh Chaplin 3 lenth
peter Couper 6 lenth
James Barker 4 lenth
Hugh Smith 2 lenth
John Bointon 2 lenth
at north sid Gorge Kilborne 2 lenth
Bachelor feild fence Gorge Kilborne on lenth
Joseph Jewet 3 lenths John grant 1 lenth
Hugh Smith 2 lenths Will Bointon 1 lenth
Richard Clarke 4 lenth
at the sid by leuetenant
Will Stickney 1 lenth
Peter couper 2 lenths in his street fence
Hugh Chaplin on in the same fence
John dreser 2 lenth in the street fence
Richard Clarke 2 lenth in the same
at north sid of Bradforth street hill
Will Stickney 10 lenth and in the same fence
leuetenant 1 lenth

Thomas Dickanson
Wiliam Jacson

Cowes in 53

		heifers
Richard clarke	3	1
John Dreser	4	
John Grant	3	1
Petter Couper	4	1
John Burbanke	3	
Thomas Pallmer	3	1
Will Jackson	4	
Hugh Smith	4	
John Trumble	5	
John Bointon	4	1
Thomas Dickenson	3	
Hugh Chaplin	4	1
Max Jewett	4	2
Richard Wickam	4	1

John Pickard	4	1
Vxor Crosbie	2	
Sam Plats	2	
Will Bointon	4	2
Will Hobson	3	
Leauetennant	6	
James Barker	3	
Samuell Stickney	3	
Will Scalles	3	2
Leanard Harriman	4	2
Gorge Kilborne	3	3
Matthew Boyes	5	3
+ + Brokelbanke	3	
Deacon Mighill	6	2
Elder rainer	6	
Will Stickney	5	1
widow Grant	2	1
	116	

Paid the heards men for 12 weeks kepeing
Charges besids paid
due to Gorge Kilborne for burneing woods 4^s—4^d
to Richard Wickam paid kepeing 1^s—4
due to Gorge Kilborne 4–4–6 due to John Grant 4–4–6
due to Richard Wickam 0–5–0
Cowes went out vnder the keepeing of Gorge Kilborne &
John Grant in yeare 53 vpon the 25 of aprill
Young cattell vnder the keepeing of Andrew Hiden
vpon the 26 of same mth
Cowes at the east end of towne vnder the keepeing of
Jonathan plats on the 21 of the same mth
Callues giuen in
Inprimis Richard Clarke.......1
John Burbanke.......3
John Dreser.........2
Peter Couper........1
Leiuetenat Remington.3

Charges for Cattell this yeare by John heseltine for corne
to toll of the boar   +   +   +   one day his
man helpe. to seck ouer the cattell with andrew now
at latter end of year........................... 1 – 2 – 6

John Bointon a day at pen minding Cattel on day drive.
    to farme and boy 1 day........................   1 – 6
Samuell Mighill 1 day and halfe......................
and deacon Mighill a day and horse..................
Hugh Chaplin 2 dayes kepeing at farme..............
3 dayes seeke. catell John Pearson on day ....
John Mighill on day Keping........................ o – 3 – o
Will Wild 7 dayes halfe and his boy 6 dayes..........
Richard Clarke 1 day at pen Samuel Stickney a day at
    farme..   2

William Hobson John Pickard Thomas Dickinson William
Tenney John Smith Are chosen to order the affaires of the towne
for the yeare ensuing vpon the 16th of December 1653
    ffor Counstable Thomas Leauer
    for marshall Thomas Tenney
    for ouerseers James Bayley John Person John Bointon Petter
Couper
    ffor pinder Charles Browne
    for calling towne meetings Thomas Teney
    ffor warneing John Trumble Tobiah Collman John Tenney

At a towne meeting Held the 16th of 10th mounth 1653 granted
and voted that John pallmer should haue that acre of Salt marsh be
it more or lesse lieing beyond his deuision of salt marsh by the
Creeke commonly called Shad Creeke bounded by the Creeke on
onsid and on the Riuer by the other side. He paying to the towne
the true and just some of 20 shillings
    At a towne meeting Held the 16th of 10th mounth 1653 granted
vnto John pickard that in concideration of one acre and 10 rod of
land by him bought of Icaac Cousens, that falls with in the bounds
of Ipswich and ther for cannot be assured him, it is ther for Agreed
vpon by the towne that thomas mighill and John Smith should in
the behalfe of the towne lay out a parcell of land lieing at the
southeast corner of that feild that lieth beyond the far end of the
West end oxpaster as alsoe to lay out a grant of two acres giuen
vnto the acre and halfe lots by the towne the which percells of
land the afore said men shall lay out vnto the said John pickard
either of that land or meadow by it acording to ther discresion as
also to lay out to him at the same place for 3 quarters of and acre
that is a wanting to the acre and halfe lott he bought of the same
Icaac Cousens

At a towne meeeting Held the 16th of the 10th month 1653 Granted and voted that hugh Chaplin should haue that acre of land that was laid out by the men Chosen for laying out that deuision of land to make vp the greater lotts equall to the acre and halfe lots lieing at the north sid of the plaine at the end of the west end ox paster and this is giuen vpon concideration of the defaults of his home lott

At a generall and legall Towne meeting held the 2d of the 11th month 53 it was agreed that Joseph Jewet Thomas Mighill Mathew Boys Thomas Dickinson and John pickard shall vew and proportion all the lands apoynted for a uillage within the bounds of Rowley vnto the inhabitants of the same towne acording to purchase : the selected men aboue said shall like wise butt and bound the said uillage and make report of it vnto the towne and soe it may be Recorded

agreed with andrew to mend pentucket fence and make it substanciall and is to set vp or leaue by ye fence side 200 posts and 300 railes all new both posts and Railes and we promised him six pounds fiue shillings for soe doeing and is 6 – 05 – 00

it is ordered that if any steeres or oxen be kept at home this 54 and not for drawing or working if they be found with the Cows it shall be lawfull for any man to impound them and the owner of the said Cattle shall pay 6d a beast vnto the party impounding for euery beast of his soe impounded

at a generall and legall towne meeting held the first of June 54 leeftenant Reminton an william Hobson were added vnto that Comittee of the six men formerly Chosen for the laying forth of all + + + for the making up of the former deuisions which is still wanting

at the same meeting Thomas Abbot added vnto the Comittee for laying out the farmers land at pentucket : alsoe James Barker added to Deacon mighill for the hearing delinquents Causes

Wheras we haue from time to time great damage Done by newbury Catle at the farme comonly called Mr Dumers farme notwithstanding any provision that hitherto haue bene made for the prevention wherof now it is ordered that the fence shall be made

vp to turn all orderly Cattle by the twenty fift of march next insueing and that the ouerseers for that farme shall veiw the same
withing one day or two after: and this fence shall be made with a
three rail fence substanciall and strong by the twenty fift of the
second moneth and the ouersseers shall view it as soun after this
day as before only At this second time ther they are to try the
fence both posts and rails by shaking and if any mans fence ther
vpon fall: they shall prop it vp and that night giue notice vnto
the Delinquents which if they repaire it (the next Day or the Day
folowing if that Day be saboth) then they shall not for that time
be fined and if any be Defectiue hering they shall for euery lenth
of rails not acording to this order be fined one shilling the ouerseers shall veiw at other time when they shall hear of any fence
Downe

Moreover it is ordered that if any Swine shall come into the
farme caled Mr Dumer farme or feild called the northeast feild not
being suficently yoaked and ringed that is to say 2 foot one way
and twenty Inches another they shall pay two shillings poundage
each hog or doubl dammage at the damnifed partys choyse

for all other feilds and inclosurs whering hurt is done by swine
if the swine be not suficently yoaked and ringed as before mentioned
then the swine shall pay half the Damages and all necessary charges
about the poundinge and the other half of the Dammage shall be laid
vpon next defectiue place of fence wher the hurt is done vnles y^e
place befound wher they came in and it shall be laid vpon them

June the 13 daye
Vpon information of the great and vnnaturall Abuse of some
Mail Asses with mares especially one of William Scails to the
dammage of Diuers persons among vs: it is ordered and this day
declared that the abouesaid Asse or any other known to vse the
forsaid practizes (after the select men or the maior part of them
shall haue giuen warning to the owner or owners of the said asse or
asses) shall be found in cow comans or any other comman pasturs
farther off or ner the owner or owners of any such asse shall 5
shillings by the day half to the towne and half to any that doe
impound the said asse or asses and if such persen cannot pound the
asse or asses if they bring in testymony that the asses or asse wer
seen in any The Comans abouesaid the Whol fiue shall be paid as
if they or he had beene impounded

At a generall and legall towne meeting held the 14th of the 4th month 54 it was granted vnto James Barker that the meadow laid out vnto him in the meadow Comonly Called the great meadow for his halfte proportion of a two acre lott bought of Nehemiah Abbot : that it shall stand good to him as it was laid out by Thomas Mighill and Mathew Boys as well as if it had beene done legally by fower men as otherwars prouided

this order made the 24th day of the 5th month 54 ffor preuenting of present dammage by hoggs it is ordered that all maner of swine which shall be found in any Corne or meadow wheresoeuer they shall be liable to pay double damage notwithstandinge any order or Custome to the Contrary except they be sufficiently yoaked and ringged : which yoake shall be one foot and halfe vpward and one foot and eight inches the Cross barre for euery hogg of a yeare old and for others ether yunger or elder proportionably acording to the descretion of the ouerseers

Whereas there is a great number of hogs in the towne and great damage done by them both on the comons and other whear the select men hath maid a stint of hogs for this year as followeth that the great lots shall haue libertie to keep twelue hogs and breed vp ten younger the tow aker lots hath libertie to keep ten and to breed vp six and the half two acker and all vnder hath libertie to keep six hogs and breed vp foure and thes younger sort is to Come into the former number when they are half a yeare ould if any of our inhabetants exeed this number they are to pay for euery hog soe keept fiue shillings half to the informer and half to the vse of the towne onely the man that keepeth the ordinary shall haue libertie to keep a doubl stint also all hogs is to be ringed constantly or cut sufishantly twice in the year this order taketh place the first of aperill and such as cut shall cut the first of aperill as they doe that ring and also they shall cut the second time the first of Jewly and in case any faill herin they are liable to pay one shilling six pence for euery hog not so ringed or cut

also it is ordered that if any hogs or pigs shall be found in any field where there is corne the said hoggs or pigs is to bee pounded and the owners of such hoggs or piggs shall be liable to pay for euery hogg or pigg after they bee 6 m[th] ould soe impounded one shillings also it is agreed that none of our inhabitants shall neither sell let nor give any of their gates vpon the Comon to any other for the hoggs to goe on vpon the forfit of fiue shillings 11 pence   +

For the present incorigmen of thosse of our neighbours and the
Towne whear they ordenarely leav the towne haith maid an
order that they shal pay halfe whear they leave and the other
halfe to our ministre until such time as they mantane a
ministre of them selues which when they doe our town haith
+ + them by the said order which is more then the law
Reqireth of us or we can obtane of our neighbors that cum to leav
with us which ar more then they are

Andrew Receeved at marchants...................... 7–00 – 0
by Richard longhorne .... 0–14 – 2
by John dreser.................................... 0– 1 – 4
by Ezeakell northend...... .... 0– 6 – 8
leauetenant Remington............................. 0– 3 – 8
                                                   ————————
                                                   8– 5 –10

for keepeing 27 weakes............................17–14 – 2
for fence seting .... 0–13 – 7
for + + + ——6 day...................... 13 – 0
for cowe driven and seaken Catell.................. 8 – 0
                                                   ————————
                                                   19– 8 – 9

    Giue to andrew–11–2–11
    The young catell comes to 1^s–10^d apeace

Towne Charges for the yeare 1654

Imp^s Joseph Jewet he paid to Ensighne howlet last yeare o– 9– +
    for newbery line 3 days and Carying a letter...... o– 6– 6
    for deputyship.................................16–15– 6
for Maxy Jewet deputyship 12– 3– 0
for nickolas Jackson 2 days and half at meeting-house...oo–04– 2
Richard Swan for Andiuer line...................... 0–10– 0
    for going to pentuckit......................... 0– 2– 0
    for newbery line and one day Court............. 0–04– 6
    for deuiding newbery fence..................... 0–01– 0
william law one day................................ 0–01– 0
John pearson for newbery gate 0–05– 0
    for uewing fence............................... 0–17– 4
    for doures windows meeting house.............. 0–01– 6
for James bayly uewing fence 0–15– 8
    for 2 days at Court............................ 0–02– 0

Charles Browne for a foxe........................... 0–02– 0
Richard lighton for underpinning meeting.............. 0–04– 6
Thomas Abbot for 10 foxes one wolfe 2–05– 0
    for 5 days at Court one day newbery line......... 0–07– 0
Thomas Tenny for warning.......................... 0–03– 0
    uewing fence and a foxe 0–04– 6
francis parrat one uoyage to Salem and a day and halfe
    newbury line.................................. 0– 7– 4
John Tod when ye indians molested vs at Spring was
    +   +   +   + ... 0– 5– 0
Henry Rila for being a solder....................... 0– 4– 0
Jonathan plat for ye same........................... 0– 6– 0
John Smith for geting water for ye young catle and other
    worke 0– 7– 0
Willia Tenny for warning towne meeting and other worke 0– 8– 0
Peter Covpr for vewing fence........................ 0– 9– 0
John boynton for ye same worke...................... 0–14– 0
John Trumbel for warning towne meetings and for scole-
    ing and 1 day at court.......................... 0– 8– 0
Thomas Dickisson for   +   +   and carring a let-
    ter 2 newbery and other worke................... 0– 4–
Hve Smith for court............................... 0– 1– 6
James Barker for court............................. 0– 1– 6
John pickard for worke 0– 3– 0
Willia Hobson for his horse going to ly out ye 300 acers.. 0– 2– 6
    for writing orders and other worke.............. 0– 7– 0
for ye five men..................... .... 5– 0– 0
John pickard for warning towne meetings.............. 0– 2– 0
                                45–13– +

Thomas Dickison Ezekiel Northen John Pickard Willia Law
William Tenny Are chosen to order the affaires of the towne for
the yeare ensuing vpon the 12th of December 54

Those that are chosen to iudge defects of them that are fined
for not coming to towne meetings Levetenant Reminton James
Barker Richard Swan Thomas Lever 12 December 54

Richard Swan & Thomas Tenny are chosen for overseers for
the plaine

    for Counstable Willia Asa
    ffor marshall John Tod

ffor overseers Hue Smith John Boynton Marke Prime Edward Hasen

for Pinder Andrew Headen

ffor calling towne meetings William Asa

for warning towne meetings John Trumble Tobiah Collman John Tenny

we the select men hauing taken into Consideration the great damage we haue years done by swine and Conseauing they might be much better in some other place ferther of from the towne we therefore haue thought good to declare and hereby it is ordered that if aney hoggs shall be found with in thre miles of the towne after the first day of aprill next insuing which will be in the yeare 55 not being suffisiently yoked and ringned as in the former order about hoggs they shall be liable to pay if they exceed not thre 1^s-4^d p hogg if aboue thre 1^s p hogg fourpence to the keeper of the pinne-fold the Remainder to him that shall impound them

Wheras there is great neclect in coming to private meeting for ye ordering of oxe pastures or feillds or other nesseary occasions wch are to be consulted about for the good of the whole it is therfore ordered that when any one doth warne such a meeting with the consent of another seing need of the same if any soe warned neclect to come at the time appoynted he shall be liable to pay 1^s : a time and it is further ordered that the maiger part of them that doe meet shall haue power to order what they mett about as they see meet

Wheras there have bene great danger of great damage by foule Chimnies it is therefore ordered that the second day after the pub-licatiō heroft all thached Chimnies in the towne shall be swept and all thached houses shall be swept that day fornight and ol clap-board houses that day month and brick chimnies on the same day alsoe and this to continve till the first of may, and in case any be defective herin they shall pay for every default 1^s and the overseers are reqvered to vew the day after and to give in defects as in cases of other orders

further it is ordered That euery man shall haue A sufficent Ladder about his house reared vp to ye chimney for preventing of ffier and if any bee defectiue hearing he shall be Liable to pay Three shillings and the ouerseer shall as duely look to the suficency of y^e

ladders as ye doe ye chȳmeys & if any two of ye select or other inhabitants shall obserue any dwelling hous without a lader acording
to order ye ouerseer shall pay 5 shillings

Johnathan Plats hath ingaged himself this 11th of the 2 moth
55 to keep the cow herd of the north east end of Rowley vpon
the tearmes following in p^{t}ms he is to haue wheat or buter wheat at
5^s a bushell and butter at 6^d a pound for the first pay and for the
last pay half rie and half in indian corne as mr Jewet will tak it he
is to haue 2^s 2^d a day and in case Jonathan Plats se gods providenc
calling him out of the towne he is to giue the 5 men 1 weeks warning to place anothr herds man also he is to haue 3 cows free

Jonathan Pllatts
Ezekiel northen
Will Law
Williā Tenny

By the men aponted to sell trees in the towne streets and of
them hath Jo pickard bought sixe trees befor his dooer also Ezekel
northend thre before his dooer also John palmer one before his
dooer al which haue maid pay^t to the towne for the said trees

The select men hauing taken into Consideration the great abuse
of falling smal and young trees much practised in this towne:
haueing our Commons lying full of other fierwood wasting and
alsoe Cumbring the Comons haue therefore ordered that whomesoeuer shall fall any tree or trees after the publication of this Order
within one mile and a halfe of the towne or any part of the same:
being within our libertys: excepting for building or Railes they
shall be liable to pay for euery tree soe felled fiue shillings p tree:
one halfe of which shall goe to the use of the informer the other
unto the use of the towne: provided this order shall not extend to
the Swampe lately granted to John Tod for a pastuer for the
ordenary nether the warehouse pastuer

The select men takeing into Consideration the ouer small
number of Bulls alotted by the former order in that Case prouided
haue thought meet to Change the deuisions that a greater number
of bulls may be prouided: all former orders Conserning bulls are
hereby repealed: and for the futuer it is ordered and now declared
that there shall be Eleauen good and suficient bulls prouided: uiz

from Richard Clarkes to and with william Jacksons one: from Hugh Smiths to and with deacon Jewets one: from Leonerd Harimans to and with Mathew Boys one: from Samuell Brockelbankes to and with Mr Rogers one from John pearsons on both sides of the street to and with Thomas Crosbys one from Thomas Tennys to and with Thomas Burkebys one from william Acees and francis parats to and with John lamberts one from Charles Brownes to and with Samuell plats one from Edward sawers to and with John harris one from goodman Broadstreets to and with Ezekiell Northends one from Richard longhornes to and with Richard wicams one: all which bulls shall be allowed or disalowed by the magor part of ouerseers

It is alsoe ordered that the hier of these bulls shall not be Raised by the deuisions thus prouiding them but shall be equally laid upon all Cows and heifers exceding two yeares old which shall goe vpon our Cow Commons or at pentucket

att a towne meeting held the 20 of disember 1655 it was granted to georg kilburne that he showld haue a cow gate vpon the Comon for the acker and a half of land he laid downe vpon the new plaine liing betwene the pine hills and batchlers plain

att a towne meeting held in Jenevary 1655 a cow gat and a half was granted to leavtenat Reminton for his land vpon the plain lieing beyond the pine plain joyning vpon elder rainers midow also James barker had a cow gatt granted for the land he laid down vpon the same plain wher leavetenats was

also adrew hedon had one cow gate grantd him for the land fomerly giuen him vpon the aforesaid plane

James Barker hath laid downe his middow in long midow and hath middow grantd to him by the towne and laid out for him by the men apointed behind an Iland that is aboue newbery gate

Trees sould by the men appointed for that work as followeth to Jo: pickard 6 tres to Ezekell northend 3 tres to Jo pallmer 1 tree for which thy haue paid   +   +   +

+   +   +   +   +   +   +   +   +   +
+   +   +   +   +   +   +   +   +   +
Williā Hobson for firewood........................... o – 3 – o
Thomas Abat for one foxe more..................... o – 2 – 6
Richard Holms for p^t of one day................ .... o – 1 – 6

Abraham Jewit for yᵉ yong   +   + ... 0 – 0 –10
Thomas Abbat for being a soulger.................... 0 – 2 – 1
ffor the ministry faling short........................ 0 –16 – 0
                                                    _____
                                                    47 – 1 –10

    Whereas much public   +   +   +   +   +   +
vpon the select men and a   +   +   +   +   +   +
falleth in that is burdensome to .   +   +   +   +   +
the beter under goeing and performeing of the same it is ordered
that they shall haue power to + + vpon euery man by house
row on day begining at Edward Hasens and soe round about
to Mʳ Nelsons takeing both sids of the hieway together for
the east end and for the west end begining at Richard Clarkes
and soe round both streets to Mʳ Rogers except Elders Deacons
ouerseers and Heardsmen and if any man Refuse haueing 2 dayes
warneing he shall be liable to pay 3ˢ – 4ᵈ to the vse of him that
doth the worke

    Bee it known vnto all whō it may concern that Jonathan Plats
and henery Riley doth ingag themselus to keep the cows of the east
end of Rowley this sumer insueing being 56 and is to haue for their
wages as followeth 13ˢ by the week their first pay in wheat and
butter and the latter pay 40ˢ in wheat and the rest half in rie and
half in indian their wheat att 4ˢ 6ᵈ a bushell rie att 3ˢ 6ᵈ a bushel
indian at 2ˢ 4ᵈ a bushell each of them is to haue two cows free :
gats on the comon and rats to the hirds man

                             Jonathan Platts
                             his mark
                    henrey + Riley

thes two aboue hired by Richard longhorn and William Law this
31 of Jeneway 1655
                         Richard longhorne
                         Wiliā Law

                      1656
    laid for reparation of meeting house the whole sum of XXIX
pound 2ˢʰ 1ᵈ June the 13 day

+   +   day 11 month 1656

at a leagell towne meeting were chosen for towne office as folowing

For fiue men Rich Swane Jo trumball Tho: dickensō Wiliā Stickney Wiliā Lawe

for ouerseers Wiliā Jacksō Rich clark Jo Jōsō Tho abbat

for cunstabl Jo Pickard

for marshal Jo Pickard

a clark to call town meeting Tho leavr

to warn tow meeting Jo trumbal Williā Stickney tho leavr Wiliā Law

for a pindr Tho abbat

to Jugd of such are delinquents at town meetings leatnat remtō Jams barker Wiliā asa and Tho leaver

the towne charges this year is........................ 24 . 5 . 8

the rat laid to answer thes charges is................ 25 . 14 . 8

Levetenant Broklebanke and Corperall Northen was chosen to lay out a country hy way betwixt Topsfeld and Meremak according to Law

Also Ezekell Northen and John Person was chosen to run the Lyne betwixt Nubery and Rowly

The latter rate for the meeting hous the whol some of sixtene pounds which was paid to thomas wood in october 56 also euery famely paid to mr Jewet for nails for the meeting hous–0–1–6

att a leagall towne meeting held the 3 day of the 12 mo[th] 1656 it was agreed by the towne that all male childrin shall pay to the scole men when they are 4 years ould till they Come to be 8 years ould also it was agreed at the same meeting that wiliā bointon shud haue fiue pound lent him out of the churches stock towards the building of an end to his hous vpon this condion that if he keep the scolle seuen years this fiue pound is to bee void but in case he leaue the scol before seuen years be out the said hous end is to be prised by two indiferant men and the one half of the pris of the said hous end soe prised shall the said wiliā bointō is to returne to the church againe

Item it is ordered and agreed by the select men

It the forty shillings the Deacon pays for Teaching is thus Distributed

to Charles Browne...................... 0 –15 – 0
to John Remington...................... 0 –12 – 0
to Richard Lighton.:.................... 0 – 7 – 0
to George Kilborne..................... 0 – 6

At A General and legall Towne meeting in the yeare 1656 granted to Andrew Hidden one cow gate in Lue of 4 acers of land that he laid Downe, beyond long medow bridge

It was agreed and voated at a leagall towne meetting in the yeare 1656 That John Lambert Richard longhorne John Boynton petter Cowper John Brocklebanke and Lenard harryman should haue all the land and medow from Thomas Dickinson staks to the Riuer. which was neuer yet laid out: for the space or full tearme of seuen paying yerely 40 shill per anum for the same

Whereas it doe apeare that yearly men doe mowe on the towne Comon without any order from the towne or the select men thereof and also that the select men haue need of the dispos thereof for the incorigement of herdsmen or of others that the towne haue need to incorige we therfore doe order that no inhabetant in our towne shall mowe in any place of the townes Comon without leaue from the select men or the maier part of them and in case any man shall mowe in any part of the townes Comon without libertie as afore said for euery load of grass so cut he that cuts it shall pay thre shillings one sh of which shall goe to the informer and the other two sh to the vse of the towne prouided that he that maketh use of the grass shall not be the informer

also it is agred by the select men that all the persons in the towne hauing ratable estat shall giue in the same as they shall be apointed by the select men both for time and place and in case of neglect herin thay shall be rated acording to the discresion of the select men

Vpō the 17 day of the 2 moth 1657 Jōthan plats and John mickell hath ingaged themselus to keep the cows this sumer at the east end of the tow for which wo they are to haue 13sh a week thir first pay in wheat and butter the later pay half wheat and half other corn at the pris curant

att a leagall towne meeting held the 28 day of the 10th mōth 1657 it was by the town agred and voted that all the inhabitats of the said towne of Rowley should haue an eaqell share of plumiland.

Memorandū here foloweth the Entry of some Landes that were laide out Anno dom : 1652 and since that time but are now entered 1657

Laide out by Thomas Mighel Francis Parrat Mathew Boyes Richard Swan Thomas Dickinson in the 4th month 1652

To Humfrey Reyner fifty 50 Acres of vplande more or lesse situate neare the Penn where yonge Catle had bene Keept butting on some Medow laide out for Thomas Mighel on the Northeast and the Southeast butting on the hy way to the Pen or to Auerill and the rest Joyning vpon the Cow Comon

Ite   laide out for Humfrey Reyner one and twenty Acres of Medow more or lesse lying and being by the Riuer that runeth North easte from a paund where vpon it Butteth and lying along on both sides of the Riuer till it come to Joyne vpon some Medow laide out for Thomas Mighel vpon the north east ende

To John Rimington Senior laide out twenty fiue Akers of Medow which he purchased of Mr Ezeakiel Rogers, in the Craine Medow fourteene Akers South of the Riuer or Brooke the southeast butting vpon the vplande and south west butting vpon a paunde

To John Remington Senior   of vpland that he purchased of Mr Ezekiell Rogers lieing on the plaine Commonly Called Andevor plaine bounded on the north east by land laid out for Mr Thomas Nelson Now in the possesion of Ezekiell Northend on all parts else Bounded by the Common land

To John Rimington Senior two Akers more or lesse in the Marsh feilde butting on the west vpon Richard Swan Medow on the South butting on the Causey on the North butting on James Barker and on the Easte vpon Williā Hobson his Medow

Ite   three Acres of Salt Marsh more or lesse lying vpon the sunn side of the greate Ilande Abutting vpon the North and West vpon William Asee his Medow buting on the South vpon a great Creeke toward the Hogg Ilande Butting vpon the East on Abel Langley Medow.

Entrys 1657 and 58.

Ite   To John Rimington Senior fiue Akers of medow more or lesse in the medow caled the great Medow Abutting on the South end vpon Jeremiah Elsworth medow and the rest round butting on the vplande

Ite   layd out for Richard Swan one Aker more or lesse in the Marsh feild Abutting vpon a causey on the South butting on the vplande on the west and butting on the northwest vpon Thomas Barker medow going with a coue that cometh into the vplande that Joynes on the hy way to Sawiers Ilande

To Thomas Dickinson foure Akers more or lesse laide out for him and lying northeast of Prospect Hill and purchased of Joseph Jewet on the east abutting vppon the Lands of the said Thomas Dickinson the east end butting on the Cōmons and the west end of it butting vpon the lande of Thomas Palmer and the lande of John Burbanke

It laide out for Thomas Dickinson one Aker of vplande in the Marsh feilde towards the Cow Bridge butting on the South vpon James Barker vplande butting west on the Comon butting North on the Rough marsh vpon the Easte butting on Thomas Dickinson owne lande

Ite laide out for Jeremiah Elsworth in the Great medow eight Akers more or lesse butting on the west vpon the lande of George Kilbourne that he purchased of Mathew Boys and North side of it butting on the Medow of Maximilian Jewet.

Ite laide out for Thomas Leauer one hundred and seauen rod fowre and twenty whereof was added vnto his lot of three Akers neare the field Gate and the rest was Joyning vnto his lott next to Nubery way in the north east feild :

Item acording to the apointment of the towne and there Grant vnto Thomas Leauer, laid out By Richard Swan and John lambert for want of measure of medow in his Sathwell Ground, a percell of Ground towards halfe an acre of the common Ground that Joyneth on the farther side of that Ground that was formerly laid out as apeares in Record to Mr William Bellingham neare vnto Satchwells meadow but now in the possession of the abouesaid Thomas, by purchasse abuting on the north of a percell of swampy meadow laid out to daniell harris now in the possesion of John Grant

Certaine parcells of medows laide out about the yeare 1646 To Sebastian Brigham to Thomas Mighill to mr Thomas Nellson and to mr Vmphrey Ranor which medow doth ly vpon the brooke, beyond the straits :

Inprimis to mr Thomas Nellson fiue Acres of medow be-gininge at a littell Brooke which lieth a littell below the straites bridge, and runneth into the straits brooke, which medow from that littell Brooke lieth on both the sides of the straits Brooke to a company of Rocks at long hill end.

Laid out vnto Ezekiell Northend A percell of land in Consideration of land that was due to the Right of an acre and halfe lot of thomas miller and should haue bene laid out in the marsh feilld as other such lots had ther but not haueing any vpland ther it was laid out to the said ezekiell northend that purchased his right on the East Side of the mill Riuer beginning not fare below the enteranc of bachelor Brooke into Simonds brooke or ther mill Riuer streigh against the south west side of his land that lieth ouer against it on the west side of the said Riuer and soe it Runeth northerly to a Small tree marked at a Small Swampe side at the turne of the Riuer wher the riuer runeth Close to the banke of vpland and from thence downward alonge by the Riuer side till it Come to another marked tree that directs his line Streight to the Riuer wher the Riuer turneth away from him toward the north east

It is ordered that all mens Medowes and vpland in ther Devisions that are laid out: or shall bee laid out this year shall be bounded with staks and stones at the corners and at the said Corners a hole shall bee made about afoot widde into which the ston shall be laid and the stak beeing about the Thicknes of A mans legg shall be strvck into the said hole and if any man fail in bovnding his propriatie as is here ordered between & the last of the seventh moneth he shall pay for euery such defect 5 shillings

It is ordered that if any cow or cows doe goe vpon the cow commons they shall pay 1ˢ a head for euery weeke that they doe goe vpon the commons vntill they doe giue notice vnto some of the fiue men that they haue disposed of them some other way

It is order that all those who haue any Cattle to be kept at any of the Towne heards shall Giue in ther names with The Number of ther Cattle vnto some of the Select Men at or before the sixt Day of the Second Moneth: And if any Catle be found before any heardsman not Giuen in as abouesaid the owner therof shall pay for euery such Beast two shilling six pence:

It is ordered that such as doe any publike service for the Towne they shall bring in ther bill of charges vnto the Prudentiall Men with in one yeare or else they shall be voyd else they shall loose four pence in the shillinge.

At a legall Towne meeting John Pickard Ensigne Brockelbanke and Richard Swan were chosen and had full power given them for to agitate and determine the differance which is betwene

Ipswitch and the towne of Rowley concerninge the line, with such men who they shall appoint for that end, and what they doe to be accounted a finall issue :

Lands giuen at a generall and legall towne meetinge held the second of March : 1658 :

Granted to Mr Philips a farme about Johnsons crecke to be vewed and laide out, by Elder Rainor, Mr Joseph Jewett, and Samuell Brockelbanke. on this Condition he liue and die hear or the Church aproue of his remoue elsewhere

Granted to John Remington a parcell of land liinge upon the hill out at the towne end, ioininge upon the side of Thomas Crosbee his lott, and upon the high way to be ueiwed and laide out by William Tenny and John Smith.

Granted to Thomas Burkbee a littell parcell of land ioininge upon his owne land that he bought of John Smith, prouided he leaueth halfe a rod by the oxpasture fence :

Granted to Henry Rily the high way that was left betwene Thomas Abbot his corner and the corner of his owne lott, prouided that he maketh and maintaneth a sufficient stile for euer for people to passe ouer too and fro.

It was Agreed and voted at a Generall and legall towne meetinge that mr Jewett should haue a thousand Acers of land in the necke, beyond the Hazeltines, and that he is to haue forty acers of medow which is to be laide out as conueniently as can be in the townes land whitch forty Acers of medow is to be for part of the thousand in the necke : in exchange for thre thousand Acers of land which is to be laide out as conueniently as can be for the towne of Rowley in the uillage land, about the bald hills :

It was agreed and voted at a Generall and legall Towne meetinge held December 20 in the yeare 1658 that Thomas Lever should come in for a proportion of an Acer and halfe Lot in the land by Merrimack

It was likewise agreed and voted at the same towne meetinge that Mr Joseph Jewet John Pickard Ezekiell Northend Thomas Abbot and John Smith should diuide euery mans proportion of Land by Merrimacke :

At the same towne meetinge it was likewise agreed and voted that Mr Ezekiell Rogers should haue a ffarme next to Mr Sammuell Philips his ffarme of thre hundred Acers or there abouts : of the whitch 300 Acers thirtie were to be medow.

It was ordered and agreed at a Generall and a legall Towne meetinge held December the 20 : in the yeare 1658 that there bee a deuision of the land by Merrimacke bounded from the greate rock to the end of Crane medow and by the village line runninge towards Andever which proportion of Land is to bee a hundred Acers to a two Acer Lot or there abouts, and the lots aboue a two Acer Lot to abate a third of there proportion acordinge to purchase, and the lower Lots to haue there proportion of that whitch the greater Lots ly downe, that is to say, halfe as mutch as a two Acer Lot, that is an Acer and halfe Lot, and the halfe two Acer Lots to haue ten Acers added, or 20 Acers Aded if the Land will reach it : and all the former Lots are to haue there proportion of Land before the lesser lots come in for a proportion, that is Lots without purchase : and they are to haue 20 Acers a peece if the land that is to bee diuided will hold out. and all the Lots aboue mr Phillips ffarme to abate 20 Ac out of a hundred exept it be a bad lott. and some beneath mr Rogers ffarme   Bradfort streete end begininge and so bringinge vp wetherfeild streete, and Holme streete and so goinge to Edward Hazons and so cominge round by John Smiths goinge vp to John Palmers and endinge at Phillip Nellsons beinge next to Newbury line

According to a Grant By the towne for the Devision of a Certaine percell of land Commonly Called merimacke land according to the seuerall Devisions of lots as it was Agreed vpon by the towne and men Apointed by the said towne for to Devide it the Devission was made as followeth by the men Apointed whose names ar here vnder writen in the yeare 1658

> Joseph Jewett
> Ezeakiell Northen
> John Pickard
> John Smith

In primis   to mr Samuell Phillips A farme Granted By the towne of three hundred Acres lieing within the aboue named percell of land but Granted vnto him befor the same land was Granted by the towne to be wholly devided and laid out vnto him by the appointment of the towne at the place or places wher it lieth Bounded as followeth on the west side By Jonsons Creeke or Brooke the south end buting vpon common land the east side bounded By a farme laid out to mr Ezeakiell Rogers the North end being in Bredth seuen score and ten Rod buting vpon the Riuer merimake only there is a highway for Carts allowed to Get ouer thwart the end next to the riuer as it may be most Convenient

Item   laid out more to m^r Samuell Phillips twenty Acres of meadow Called˙ Jeremies meadow the west side buting vpon meadow laid out to m^r Ezeakiell Rogers the east side vpon a swampe the North and south Bounded By vpland which is laid out to seuerall men Through all which lots hee is to haue a Cart way and they ar allowed for it in ther Seuerall lots ; the other ten Acres of meadow lieth with in his land

Item   laid out to m^r Ezeakiell Rogers three hundred Acres more or lesse Bounded on the west by m^r Samuell Phillips and Common land, on the east side on land allowed for seuerall Small lots on the north By merimacke Riuer haueing a Cart way throu it, the South end Bounded by a line betwene merimacke land and the land Commonly Called the village land the meadow Belonging to this farme is also thirty Acres twenty fiue wherof lieth in Jeremies meadow soe Commonly Called) Bounded by the meadow of m^r Phillips on the east and on the other three sides vpon Seuerall lots laid out to seuerall men also a litell peece of meadow about fiue Acres more or les lieing Easterly from m^r Phillips meadow all that peece of meadow is laid out to m^r Rogers except about one acre and halfe to the south east end which is bad all ther meadowes were Granted to those two farmes with Convenient high wayes to those meadowes before the rest of the land was Granted and to be theres in whose lands soeuer it falls

Item   to John Pallmer Six score Acres Be it more or lese as it lieth Neere vnto Crane meadow which hath its bounds on the east end by some Common land and vpon the west end of Samuell Brocklebankes Crane meadow the south west side by Common land Runing South west along in a Swampe and soe to the 2 Raille fence standing in or neere the midell of a percell of meadow and soe Runing along by that fence till it Come to a Swampe (Isuing out of that meadow) that Runes to the vper end of his land being ther bounded by a small Brooke or Runlet of water and bounded on the northeast alonge by the meadow

It was agreed and voated at a leagall towne meetting held march 14 1659 : That mr Phillip Nelson should haue A percell of land between his owne house and the Schole house for euery acre he hath ther it was to be for Three which was wanting of his proportion which land was to bee veiwed and laid out by John Pickerd and Richard Swan Mr Rogers likewise beeing ther at the same time

It was granted likwise to Mr Philips that his sidefence Joyning vpon the same land shall rune with a strate line :

It was likewise agreed and voated at the same towne meeting That Jonathan Plats his fence between Ipswich and Rowley line by prospect hill side should rune one a straite line which was to bee veiwed by Thomas Dickinson and Deacon Jewitt

Ther was Like wise granted at the sametime to Edward Sawier about some thirty or fortie Rodd of Rough marsh Joyneing vpon Mr Jewitts Devission of Rough marsh below planting hill and James Bally and Petter Cowper

A agenerall and leagall towne Meetting maie the 5 1659 granted that Richard Swan and John lambert should veiwe and lay out a sertaine parcell of land to thomas leauer Joyneing vpon his owne land with in the Commone field for a quarter of an acre of medow that he wanteth in sachells meadow for satisfaction for the same according as they see Cause

At a generall and legall towne meeting held the same tyme It was granted that Richard Swan and John Lambert should veiw and lay out a certaine percell of land as they shall see cause vnto Edward Hazen Joyneing to his owne land in the Common feild nere Cowbridge :

A a legall towne meeting held Jenevary the fourth 1659 it was agreed and voated that John harris is to haue a peece of land as farr as his lot goeth along by the streete vpn a strait line from his barne corner vnto Samuel Mighel house corner onely leaueing out a low place of Ground for a wattering place if that part of the towne make vse it for that end otherwise it shall Returne to him To Rune a streight Line

at a legall Towne meetting held Jenevary 25, 1659 it was granted that John pearson shold haue the land which is now fenced in beeing about 3 quarters of an acre more or les with that ground to the rever which the tenters stande vpon in Consideration of ayears ringine the bell released

at a leagall Towne meeting held the 7 of febuary it is agreed that if any man in the towne shall refus to take vp a pound of powder and pay 1^s 3^d in wheat the Day folowing he shall pay one shilings and the marshall shall haue power emediatly to Destraine for it

febuary the 13

Vpon Consideration of the Decay of vsefull timber for Cowper stuf as stands heading stuf so as allsoe of shingl and Clapbord it is ordered and this day Declared That if any person or persons from henceforth get any of the formentioned cowper stuft shingl or clapbord and despose theroff soe as it be caryed out of the Towne except in cowper ware wrought vp he or they shall forfeat to the towne for euery hundred of the formentioned stuf desposed Contrayerie to this order 4 shillings the intent of this order is to prohibit the transportation of shaken or vnpackt Cask as well as other

Aprill the 18. 1660.

it is ordered that if any younge Cattle or fatting Cattl or oxen or cowes with ther Calus be found vpon the Cowe Comans so as to disturb the Cow heard shall be liabl to pay 1.6^d the head the pounding and the heardman shall haue power to impound them euery time soe found vnles Such Cattle haue been taken into the Poul to goe into the conntry aboue the fence

Provided that if any worken oxen belonging to eyther end of the towne be driuen Away out of the way of the heard they shall not the first time they are found be liabl to this penalty if being told therof they driue them or other wise secure the next day if it be not Saboth But if they be found asecond tyme not soe driven and soe from time to time then : six pence ahead poundage

It is ordered that if any mans Catle be found vpon the Commons aboue his proportion at any time not haueing hiered gates of some other. he shall be liable to pay foure shillings six pence a beast : provided that if he shew to the ouerseers a note vnder the hand of the man of whome his pasture was hyered it shall satisfie to saue his fyne : And all that doe hire gates of the Towne shall pay one shilling six penc a gate.

It is ordered that all Common Gats and perticuler mens fence shall Be made and repared against all maner of Catle and hoggs from the first of march & before ye first of aperil and in case they be not so made and maintained vntill the last of the eight moneth they shall pay twelue pence arod besids the Just dammag done by ther default : & allso that street fences shall be made sufficient : And be maid foure foot high if it ly against corne and the fence ner ye hous next mens Corne or pasture wher hogs & Catl ly shall be counted the street fence

It is ordered that no parcell of Land shall be sould or giuen by the towne, by way of grant to any person or persons untill it bee twice published, at two legall town meeting, and granted the third towne meetinge if the towne doe see cause, prouided that it bee published thre towne meetings gradually one after a nother prouided allsoe that if sutch lands bee nere any mans propriety, it shall not be granted to his preiudice or damage without his consent. prouided likewise that all sutch land that are giuen or sold by way of grant, shall bee written in the Towns book and red at the same towne meetinge that they are Granted, this order Doth likewise include the changinge of any land.

It is ordered that there shall bee no horses nor asses left tethered in the night time in the common feild, or any way side-langeld, or hopled neither shall any person, hopell, tether, or side-langel, or let loos, any horse or asse in the day time in the common feild in the contry way except it be against a mans owne propriety, and no other, upon the same penalty that there is for the poundage of horses after the month May.

It is likewise ordered that all orders customs and priuiledges, must be renewed yearly, or else they shall be of no force.

That all future Grevance might Carefully be inheuered to be prevented at a meeting held the seuenth of may 1660 it was agreed by the proprietors of the meadow that lieth on the east side of the Brooke in Bachelors meadow that the fence Belonging to each propriety should bee made and mantained a sufficient two raille fence from time to time. and to be sufficiently Repaired yearly by the first of aprill and that there might be a just and equall proportion of fence acording to the seuerall acres it was then also agreed that John Pickard and Samuell Brocklebanke should devide it, and that the devission made that what euer proprietor doth not make and mantaine his fence sufficient by the fore named time of the first of aprill It shalbe in the poure of any of the proprietors that suffer and are agreued to be ouersseers and to fine the said defectiue fence foure pence a length of railles:

The fence Being Devided by the aboue named partyes John Pickard and Samuell Brocklebanke falleth vnto euery acre elleuen Rod and six foote and is marked as followeth begining in a swampe at the south end

John Pickard runeth north ward to stake or post marked ..   I

Petter Couper Begineth at 1 and Runeth to the marke   II

Mr Phillips Begineth at II and Runeth allonge to the marke.   III

Samuell Brockelbanke begineth at III and goeth to the
        marke..   IIII

vxor Hobson begineth at IIII and goeth about the corner to
        the marke................................   IIIII

Mrs Rogers Begineth at IIIII and goeth to the marke.......   IIIIII

Richard Wickam Begineth at IIIIII and endeth at the
        Brooke

fines at new Plain

.Peter Coper delinqent 2 lenth
        and for want of suficient bounds
Richard Wicom defective bounds
Richard Clerke defective 2 lenth
Wiliam Stickny defective 1 lenth
Jerimiah Elsworth defective 2 lenth
Thomas Dickerson defective 2 lenth
        William Jackson
        John Broklebank

fines Deliuerd to the Constable

1660   44 shall & 10
        more............0–10–4

Foxes voats that all which ar Diged shall be one shil a head &
the rest catched by trap or gun 2.6

Offecers for the towne for the year 1660 & 1661
Will Teny Constable & marshall

for Select men   for ouerseers
    M^r. Nelson   Richard Clark
    John Pickerd   William Jackson
    Will : Stickney   Richard longhorne
    Ezekill Northend   Edward hazen
    Thomas Teny

for the great plaine ouerseers Richard Swan & Will : teney
for calling towne meetings Samuell Plats
for warneing meettings for our end Thomas teney
for the other end Joh Pickerd
for pinders for our end James Bally or son John
        Sam Stickney

searlher of leyther Deacon Jewit & Joh Dresser
Judges of Delinqents Ensign brocklbank
James Barker
Will teny
James Balley

Appointed by the town at a legall towne meeting that Richard
Swan John Pickard Ezekiell Northend and Samuell Brocklebanke
should Run the line betwene Nubery and vs and Andeuer and vs
and Topsfeild and the land called the village land or soe fare as
they find it needfull to be done or them or any of them and what
they doe in the said case the Towne doe Ratefie as valid

Laid out To Thomas Dickinson one Acre of Rough marsh Be
it more or lese as it lieth in the Northeast feild joyneing to the
Country highway neere the Bridge at the east end of mr Rogers
planting lott and soe Runing downe a Gladee of meadow Bounded
on the north west by the planting lot of Gorge abbot acording as it
is agreed By Seuerall stakes and stones not being any streigh line
but seuerall lines acording as the meadow makes corners into the
vpland the north part is Bounded by meadow that Thomas Abbot
Son of Gorge abbot purchased the south east side Bounded by the
vpland

Laid out vnto James Barker a peece of meadow about one
acre and halfe be it more or lese lieing in a peece by it selfe neere
vnto the east end of that meadow that was laid out vnto matthew
Boys in the meadow Commonly Called the great meadow ; bound
by the vpland and the Brooke The which meadow was laid out
vnto him for meadow due vnto the proportion of a halfe two Acre
lot that he purchased of Nehemiah Abbot

Laid out vnto zekiell Northend one acre of marsh in the hoge
Iland marsh be it more or lese in consideration of a high way that
is used ouer his marsh that somtimes was Sebastines Brighams
below the oyster poynt downe towards Shad Creeke ; the which
acre be it more or lese lieing in the hoge Iland marsh is bounded
by marsh laid out vnto Thomas dickinson on the north west end
the north east side is bounded by a Creeke that devides it from
marsh laid out vnto John pickard on somepart and the other is by
the same Creeke devideing it from marsh laid out vnto mr Anthony
Crosbie soe that the Creeke devides it from the said John Pickard
and mr Crosbie on the north east side the south east corner is buted

against the same Creeke being noe breedth the south west side is bounded by marsh laid out to Thomas Nelson haueing Alowance for the high way Through it

Laid out vnto Thomas Nelson halfe an acre be it more or lese in the said hoge Iland marsh in consideration of a high way ouer his marsh That was the first devission of marsh laid out vnto m^r Thomas Nelson his father deceased the which halfe acre be it more or lese is bounded by the marsh of Zekiell Northends on the north east and partly by a creeke the south east end is bounded by a small Creeke or place where watter Isueth into a greater creeke the south west side is bounded by or neere vnto the ould foote way that goeth vnto hoge Iland the north west end buting against the marsh that formerly was laid out vnto Thomas dickinson now in the possesion of James dickinson his Sonn that end being a poynt and noe breeth haueing now the high way in it and allowance for it to be free

Laid out vnto m^r Anthony Crosbie fiue acres and one halfe of marsh in the hog Iland marsh be it more or lese in Consideration of marsh or meadow due vnto John Heseltine that was purchased of the said John by Thomas Crosbie his Grand father the which marsh is bounded by a creeke that devideth it from the marsh of John pickard and Zekiell Northend and a litle of Thomas nelsons one the south west side the north end is bounded by a greate Creeke the north east side and south east end adjoyneth vnto the Common marsh

At a generall and legall Towne meetinge held March the 23 : 1660 or 61, The towne of Rowley did kindly accept of the land that was giuen by Mr Ezekiell Rogers, vpon this prouiso that they payed Eight score pounds, in two years time for the purchase of the same, and that the said lands were to be purchased by the towne, by way of Rate euery one to pay according to Estates of lands, and goods, as was usuall to pay all rates.

At a Generall and legall Towne meetinge held : 4th : 8th : 61 :

It was agreed that such parcells of lands, (and no other) that were then nominated, and agreed upon by the maior part of such as were there present, should be sould for to procure pay for to pay for the lands that were giuen by mr Ezekiell Rogers, vpon this prouiso that they payed eight score pounds, in two years time for the purchase of the same.

first :   At the same Towne meetinge held : 4 : 8 : 61 : it was uoted
and agreed upon by the Towne that the Iland Commonly
called Mr Nellsons Iland should be soulde, upon these conditions, that
there should be left sufficient rome and wayes for the settinge of
hay, and that no dwellinge house should be sett up upon the saide
Iland, and that whosoeuer bought it should beare all dammages done
by cattell or horses

2.   At the same Towne meetinge it was granted and uoted that
all the common Lands towards cow bridge, and all the
Ilands towards mr Rogers his Rough Marsh should bee sould, after
all such persons were serued with land that they wanted after they
made it appeare

3.   At the same towne meetinge it was granted that John
Dresser and John Pallmor might buy a small parcell of
land liing betwene the farme house, and the ends of there owne
landes, there beinge a high way allowed thorow it.

Leutenant Brockellbanke Henry Rily Thomas Wood and John
Grant, Jachin Ranor and John Mighill, hauinge ingaged for to
make a pen for to catch wolues, had that priuiledge granted that
no boddy else should make any pen, any where upon the cow
commons, duringe the space of three years, and were to haue for
euery wolfe taken by there pen fifty shillings, payed by the towne.

Sume lands laid out in the northeast feild and farmes vn-
Recorded till now   In primis   To Thomas Abbot two Acres of
vpland be it more or lese lyeing at the east end of those Ilands that
lye as one goeth to Mr Nelsons first devission of Salt marsh and is
bounded By sume land laid out to thomas Barker on sume part of
the west end the most parts of it else is bounded by some Comon
Scirts of that Iland betwen this land and the meadow and a highway leading into those meadowes all the which Common Scirts
are now sould vnto Ezekiell Northend By those men appointed
to Sell Comon land for the raiseing mony to pay Mr Ezekiell
Rogers of Ipswich for the leagacy Giuen him By will of Mr
Rogers acording to the order of the towne

Laid out vnto Mr Thomas Nelson, deceased, as to part of the
Right of his lot acording vnto purchase ; in the yeare 16 + or ther
about ; it was laid out vnto him one hundred acres of vpland be it
more or lese as it lieth on a plaine

Sargent John Pallmor in the yeare 1661 there was soulde by leafteuant Sammuell Brocklebanke Richard Swan and Ezekiell Northen who were apointed for to sell certaine parcells of Land to pay the eight score pounds that the towne of Rowley were to pay in two years time, there was then sould thre quarters of an Acre of Land and six rods more or les in the marsh feild at the farme house where Domer dwelt. bounded southeast upon land of his owne west bounded by land of John Dreser, buttinge on the north upon land granted to Mr Thomas Nellson east by land of Robert Hunter in part and partly by land of John Newmarch. and others.

    Att A Generall And Legall Towne meeting Held 4th of the 8th month 1661

It was Agreed and voted by the towne that the Iland Commonly Called Mr Nelsons Iland should be sould, vpon these Condisions That there should be left sufficient Roume for the seting of hay. and that noe dwelling house should be sett vp vpon the said Iland, and that who soeuer bought it should beare all dammages done by Cattell or horses

It was also Agreed at the same Towne meeting and choyse made and voted that William Asee Mr Phillip Nelson and John Lambert should lay out the same Island according to the Grant of the Towne aboue expresed And according to the Trust by the towne Commited vnto them; they haue sould vnto John Bond Inhabbitant of plum Iland for the just and full Sume of twenty pounds to be paid for the vse of Mr Ezeakiell Rogers of Ipswich as part of that leagecy Giuen him by will of Mr Rogers late pastor of this Church, and is by those men laid out acording as it lieth bounded   Begining a litle aboue a dich Runing into a Creeke by the side of the Iland and Runing Round according to the marked trees there appereing   there being left sufficient Roume for the setting of hay and a sufficient way for horse and man to pase through the ILand vnto Euery mans propriety as the way lieth alRedy and free passage ouer any part of the said Iland in winter   +   for the proprietors adjoyneing the Iland to Bring away there hay and all these priueliges vnto the propritors to be Continued for ever

    At A Generall and Legall Towne meeting Held the 4th of the eight mounth 1661

It was Agreed that such persells of land (and noe other) that were then nominated and agreed vpon by the maior part of such as

were there present should be sould for to procure pay for to pay for
the lands that were Giuen by Mr Ezekiell Rogers vpon This proviso
that they payed eight score pounds in two yeares time for The
purchase of the same

At the same Towne meeting it was voted that leiftennant
Brocklebanke Richard Swan and Ezekiell Northend Should lay
out and sell all the other parcells of lands exceping Mr Nelsons
Iland And it was further agreed at an other towne meeting that all
Common lands and meadowes lieing with in the Northeast feild and
farme should be sould by those men aboue mentioned and
appointed to sell such Common lands : and according to the order
of the towne They haue sould and laid out

vnto James Bayley and Samuell Plats one acre and a halfe of
Salt marsh Be it more or lese as it lieth Bounded on the west by
other meadow of the said James and Samuells bounded on the
East by marsh of William Laws buting on north end by a Creeke
on the south end By the Riuer

To William Law three Acres be it more or lese lying on the
East side of James Bayley and Samuell Plats ther marsh abuting
as afforesaid

To Andrew Hiden two Acres Be it more or lese as it lyeth
one the East Side of William Lawes his marsh abuting as afforesaid

To John Mighill Two Acres be it more or lese but he not
paying, his grant was purchased by William Law, and payment
made by him to the towne and soe the said two Acres lieth vnto
William Law on the east side of Andrew Hidens marsh abuting as
affore said

To Abraham Jewett fiue Acrees Bee it more or lese lyeing on
the East of William Laws his marsh and lyeing part of it against
the ends of Seuerall small lots and buting on the Creeke on the
north and one the the Riuer on the south as afforesaid

To Petter Cooper Two Acres Be it more or lese lying on the
East side of Araham Jewetts marsh Bounded by the riuer on the
south on the north buting against Araham Jewetts marsh

To John Bointon Two Acres lieing on the East of Peter
Coupers marsh buting as affore said on the Riuer and on Abraham
Jewetts marsh

To Thomas Leauer Two Acres Be it more or lesse Lieing on
the east side of John Bointon his marsh Buting on the Riuer on the
south and the North end Buting on Abrahams Jewetts marsh

To Thomas Tenney and William Tenney foure Acres and three quarters Be it more or lese lieing on the east side of Thomas Leauers marsh Bounded by a Great Creeke on the south east the south and North ends Buting as afforesaid: There Being a Cartway allowed Through all These meadowes for feching hay

To William Tenney fiue Acres of vpland Be it more or lesse Lieing on the west side of Mr Humpray Rainers planting lott the south end buting on lands of the said William Tenney the other parts Bounded by the Rough marsh Through which land they ar to haue a Convenient way to lead away ther hay

To John Jonson those Ilands that lye with in and adjoyne to his salt marsh that was Richard Thurrells Being neare vnto Shad Creeke

To Ezekiell Northend foure acres of vpland Be it more or lese as it lyeth Bounded on the northwest By a Cart way leading to Mr Nelsons first devission of said marsh on the South Bounded by the meadow of Thomas Nelson and Thomas Barkers now Mrs Rogers and on some land laid out to William hobson

To Thomas Leauer one acre of swampe land adjoyneing vnto the land of the said Thomas that lieth on the East side of the land that was Mr William Bellinghams neare vnto satchwell meadow, on the north and east Bounded by land of Thomas Remington the south end abuting on the high way

To the said Thomas Leauer Twenty Rod ofland be more or lese adjoyneing to the south east side of his planting lot neare to the further end of it the south east side of it joyneing to the Country way

To the said Thomas a little hill at the further end of his said planting lot adjoyneing to the Contry way

To Thomas Remington one Acre of swampey meadow land be it more or lese on the east and north of Thomas Leauers land adjoyneing vnto lands of the said Thomas Remingtons that he purchased of Mr Anthony Crosbie on the east side, and the west part bounded By meadow of John Grants, the north end adjoyning on Mr Nelsons Satchwells meadow

To John Lambert a litle peece at the east end of his home lot to make his fence streight with the end of Thomas Remingtons home lot

To Mr Anthony Crosbie a small percell of vpland on the east side of the high way at the south end of the Cowbridge Causey the south part of it buting against land of vxor Smiths the other parts or north end buting against meadow of the said Mr Crosbes

To the said Mr Anthony Crosbie and other small percell of land adjoyning vnto his acre and quarter of meadow that was formerly laid out vnto Robert Heseltine in satchwell meadow the west side of it joyneing vnto the Common fence the north end buting against a high way the east side bounded by Common land

To Samuell Brocklebanke foure Acres be it more or lese lieing at the East end of the land he purchased of Matthew Boys not fare from the west end of the towne buting on all parts else on the oxpasture that lieth in Common.

To John poure of Nubery Neecke That percell of vpland Commonly Called The Ilands beyond the Cowbridge meadow being by Estemation about thirty Acres of vpland be it more or lesse as it Lieeth Bounded on the south by meadow Commonly Called m^r Rogers his Cowbridge meadow and other small percells of meadow belonging to seuerall men ; bounded on the west by meadow of william Teenney and others bounded on the north by the fence Betweene Nubery Neecke and the towne of Rowley on all the north part excepting on that place where ther is a percell of meadow belonging vnto and in the possesion of James Barker of Rowley that lieth betwen the fence and his vpland the East parts of it bounded by Comon vpland and meadow belonging to the Towne of Rowley only the said John poure is to goe a litle way in to the said meadow that appears to be Common acordingly as it is staked out and if in any part wher the stakes doe stand it apeears to be inapropriated then he is to haue his bounds by the meadow Through which percell of vpland those men that haue theire meadowes lieing beyond it and haue need of a high way are to haue a ssufficient high way for the Carting of ther hay away and if ther be any differance about the place of the way they are to Chuse two Indifferent men for the deciding of it the one chossen by one party and the other chosen by the other party that soe it may be laid out wher it is least preiudiciall vnto the said John poure and further its agreed that they may come ouer that way that the said John pouer maketh ouer his meadow to Carry away his Corne of his land to his house in Nubery neecke vntill they come to the fence betwene vs and the neecke and then they are to keepe ther way within the fence that soe the said John poure may not suffer any damage by ther pasing through his fence into the neecke. it is also further Agreed vpon ; on the saille of this aboue said land that the said John poure is both he and his sucksessers for euer, to free the Town of Rowley from all that fence that the Towne formerly

maid betwene the neecke and our land soe fare as his land doth lie
against it and also to make and mantaine a sufficient fence betwene
his land and the seuerall persells of meadow that lieth about his
land for euer soe as the proprietors may be as litle damnefied as
maybe nor the land with in which those Ilands lie be prjudised by
his Improueing the said land by feeding nor that he nor any of his
heires or sucksesers that for time to come shall haue any poure or
liberty (for euer) to feed this land or any part of it in Common
with land of Rowley in which it lieth

To John Dreser senior a percell of vpland at the northerly end
of m^r william Bellingham fiue acres of land in the marsh feild
wher m^r dumers farme house stood the northerly end of it buting
against m^r nelsons land also to the said John dresser a percell of
vpland at the south end of leift John Remingtons Rough marsh
at the Cowbridg^e bounded by Edward Hassen land william
Laws land and Richard longhornes land to the oxpasture fence in
which land ther is to be left sufficient and Conuenient wayes for
men to Cary away ther hay that haue ther meadow lying against it

also To Leonard harriman and Henery Royley all That Tract
of land in the marsh feild towards the Cowbridge both vpland and
meadow That formerly was not laid out lieing on the west side of
Thomas dickinsons land in the marsh feild all that land is sould
vnto the said Leaonard and henery except one acre joyneing vnto
the west side of the foresaid dickinsons land which acre is bounded
by the Rough marsh at the north end the south end buting against
a cartway all the rest of the land toward the Cowbridge is the said
Harrimans and Royleys on both sids of the high way bounded on
the east side by Edward hasens land on the north side of the high
way and on the south side of the said high way bounded on the
East by James Barkers land that formerly was laid out vnto m^r
Edward Carlton on all parts else it is bounded by seuerall mens
meadowes Round about through which land ther is allowed to be
sufficient and Conuenient Carting wayes for men to Cary away
there hay to the towne prouided; that they be as litle to the dammage of the proprietors as may be

also To Thomas Dickinson a percell of vpland that lyeth with
in his fence that fenceth The meadow that he bought of Thomas
Nelson that lyeth on the brooke a litle beyond the Straits

Lands Laid out in The yeare 1652 and Since
That time But Now Entered 1661

Vnto Thomas Mighill thirty three Acres of vpland at the place Called the Pen where young cattell were formerly kept Bounded on all parts By the Towne Common except where it Toucheth on meadow laid vnto the said Thomas

Also laid out vnto the said Thomas mighill fifteene Acres of meadow Be it more or lese that is all the meadow Commonly Called the Spruce meadow lieing neer vnto and adjoyneing vnto the afforesade land at the north west Corner being the south east part of the meadow also one other part or percell of meadow lieing and touching on the south east Corner of the afforesaid land also another percell of meadow lieing more southerly (into which the last percell of meadow mentioned doth Isue) bein Bounded on the North by vpland purchased now by John Brocklebanke (in whose possesion all the afforesaid vpland of Thomas mighills thirty three Acres and fifteene Acres of meadow is.) bounded also on the south By land laid out to mr Humpray Rainer and on the west by the pen Brooke also one other percell of medow that lieth with in the Bounds of the thirty three Acres of vpland at the north east side neere vnto the north east Corner Bounds of the said land

Sould vnto John Brocklebanke By the men appointed by the Towne To Sell Land for the Raiseing pay to pay the Leagacy Giuen vnto mr Ezekiell Rogers of Ipswich By mr Ezekiell Rogers late pastor of This Church of Rowley for the purchase of those Lands Giuen vpon The Condision as it Spacefied in the will of the said mr Ezekiell Rogers; Sould vnto the said John Ten Acres of vpland Be it more or lese as it lieth on the South of the pen land laid vnto Thomas mighill as is aboue expresed; adjoyneing vnto the said land at the end where the pen house stoode one part of it and the south part joyneing to the north side of the meadow the west and north part of it Bounded by the Common and vpon the Brooke that parts Betweene it and Samuell Brocklebankes land the east side adjoyneing vnto the meadow that lieth at the south east Corner of the aboue said land that was laid out to thomas mighill also an other part of the ten acres lieth betwene the two percells of meadow Bounded by Common land next toward the towne Through the which Ten Acres The Towne hath Reserued a sufficient and Conuenient high way for driueing Cattell and Carts as they may haue ocation to make use of it

Laid out vnto Samuell Brocklebanke land that he purchased of William Hobson fifty Acres and also land Belonging to his owne lott and to the lott he purchased of matthew Boys twenty two Acres all which seauenty two Acres of vpland lieth on the west side of the Brooke Called the pen Brooke the said Brooke Being the East side Bounds the north end Being Bounded By a high way Reserued wher Cattell vsed to Goe ouer the Brooke to the pen land laid out to Thomas mighill the west side adjoyneing to the way that leadeth to Andeuer only the north west Corner Goeth ouer the high way that now is in use and the high way is to Run all alonge the west side about the Corner the south end Bounded By the Common Land Belonging to the towne from the Brooke Neare vnto mr Humphray Rainers meadow Runing on the South side of a swampe vntill it come to an other Swampe Through which it Runeth vntill it come to a marked Tree at the North side of that Swampe Neare vnto Andever way that Tree Being the South West Corner of the abouesaid land

Laid out vnto Mrs Mary Rogers   Acres Be it more or lese as it lieth on the South Sid of the pond Called (Commonly) pentuckit pond the East end Bounded by A high way leading to Andeuer the South and west parts buting against Common Land this land is the land due vnto The lot was Thomas Barkers for land that was due at The towne to make vp the said Thomas Barkers lot proportionable to the lower lots according to purchase

Laid out also vnto the said Mrs Mary Rogers for hir proportion of land due vnto the lot of the afforesaid Thomas Barker in the land Commonly Called merrimacke land Three hundred and Seauenty Acres be it more or lese lieing and being on the north sid of the pond Comonly Called pentuckit pond bounded by the said pond and the Brooke Coming into and Isueing out of the pond on the south and on part of the east end vntill it adjoyne vpon some land laid out vnto Ezekiell Northend and soe it Runeth along by seuerall marked Trees northerly vntill it leaue a small percell of meadow on the East of it vnto which meadow it joynes acording to the seuerall marked Trees and soe after haueing cleared that meadow it Runes downe The swampe easterly vnto a Tree marked neare the brooke Called Craine meadow Brooke the brooke acording to that linne being the east bounds at that end the north side buting against Common land The west bounded by the ends of seuerall lots that Rune to merrimacke the south west corner being the great Rocke that also is the Corner of the village land and of

merrimacke land the north west corner of the said land being the
south east Corner of Thomas Crosbies merrimake land is a pine
Tree marked for the head of those lots

Laid out vnto Ezekiell Northend as part of merrimacke land
Belonging vnto his Two Acre lot and for part belonging vnto
Thomas Abbots lot Thirty Acres Be it more or lese as it lieth on
the East side of the land of m^rs Rogers the west and northerly
sides of it abuting against the said land of m^rs Rogers the south
side bounded by The Brooke Comonly Called Craine meadow
Brooke and by meadow laid out vnto francis parrat now in the possesion of the said Ezekiell and by some land lyeing on the west
side of the said Brooke belonging to Richard swan The Brooke
being The South and East bounds of the said lands excepting
where the afforsaid land lieth vntill it adjoyne vnto the land of
m^rs Rogers

At A Legall Towne Meeting held the 11th of the 8th month
61. It was Agreed vppon by the maior part of the Towne. that all
Common Land meadow and vpland. Lying with in the North
East feild and farme should be sould for to procure pay for the
Land giuen by Mr Ezekiell Rogers: vpon proviso by: Leauetenant
Brocklebanke Richard Swan & Ezekiell Northen: being ap-
poynted by the towne to sell such Comman Lands.

At a legall Towne meting held the 31 of 8th 61 it was
granted to John Johnson that the men apoynted to sell land in the
comon feild should sell To him a parcell of land lying on the other
side of sandy bridge joyning to his owne meadow allowing
sufficient for high wayes thorue it

	£	s	d
The Towne Charges for the yeare :61 is	31	08	3
The Rate to Releaue for Disbursment to defray the	£	s	d
same Charges is................................	32	9	2

At a generall Towne Meetinge held the 7th 10: 61 were chosen
Towne officers for the Towne of Rowley for the remaninge time
of· 61· and 62

Inprimis John Todd for Constable & marshall.
for Select men. Richard Swan Thomas Tenny Ensigne Brockellbanke John Dresser Abell Langly

Ouerseers for this year John Burbanke Richard Clark Edward hassen & Richard holmes

For newbury fence John Johnson John Lambert

ouerseers for pentuckit sid John Gage and henery Kingsbury for fences and highway

ouerseers for ye great plaine Will. teny and James Bally Clarke for calling towne meetting Samuell Plats

for warneing towne meeting Joh Drusure at midl of towne & ye end & Richard Swan & Tho teny for east end

for Pinders John Spofferd Joh Grant & Thomas Burkebee

Searcher of leather Deacon Jewitt & John Druser

Judges of delinquents left broklbanke James barker Will teny James bally

At a legall Towne meeting Held the 4th of Jenuary 1661 & 2 it was agreed vppon and voted that John Bond should haue Six Acres of land layed out at the Iland caled Mr Nelsons Iland as convenyently as it could for the proprietors thier belonging alowing for the said Six Acres 12 pounds and to haue eight pounds of his purchase Returned for the Remaineing part of the Iland that was formerly sould to him

It was also agreed at the same Towne meeting that Richard Swan leat Brocklebanke & Ezekiell Northen should layout the said Six Acres of land according to their Decresion and see to the Returning of the a boue said Eight pounds. and what ever they doe in this Case shall be accounted a valid act.

At a legall Twone meeting held the 28 of Jenuary 61 it was agreed vpon and voted that Mr Nelson Thomas Leauer John Pickard leauetenant Brocklebanke & Ezekiell Northen should be joyned together with the Select men for that present yeare to Conseder of and order the apprizing of Housing Lands Catell and things of the like Nater as also to Conseder of orders for Confirming of same and Nuling of such as may be thought to be of noe vse : according to their descrsion

At the same Twone meeting it was granted and voted that Mr Phillips should haue nine gates stated to his Lott.

At the same Twone meeting it was also voted that the houseing and land giuen by Mr Rogers to the vse of the Twone of Rowley after the Decease of Mts Rogers should bee freed of all Rates Arising in the Twone Dureing the time of hir Life

A Survay of The Seuerall Gates or Commonages belonging vnto The Seuerall Inhabbitants of The Towne of Rowley as They are Now in possesion haueing Beene Trancefered and Sould from one To another since the Begining of the Said Towne and soe diverted from that first order and stint that was Then made wherby they were proportioned vnto the seuerall Lots acording to the purchase and devission that Then was made

By order and appointment of The Towne Taken (By the Select men Richard Swan Thomas Tenney Abell Langley John Dreser John Brocklebanke with Samuell Brocklebanke joyneing with them) vpon the fourth of february 1661 That there may be a True Record of them acording to ther prsent state they now are in which is as followeth

In primis The Towne did Grant and Giue vnto Mr Samuell Phillips vpon The Said Towne Commons Nine Gates

There Belonges To William Acie; his Lot foure Gates and one halfe and more That he purchased of Mr Joseph Jewett Two oxe Gates purchased of the towne one gate and one halfe gate

To James Bayley his lot and halfe a gate purchased of the Towne Two Gates, purchased of Mr Anthony Crosbie Two Gates purchased of Mr Joseph Jewett of them that belonged to Mr William Bellinghams lot Two Gates and a halfe purchased of Mr Jewett as belonging To Mr Edward Carltons lot One Gate purchased of Towne one halfe gate

To Thomas Leauer his lot and halfe one Gate he purchased of the towne Two Gates, purchased of Mr Joseph Jewett of them That Belonged to Mr William Bellinghams lot one Gate : and of Mr Jewetts owen propriety Two Gates; also purchased of Mr Anthony Crosbie one Gate

To John Pallmer as to a halfe Two Acre lot Two Gates And one quarter, purchased of Mr Joseph Jewett of Them that belonged to Mr William Bellinghams lot Two Gates; purchased of Mr Sewall Senior one Gate purchased of Danniell Harris one Gate And of William Hobson halfe one Gate purchased of the towne one quarter of a gate

To William Tenney as to his acre and halfe lot and halfe .

a gate purchased of the towne two gates.......... 2 Gates purchased of Mr Edward Carlton that he had of the towne for Consideration of mony lent........... 1 Gate

William and Thomas Tenney purchased of Mr Phillip
    Nelson .... 2 gates
and of John Harris one and of Thomas Crosbie one.... 2 gates
William purchased of the towne one gate............. 1 gate

To Richard Holmes as belonging to a halfe two Acre
    lot two gates and one quarter and A quarter pur-
    chased of the towne........................... 2 and halfe
purchased of Mr Edward Carltons that Mr Jewett as his
    Aturney sould halfe one Gate.................. one halfe
purchased of John Jonson of Richard Thurleys pro-
    priety... 2 gates

To John Jonson left of his two Acre lot that was
    Richard Thurleys one Gate and a halfe.......... 1 halfe
and as belonging to the lot that was Edward bridges.... 1 halfe
purchased of the Towne one Gate................... 1 gate

To Edward Hassen his halfe two Acre lot that he pur-
    chased of John Smith two gates and one quarter. 2 one quarter
purchased of John Tod one Gate .... 1 Gate
purchased of the towne one and of Thomas Crosbie one 2 gates
purchased of Thomas Nelson one, and one that he had of
    the towne for land he laid downe.............. 2 gates

To Gorge Kilborne as belonging to his Acre and halfe
    lot and halfe a gate purchased of the towne....... 2
    as also one gate he had for land laid downe at new
    plaine... 1
purchased of Mr Jewett by exchainge of village land... 2

To Thomas Pallmer as to his Acre and halfe lot and
    halfe a Gate purchased of the towne............. 2 Gates
purchased of Mr Phillip Nelson one Gate............ 1
purchased of Thomas Nelson two Gates.............. 2

To Richard Longhorne as to a halfe two Acre lot pur-
    chased of John Newmarch two Gates and one
    quarter .... 2 one qur
purchased of Mr Phillip Nelson one Gate............ 1
purchased of Samuell Mighill two Gates.............. 2
purchased of The Towne three quarters of on gate..... 3 quarts

To Abraham Jewett as purchased of Thomas Nelson
  Two Gates.................................... 2 gats
  purchased of the towne one Gate................... 1 gate

To Thomas Nelson as Reserued to himselfe Seauen
  Gates and one quarter......................... 7 quarter

To John Pickard as belonging to the two Acre lot that
  was vxor Crosbies foure Gates and one halfe...... 4 halfe
also as to the priuelidge belonging to and acre and halfe
  lot Giuen by the towne to Isaac Coussins and
  what the said Isaac purchased of the towne two
  gates and one halfe........................... 2 halfe

To Richard Clarke as to an acre and halfe lot that he
  purchased of Thomas Elathrope one gate and a
  halfe .... 1 halfe
purchased of the towne one gate and one halfe gate.... 1 halfe

To William Law as belonging to a halfe two Acre lot
  that he purchased of John Newmarch two gates and
  one quarter.................................... 2 quarter
purchased of the Towne three quarters of one gate..... 3 quarters

To John Burbanke as to his Acre and halfe lot and halfe
  a gate purchased of the towne two gates.......... 2 Gates
purchased of Mr Phillip Nelson foure Gates........... 4 Gates

To Leaonard Harriman as belonging to the Acre and
  halfe lot that was John Spoferds and what was purchased of the towne two Gates .... 2 Gates
purchased of Ezekiell Northend three Gates.......... 3 Gates

To Thomas Burkbie as purchased of Mr Joseph Jewett
  three Gates .... 3 Gates

To Ezekiell Northend as belonging to a halfe two Acre
  lot purchased of Thomas harris and a halfe two Acre
  lot purchased of John harris foure and a halfe
  purchased of francis parrat one gate purchased of
  Mr Anthony Crosbie foure and a halfe purchased of
  daniell harris one gate purchased of william hobson
  one gate purchased of Thomas Nelson one purchased of Mr Phillip Nelson one and purchased of

Thomas miller three two of which three the said
miller purchased of m^r Jewett all these seauenteene
gates appeared vnder hand and sealle of from which
the said Ezekiell hath sould to seuerall men soe
that ther is left Remaineing vnto himselfe Eleuen
Gates .... 11 Gates

To Andrew Hiden as by land laide downe by way of
exchainge the which land was giuen by the towne
vnto the said Andrew, one gate purchased one gate
of Danniell Rouse .... 2 gats

To Thomas Dickinson as belonging to a two acre lot
foure gates and one halfe..................... 4 halfe
purchased of william hobson two Gates.............. 2
purchased of Mr Phillip Nelson one gate............ 1

To Charles Browne as to an acre and halfe lot and giuen
by the towne to be at cost to beate the drum for the
benefit of the towne two Gates.................. 2 gates
purchased of the Towne one Gate................... 1 gate

To vxor mighill as Remaineing to hir of a three Acre lot
nine Gates and one halfe....................... 9 halfe

To vxor Smith as to a two Acre lot that was purchased
of Mr John Miller foure Gates and one halfe...... 4 halfe
purchased of Mr Jewett one Gate and a halfe......... 1 halfe

To John Trumble one gate that was giuen to his father
in Relation to keepeing of a Scoolle............. 1 gate
purchased of the Towne one gate................... 1 gate

To Abell Langley as to a two Acre lot giuen him by
Robert hunter foure Gates and one halfe......... 4 halfe
purchased of Mr Jewett one Gate and a halfe......... 1 halfe

To Nicholas Jackson as giuen by the towne one gate
and two gates that he had by his wife that were
purchased of Thomas miller Acre and halfe lot.... 3 gates
purchased of the Towne two gates.................. 2 Gates

To Thomas Tenney as to an acre and halfe lot and one
gate giuen by the towne two and a halfe.......... 2 halfe

purchased of francis parrat one gate.................. 1 gate
purchased of the towne one halfe gate............... halfe gate

To Elizebeth Tenney allias parrat as belonging to fran-
    cis parrats two two Acre lot seauen gates vnsould.. 7 Gates
purchased of william hobson Sixe gates.............. 6 gates

To William Jackson as to his Acre and halfe lot and
    purchased of the towne two gates................ 2 Gates
purchased of Mʳ Joseph Jewett one gate.............. 1 Gate
purchased of the Towne one Gate.................... 1 Gate

To Thomas Wood as purchased of nehemiah Jewetts
    gardion with the house that somtimes was Mʳ
    William Bellinghams two gates.................. 2 gates
purchased of the Towne one Gate................... 1 Gate

To Henory Royley as giuen by the towne two gates.... 2 gates
purchased of Mʳ Anthony Crosbie two gates .... 2 gates

To John Grant as Giuen by the Towne to his mother
    Jane Grant one Gate.......................... 1 Gate
purchased of The Town one Gate................... 1 Gate

To Edward Sawyer as Giuen by the Towne one Gate.. 1 Gate
purchased of The Towne two Gates................. 2 Gates

To Richard Swan as belonging to his two Acre lote
    foure gates and one halfe gate............ .... 4 halfe
and as by purchase of one acre and halfe lot of Thomas
    Lilforth one gate and one halfe gate............. 1 and halfe
purchased of Mʳ Thomas Nelson one gate giuen the
    said Mʳ Nelson by the towne for forbearance of
    mony lent for the use of the towne............. 1 Gate
and as by priuelidge of marriage belonging to one acre
    and halfe lot and halfe a gate purchased of the
    towne that were John Trumbles 2 gates as also one
    Gate more the said John Trumble purchased of Mʳ
    Joseph Jewet .... 3 Gates
also as to the halfe two Acre lot that was micaell
    Hobkinsons two Gates and three quarters.... 2 and 3 quarters

To John Tod as to one halfe two Acre lot that he pur-
    chased of William Harris Reserued vnsould one
    Gate and one quarter of a gate................ 1 and quarte

and for land purchased of Mr Carlton and exchainged
with the towne for one gate..................... 1 gate
purchased of the towne one Gate and three quarters of
a gate..................................... 1 3 quarters

To Maxemillion Jewett as to his two Acre lot foure
Gates and one halfe gate..................... 4 one halfe
purchased of Mr Phillip Nelson one gate............ 1 Gate
purchased of Mr Joseph Jewett halfe one gate...... halfe one gate
purchased of william hobson and assured by his wife as
administrator one gate....................... 1 Gate

To James Barker as to his Acre and halfe lot and halfe
one gate purchased of the towne two Gates ....,. 2 gates
purchased of william wild as to his acre and halfe lot
two gates................................. 2 gates
purchased of Danniell Harris two gates .... 2 gates
and by exchainge of land with the towne one gate...... 1 gate

To John Pearson as purchased of the towne one gate.. 1 gate
purchased of Thomas wood two Gates............... 2 gates
purchased of Thomas Crosbie that belonged to John
Heseltines lot two Gates...................... 2 gates
also purchased and injoyed by leafe from Mr Richard
Dumer of Mr Thomas Nelsons propriety belonging
to Mr Nelsons Childeren in England Mr Dumer
being excequtor; foure Gates .... 4 Gates

To John Mighill as purchased of Ezekiell Northend one
gate purchased of Mr Jewett one Gate purchased of
Thomas Nelson one gate..................... 3 Gates

To Dorrity Chapman as belonging to the halfe of a two
acre lot was Gorge Abbots being the right of hir
former husband Thomas Abbot deceased belonging
to his propiety in the north east feild two gates and
one quarter of a gate.................. 2 gates one quarter
and one gate that the said Thomas purchased of M^r
Joseph Jewett............................... 1 Gate

To William Stickney as to his Acre and halfe lot and
one halfe gate purchased of the towne two gates... 2 gates
and as by gift from the towne one gate.............. 1 gate
and more purchased of the towne three gates......... 3 gates

To John Scalles as belonging to the two Acre lot that
was John Jarrats his by right of mariage foure
gates and one halfe gate .... 4 one halfe
and as belonging to his owen Acre and halfe lot and
halfe one purchased of the towne two gattes ...... 2 gates
purchased of the Towne one halfe Gate .... halfe gate

To Mrs Mary Rogers as belonging to the foure acre lot
that was hir former husbands Thomas Barker
Twenty gates and one halfe gate................. 20 one halfe

To Richard Lighton as by gift from the towne one gate. 1 gate
purchased of the Towne one gatte................... 1 gate

To John Bointon as belonging to his acre and halfe lot
and halfe one gate purchased of the towne two gates 2 gates
purchased of the towne two Gates.................. 2 Gates

To Mr Phillip Nelson as Reserued vnsould of his part of
the proprietie of Mr Thomas Nelsons lot his father
deceased Eight gates and one quarter of a gate
....8 gates one quarter

To William Scalles as to his acre and halfe lot and halfe
one gate purchased of the towne two gates........ 2 gates
purchased of the Towne one Gate .... 1 Gate

To Jaehin Rainer as belonging to the part of a two Acre
lot he purchased of Leiftennant John Remington
foure gates..... .... 4 gates

To Samuell Plats as purchased of Mr Joseph Jewett
three gates................................... 3 gates
purchased of the Towne one Gate.................. 1 Gate

To Marke prime as purchased of Mr Phillip Nelson one
gate purchased of John Jonson belonging to
Richard Thurleys lot one gate purchased of M^r
Joseph Jewett of from Mr Carltons propriety. he
being atturney three Gates..................... 5 gates

To John Dreser as belonging to his Acre and halfe lot
and purchased of the towne halfe a gate two gates. 2 gates
purchased of the towne two Gates.................. 2 Gates

To Samuell Brocklebanke as to a two Acre lot was his
      mothers foure gates and one halfe gate .... 4 one halfe
as to a two acre lot he purchased of mathew boyes
      Reserued two gates and one halfe gate............ 2 one halfe
purchased of daniell harris one gate................. 1 gate

To John Brocklebanke as purchased of Samuell Brock-
      lebanke two gates.............................. 2 gates
purchased of liftennant John Remington two gates..... 2 gates
purchased of The Town one gate..................... 1 gate

To William Boynton as to his acre and halfe lot and one
      halfe gate purchased of the towne two gates....... 2 gates
purchased of The Towne two Gates.................. 2 Gates

To Vxor Hobson as to a three acre lot of hir fathers
      Mr. humphray Rainers and to a two Acre lot he
      purchased of Mrs margery Shoue Eighteene gates.. 18 gates
and as Remaineing vnsould of the Right of a foure acre
      lot that hir husband william hobson purchased of
      Captaine Sebastin Brigham twellue gates........ 12 gates

To moyses Brodstreet purchased of John Pallmer that
      was of Mr Nelsons propriety two gates and one halfe
      gate .... 2 an halfe

To Mr Ezekiell Rogers foure acre lot twenty two Gates
      and one halfe gate...................... .... 22 gates one halfe

To Samuell Mighill Resurued of them he had of his
      fathers propriety two gates purchased of Mr Joseph
      Jewett of the Right of Mr William Bellinghams lot
      two gates .... 4 gates

To John Harris as belonging to a halfe two Acre lot two
      gates and one quarter purchased of Ezekiell North-
      end that were Mr Anthony Crosbies two gates pur-
      chased of Mr Jewett one gate.............. .... 5 one quarter
purchased of the town three quarters of one Gate...... 3 quarters

To Jeremiah Elsworth as belonging to the Acre and
      halfe lot of hugh Smith and halfe a gate purchased
      of the towne two gates...................... .... 2 gates

purchased of M^r •Jewett assured by the excequtors two
gates... 2 gates
purchased of Thomas Nelson three gates.............. 3 gates

To John Lambert as belonging to a two acre lot and one
his father purchased of the towne fiue and a halfe.. 5 one halfe
purchased of Thomas Barker two gates.............. 2 gates
purchased of the towne one halfe Gate.............. halfe gate

To petter Couper as belonging to his acre and halfe lot
and halfe one gate purchased of the towne two
gates... 2 gates
purchased of Leiftennant John Remington one gate.... 1 gate
purchased of the towne two Gates.................... 2 Gates

To Richard Wickam his acre and halfe lot and one halfe
Gate purchased of John Tod...................... 2 Gates
and as from The towne for worke done for Mrs Margery
Showe when she was in hir Illnes.................. 2

To Jonathan Plats purchased of the Towne two Gates.. 2 Gates

To Daniell Wicom purchased of Thomas Lambert..... 2 Gates
To Danniell Wickam purchased of The Towne two
Gates.. 2 Gates
To Daniell Wicom purchased of Thomas Remington .. 2 gates

To Thomas Remington purchased of The Town two
Gates.. 2 Gates

To Samuel Stickney purchased of The Towne two
Gates.. 2 Gates

At a Legall Twone meeting held the 16th of febuary 1661 it
was agreed vpon and voated that Oure Neighbours now liueing at
pentuckett should haue all ther Rateable estats Rated to the ministry Rate according as oures in the Twone are and that the one
halfe of it the Rate should be payed to the vse of the ministry heare : and the other halfe should bee payed to the vse of M^r
Ward : minister at Haverill

This vote above writen is agreed vpon only for this present
yeare 1661 :

At the same Twone meeting it was agreed & voted that the
select men for that yeare should have power to dispose or lett the

land that was Mʳ Rogers. being purchased for the ʋse of the ministry that they should lett the same for þe Tearme of seauen yeares

At the same Twone meeting it was also agreed and voted that William Stickney should have three gates vpon the Commanes layed out to him att the Rate of thirty shilling a gate as part of payment of that fiue pounds that is due to him from the Twone vpon the account of sume mony that was left by Goody Hunter

At the same Twone meeting it was granted and voted that Jerimiah Elsworth should have a quarter of an Acre of land laid out to him at prospect hill end joyneing vppon his owne land that he bought of Nathanill Elythorpe as the men apoynted for that purpose shall Judg meet wheare he desires it.

At the same Twone meeting it was also granted and voted that Deacon Jewett should haue a way layed out to him from Bradford street to his land laying one the fore side of prospect hill

	Gate						
Clarke	1	dreser	2	Tenney	1	plats	1
Jackson	2	plats	2	Bayley	—	Tenney	—
Couper	2	Grant	1	Browne	1	Scalles	—
Jackeson	1	Thomas	1	Remington	2	Heedon	1
Wickam	2	Tod	1 3 qrts	Harris 3 qrters			
Trumble	1	Law	3 qrts	lambert	—		
bointon	2	Jewet	1	Jonson	1		
bointon	2	Sawyer	2	Ace	1		
Scalles	1	pallmer	qrter	Stickney	2		
Brocklebanke	1	longhorne	3 qrtrs	lighton	1		

of the negitiue vote

    Thomas Leauer

    Thomas palmer

At a legall Towne meeting it was Granted and voted that those men whose names ar aboue writen shall haue liberty of the towne to bye if they will that number of Gates set downe to them paying thirty shillings a Gate and soe proportionally for lese or more then one Gate vnto mʳ Ezekiell Rogers of Ipswich in Corne and Cattell prouided that the deuision of land to be laid out be acording vnto Gates euery Gate one Acre of land : and if any think not good to bie any Gates then those Gates to Remane in the towne and not to be transeported from one to another

At the same Towne meeting Held this 17ᵗʰ of february 1661 it was Agreed and voted that ther should be laid out a certaine proportion of land acording vnto the Gates or pertickuler commonages as they are at this time belonging vnto the seuerall inhabbitants and the deuision to be vnto euery one Gate one acre

It was Agreed and Voted that after this deuission of land laid out ther shal be noe more deuissions of land on the towne Commons nor noe more Adission of Gates nether by Giueing leting or selling except it be for the nessesery of the towne to accomodate teaching elders

ffebuary the 25th : 61 : 62

The select men for this present yeare Richard Swan John Dreser Thomas Tenny Abell Langhley John Brocklebank Being Impowered by the Twone for to let or to dispose of the land that was Mr Rogersis being pnrchased for the vse of the Ministry They haue Accordingly disposed of the same for the Tearme of Seauen yeares : as foloweth

Impr :   To Wiliam Stickney And Samuell Stickney the one halfe of the said land vpland meadow & Gates or Commanages theire to belonging vppon those Condisions or Tearmes folowing viz :   That they pay for the same the full and just sums of fouer pounds tenn Rent by the yeare. to be payed in Corne and Cattell for the vse of the ministry & to be payed at the Time the ministry Rate or Rates is payed.   And the abouesaid psons by vertue of this Agreement shall be Rate free for the land let to them And alsoe the Aboue said William & Samuell are heare by Ingaged to lay vppon the saide land Twenty loads of Dunge Every yeare Dureing the Tearme of Seauen yeares & make & maynetaine the proportion of fence belonging to the part of land above let for the tearme of yeares abouesaid

In witnes wheare of the abovesaid William & Samuell

Sett to theire hands.

William X Stickney
his marke

Samuell S Stickney
his marke

The Sellect men whose names are aboue writen and Impoured by the Towne to let out the land that was Mr Rogers giuen vnto the Church and towne as appeares by the condission in his said will They haue let vnto Thomas wood one halfe of the said land and meadow and halfe the gates or commonages belonging thereto vpon

the condisions and Tearmes following (viz) that he is to pay for the said one halfe the full and just some of foure pounds tenn shillings by the yeare dureing the terme of sixe yeares next ensueing the date hereof to be paid in Corne and Cattell for the vse of the ministry at the time that the ministry Rates is to be paid and by uertue of this Agrement the said Thomas is to be Rate free for this abouesaid land let vnto him and also the abouesaid Thomas doth herby ingage himselfe to lay vpon this abouesaid land that he thus Rents all the dounge that may or shalbe produced by the hay and storks that doth arise on the said land and meadow and that yearly dureing the terme of sixe years and further the said thomas is to mantaine the fence bellonging to the said land and meadow vnto which aboue expresed agrement I set to   +   +   +
the first of January 1662

Thomas   +   +

At a Leagall Towne meeting held in march 1662 it was Agreed by the towne that Leift Samuell Brocklebanke and Richard Swan; being Chosen by the towne should Together with the Townes men of hauerell Agree and determine where the highway from hauerell to Rowley should lye and acordingly being together and Considering the intollarable Charge it would be to lie alonge by the riuer wher it once was laid; haue agreed the Country way now is to lie allonge by the riuer to the Corner of John Hesseltines feild and turneing that Corner soe to the stony brooke and soe alonge ther pasture land as they vsually use to goe

Robert Stiles 2 oxen....................................
one cowe......................................
one hogge.....................................
one yearinge..................................
Lande broke up 7 Acres: unb 2 Acres.........
a house and sellar............................

March the 7th: 62:

It ordered that all the fence against the Northeast feild shall bee maide suficent against Catell by being ditched against the fence with a ditch of a bout two foot in bredth & a one foot deepe. begining at the bridg at the twone end beyond Mr Crosbyes. & going to the Rough marsh beyond Richard Longehornes New ground beyond the oxpasture hill Provided that wheare its not capable of being soe ditched that the fence be mayed foure foote & thre Inches high

It is like wise ordered that the order aboue mentioned shall be in force for all other places and feilds as for all the fence at Wetherfeilds street end from Jackin Rayners to Elder Rayner horse pasture. & the fence *Fences to be mayed* Against Bradford street lots lying against the *4 foot 3 Inches* oxpasture and also Bachelers playne against *highe* the oxpasture. & such places about the the aboue said feilds & at the Twones end wheare Catell Comonly hante. be mayed suficent by ditching wheare its capable by Reason of the ground for Rockes or otherwayes or for height as aboue sayed betwene this present and the last of maye ensuing vppon the penalty of 6ᵈ a Reyle length for defect heare in and + + to the like penalty for +

At A legall twone Meeting held in march 62 it was voated that left Brocklebanke & Richard Swan being Chosen by the twone Should lay out the contry high way from pentuckitt toward Rowley

At a twone Meeting held the second of June 1662 itt was ordered & declared that if any Cattell or Horses be found in the marsh feild comanly Called Mʳ Dumers farme theire being None theire present tending their owne proprietys or they be some way suficently tethered or tyed their vppon their owne propyety they shall forfeite by way of poundage fiue shillings & this order to continue inforce from the Date heare of till the last of August ensuing : & This order doth also Includ the Northeast feild to beare force Against all vnruly cattell & horses after Notice giuen to the owner that they are soe : & they keepe them not away : & if any person or persons complaine to the Select men or any two of them of the vnRulynes of any such horse or beast & the said select men or any two of them telling the owner of the same shall bee accounted suficent Notice

At the same twone Meeting it was also agreed vpon and voated that Left : Brocklebanke should be aded to John Pickard and Ezekiell Northen for to lay out a psell of land at merymacke for the making vp the proportion of the Deuisons of Richard holmes Richard longhorne & some others that threw some mistake was not maid equall at first with other proprietyes & for seteling and Righting some bounds in diferance thire

At a Twone Meeting held the 19ᵗʰ June 62 :

It is ordered and declared that if any person or persons doe put any catell or if any be found vpon the Cow Commans that are not working catell but being Cowes or young cattell they shall bee Rated to the Cow heards & be lyable to pay for quantyty & qualyty as the Rest of the cowes belonging to the Cow heard are

Provided that such cattell as haue beene giuen in to the young Cattell heard & stray from thence vpon the Cow commans shall not bee lyable to this order. if they pay to the young cattell heard as the Rest belonging to that heard doe.

At the same Twone Meeting it is ordered that noe person or persons shall cutt any grass vpon any coman meadows in the Cow Commans farme or else wheare belonging to the Twone of Rowley with out the consent of the Select men or the Major part of them vppon the pennalty of foure shillings the Loade :

		£
The Towne Charges for the yeare 1662 is............	19 – 8 –10	
more aded to the aboue Rate Sam plats.............	0 – 4 – 0	
dan wickam............	0 –10 – 0	
will bointon............	0 –02 – 0	

The Rate and mony put into the Constable hand for the £
defraying of the abouesaid Charges is ....21 –14 – 8
more put into the Constable hand by John Bointon for
his Rent of hog Iland.................... ...... 0 – 6 – 8

+   +   +   +   +   +   +   +

Tho burkby	0– 5–11	Charles browne	0–07– 0
Rich Swan	0–18–10	Abell Langley	0–09– 9
Tho Tenny	1–00– 3	Marke Prime	0–10– 2
Tho Leauer	0–10–11	James Baly	0–14– 7
John Scales	0–09–01	Rich Langhorne	0–15– 8
Will Ace	0–13– 8	Edward Sawer	0– 6–11
Sam : stickney	0– 4– 6	Rich Holmes	0– 8– 6
Judith Lumm	0– 1– 7	Sam Woster	0– –8 3
Rich Lighton	0– 5– 8	Henry Riely	0– 8– 8
Benja Scott	0– 8– 1	Andrew hiden	0– 4– 3
Ed hason	0–10– 2	Will Law	0– 9– 4
John Johnson	0–10– 4	John palmer	0–15– 5
Vxor Smith	0– 7–11	John harris	0–12– 3
Tho : Remington	0– 8– 5	Sam mighill	0–07–10
John Lambert	0–16– 5	John Grant	0–o8– 4

Sam plats	0–05–11	Jokin Rayner	0– 5– 1
Tho: wood	0–07–03	James Barker	0–14–10
John Pickard for Ne-		Will Stickney	0–19– 4
hemiah Jewitt house		Will Scales	0– 8– 8
& land	1– 3	John Brockle[bk]	9– 6
Ezekiell Northen	0–15–10	Sam Brockle[bk]	0–15– 6
M[r]. Nelson	0–15– 7	Vxor mighill	0–12– 0
Tho. Nelson	0–15–00	Vxor Hobson	1–00– 0
John Spofard	0–14–10	M[rs]. Rogers	1–06– 4
John Pickard	01–01–04	Jon Person	1– 5– 7
Willi boynton	00–11– 9	Rob: Heseltine	0–15– 2
Jonathan Plats	0–04– 5	good Starling	0–03–10
Abraham Jewit	0–08– 2	Henry Kingbury	0– 9– 2
John mighill	0–04– 9	Corp gage	1– 9– 8
John Dreser	01– 2– 3	Vxor grifin	0– 3–11
Will foster	0– 8–11	Dan bradley	0– 6– 8
Rich Wickam	0– 5– 6	Georg Hadley	0– 7– 3
Rich: Clarke	0– 7– 3	Rob: Andrews	0– 9– 3
Nicol: Jackson	0– 9–10	Rob: Smith	0– 6– 9
Peter Cooper	0–14–00	Abram Redington	0–14– 3
John Burbanke	0–11– 7	Rob: Stiles	0– 6– 9
Tho Palmer	0–14–05	Jos: bigsby	0– 9– 5
Will Jackson	0–13–06	Good Pebody	0– 0– 5
Jerimiah Elsworth	0–15– 6	Good H + ley	0– 1– 1
John Trumble	0–06–07	Jo[n] Cumings	0–10– 0
Danill wickan	0–08– 6	Jo[n] Bond	0– 5– 5
		Rob: Rogers	0– 5-- 5
	26–17– 7	Goodd Hardy	0–13– 7
Jo[n] Boynton	+ + +		
Vxor Dickinson	1 + +		19–11– 7
Deacon Jewett	1– 5 +		26–16– 7
Leno: Harimon	0– 8– 9		46–08– 2
Georg Kilborn	0– 9– 1		

Robert Hesseltine and Corperall gage are appointed to be ouerseers at pentuckit for the high wayes betwene Andeuer and them and also to take care of there fences there

Richard Swan William Stickney & William Jackson Being Apoynted by the Towne to sell Trees in the Twone street to such as desire them to stand for theire vse Against their houses or Land

They haue sould to John Pickard a small percell of young Trees vppon the west side of the path over A gainst his Now

dwelling House att Murlay feild as many as groweth vppon fourteene Rods of ground as the trees are marked

At a Legall Twone meeting held the 26th of September 1662:
it was agreed and voted that Leue Brocklebanke Richard Swan &
Ezekiell Northen Should Lay out Land for any such men as maide
it apeare vnto them they wanted Land to make their Deuisions
equall according to purchas with the Rest of theire Neighboures

At a legall Twone meeting held the 26th of November 62:

It was agreed & voted that vxor Dickinson should haue a
percell of land Joyning to hir lot at the end of bradford street
layed out to hir vppon the account that the other land is. that is to
be layed out an Acre to a gate vppon the Cow commans is Provided it be not to the prejudice of the Neighbours adjoyning nor
any high wayes & that it be layed out for quantyty according to the
Discresion of the men appoynted by the towne for that purpose to
lay it out and to heare and determine the objections & complaynts
of Neighbours against it and then lay out if they see cause.

It is further ordered also that any other person may have the
lik liberty to haue som small perceles of land Joyning vpon their
owne land in bradford street or else wheare in the twone vpon the
fore said account. according to the discresion of the men appoynted
for that purpose. provided that it be not prejudicall to their Neighboures nor high wayes nor any ordynary watring places

At the same twone meeting it was agreed and voted that
Richard Swann Leuietenant Brocklebanke Ezekiell Northen &
William Stickney being chosen by the twone. should lay out the
land formerly agreed to be layed out to eury gate vppon the commans one Acre of land & that what the said persons or the major
part of them did in that case should be accounted a valid act

At the same twone meeting it was also granted and voted that
John Spoferd should haue foure Acres of land layed out to him in
that deuision of land an Acre to a gate vpon the Cow commans

At a Legall Towne meeting held the 17th of february 1661
It was agreed and votted that there should be laid out a certaine
proportion of land according to the Gates or particuler Commonages as they are at this time belonging vnto the seuerall inhabbitants and the devission to be vnto euery one gate one acre of
land

At A Legall Towne meeting held the 26th of Nouember 1662 it was agreed and voted that Richard Swan Samuell Brocklebanke Ezekiell Northend John Pickard and William Stickney should laye out the said land formerly Agreed to be laid out to euery gate one acre of land and that what the said persons or the maior part of them did in that case should be accounted a vallid act

According to the foresaid agrement of the towne and also acording vnto the order and agrement of the towne for the beginning of the said devission The east end of the towne to begin : the furthest of at the Neerest land and to haue each man his halfe proportion of land laid out first it was laid out as followeth

Imprimis To Moses Brodstreet one acre and a quarter be it more or lese lieing on the east side the mill Riuer bounded on the north east side by land formerly laid out vnto m^r Thomas Nelson at present possesed by John person the south east end abuting on the Common the north west end abuting on land laid out to John person

To Samuell Mighill two Acres be it more or lese lieing on the south west side of Mosses Brodstreet his land buting as afforesaid

To Nehemiah Jewett one acre of land be it more or lese lieing on the south west side of Samuell Mighills land abuting as afforesaid

To John Grant one Acre be it more or lese lieing on the south west side of Nehemiah Jewetts land abuting as afforesaid

To John Harris three Acres be it more or lese lieing on the south west side of John Grants land abuting as afforesaid

To John Pallmer three Acres and a halfe be it more or lese lieing on the south west side of John Harris his land the north west cnd buting on the mill Riuer the south west side bounded by his owne second devission of land which said second devission of land he hath laid out vnto him and he accepted it as its bounded on the mill riuer on the north west end the south east end as his first devission doth abuting the Com̄on the south west side as its bounded by seuerall markes not fare distant from the way leading to the mill

On the west side of the mill Riuer Next vnto the land that John Person posseseth that formerly was laid out to m^r Thomas Nelson is laid out to Samuell plats one acre and a halfe be it more or lese lieing betwene the hill and the said land ther being left a conuenient high way betwen the hill and it on the south side of the afforesaid John person land that he purchased of Leaonard Harriman is laid out

To John Tod two Acres be it more or lese bounded on the north east by the said Persons land the south east end abuting the mill Riuer the north west end buting on a high way betwen the hill and it

To William Law one acre and halfe be it more or lese lieing on the south side of John Tods land abuting as afforesaid

To Andrew hiden one acre be it more or lese lieing on the south side of William Laws land abuting as aforesaid

To Henory Royoly two acres be it more or lese lieing on the south side of Andrew Hiden his land abuting as afforesaid

To Thomas Wood one acre and a halfe be it more or lese lieing on the south side of Henory Royolly his land abuting as aforesaid

To Ezekiell Northend fiue acres and a halfe be it more or lese lieing on the south side of Thomas Woods land abuting as afforesaid.

To m^r Phillip Nelson foure Acres be it more or lese lieing on the south side of Ezekiell Northends land abuting as afforesaid

To Thomas Nelson three acres and three quarters be it more or lese lieing on the south side of m^r Phillip nelsons land abuting as afforesaid

To Edward Chapman as belonging to the right of his wife somtimes Dorrity Abbot one acre and halfe and halfe a quarter bounded on the north east by a percell of land that was left in comon betwen the land of Thomas Nelson and it the southeast end buting against a swampe the northwest end buting against a high way bettweene the hill and it

To Richard Hollmes two Acres and a halfe be it more or lese lieing on the south side of Edward Clapmans land abuting as afforesaid as the said Chapmans land doth

To Edward Sawyer one acre and halfe be it more or lese lieing on the south side of Richard hollmes his land abuting as afforesaid

To Richard Longhorne three acres be it more or lese lieing on the south side of Edward Sawyers land abuting as afforesaid only his end buts on the mill Riuer

To James Bayley foure acres be it more or lese lieing on the south side of Richard longhorns land abuting as afforesaid the end buts on the Riuer as Richard longhorns doth

To Marke Prime one acre and halfe be it it more or lese lieing on the south side James balleys land abuting on the riuer and high way only the said high way comes about the end and downe most of the south west side to goe ouer to Simonds meadow

On the South east side of the mill Riuer or Simonds Brooke and on The west side of a small Brooke that Issueth in to the said Brooke is laid out vnto William Tenney three acres be it more or lese bounded on the east and south by the said litle brooke and by seuerall marked trees in the swampe that the Brooke runes in and on the north end abuting on Simonds brooke or Riuer

To Abell Langley two Acres and three quarters be it more or lese lieing on the west side of william tenneys land the south end bounded by seuerall marked trees in the swampe the north end abutting on Simonds Brooke

To Marke Prime one acre be it more or lese lieing on the west side of Abell langleys land the south end bounded by seuerall marked trees in the swampe the north end abuting on Simonds Brooke

To Charles Browne one acre and halfe be it more or lese lieing on the west side of Marke Primes land the south end abuting on marke primes second deuision of land and part of the east side bouned by seuerall marked trees in the swampe the north end abuting on Simonds Brooke

To John Lambert foure Acres be it more or lese lieing on the west side of Charles Brownes land the south end buting on marke primes second devission of land the north end abuting on simonds Brooke

To Thomas Remington one acre lieing on the west side of John lamberts land (be it more or lese) buting as afforesaid

To John Jonson two Acres be it more or lese lieing on the west side of Thomas Remingtons land abuting as afforesaid

To widdow Smith three acres be it more or lese lieing on the west side of John Jonsons land abuting as afforesaid   :

To Goodwiffe Parrat (allias) tenney as belonging to ffrancis Parrats childeren six acres and a halfe lieing on the west side of widdow Smiths land buting as afforesaid (be it more or lese)

To Mr Anthony Crosbie one acre be it more or lese lieing on the west side of francis parrats childerens land buting as afforesaid

To Thomas Burkbie one acre and halfe be it more or lese lieing on the west side of mr Crosbes land buting as afforesaid

To Richard Swan Sixe acres be it more or lese one acre of it being part of his second deuission lieing on the west side of Thomas Burkebies land abuting as afforesaid only a litell part of the west side joyneth on some common land through all these aboue mentioned lots there is allowance for a cartway that soe each of them and the lots that are laid out beyond them may haue sufficient and conuenient passage with out disturbance

To Thomas Leauer foure Acres be it more or lese one acre of being part of his second devission lieing on the west side of Richard Swans land buting on the common on the south end the north end abuting on simonds Brooke

To Thomas Tenney three Acres be it more or lese lieing one The west side of Thomas Leauers land the south end buting against common land the north end abuting on simonds Brooke

To John Scalles foure Acres and twenty seauen Rod be it more or lese one hundred and seauen Rod of it is for want of the share of one Acre and halfe lot in the marsh feild part of it lieth against the west end of his Pollipod lot and against the west ends of William Sticneys and William Scalles Pollipod lots the Rest of it lieth on the west side of Thomas tenneys first deuission of land the south end buting against common land the north end buting on simonds brooke the west side bounded in a Swampe against William Acie land

To William Acie foure Acres be it more or lese lieing on the west of a Swampe against the west side of John Scalles his land the north end abuting against Simonds brooke the south end abuting against common land the west side bounded by land of mᵣ Samuell Phillips haueing a high way Through it for the lots beyond it

To mᵣ Samuell Phillips foure Acres and one halfe lieing on the west of William Acies land the north end abuting against Simonds brooke the south end buting against common land bounded by land of Richard Lightons on the west

To Richard Lighton Two Acres be it more or lese lieing on the west side of mᵢ Samuell Phillips land buting on Simonds brooke on the north end the south end buting against the common the west side also bounded against the common

To John Pearson seauen Acres be it more or lese which he acceped of in steed of nine acording to his gates or commonages fiue and one halfe of it be it more or lese lieth on the east side of the mill Riuer the south east parts of it is bounded by the north west ends of moses broadstret Nehemiah Jewett Samuel mighill John grants and John harreses first deuission of land; The north east side is bounded by land formerly laid out to mᵣ Thomas Nelson bounded on all parts else by the mill Riuer The other acre and halfe lieth ouer against it on the west side of the mill Riuer haueing aded to it a small persell that was sould vnto the said John Person and is bounded by the high way on the west the north end bounded by Nubery line the south end on land granted at a leagall towne meeting held January the 25th 1659 it was granted that John Person should haue the land which is now fenced in being about three quarters of an acre be it more or lese with that ground to the Riuer which the tenters standeth on in consideration of a years Ringing the bell Released

At The west end of the Towne is land
Laid out vpon the fore Named account of gates or
pertickuler commonages

Vnto Mrs Mary Rogers as belonging vnto the Right of Thomas Barkers Lot twenty acres and one halfe; ten whereof lieth on the south side of the hill commonly called Hunslay hill be it more or lese bounded on the south by land laid out vnto daniell wickam and John Boynton the east end buting against the common the north buting against the hill the west end bounded by land laid out to william Boynton the other ten acres and halfe lieth part at the east end and part at the west end of hir land laid out for hir as the priuelidge of the afforesaid thomas Barkers lot on the south side of a pond commonly called Pentuckit pond and on the west side of the pen Brooke

To William Boynton foure Acres be it more or lese lieing on the west side of m^{rs} mary Rogers ten Acres on the south side of hunslay hill buting against the hill on the north the south buting against John boyntons land

To Ann Mighill (widdow) Nine Acres and one halfe be it more or lese lieing on the west side of William Boyntons land the north end buting against the hill or a high way the said William Boynton is to haue to come conueniently to his land which she hath allowance for and may either allow it within or without; the north west parts of it bounded by the towne common the west and south parts of it bounded by a swampe and by John boyntons land or meadow

To daniell wickam two Acres be it more or lese lieing one the south of part of m^{rs} mary Rogers land on the south side of hunslay hill the east side and the south end buting against the towne common the west side bounded by John boyntons land

To Ann Hobson (widdow) Nineteene Acres be it more or lese part at the west end and part at the south side of fifty acres of land

that was formerly laid out vnto mᵣ Humphray Rayner neere to the
pen the south part of it joyneth vnto the common the west and
north parts joyneth vnto meadow formerly laid out vnto the afforesaid mᵣ Rayner also ten acres more or lese lying one the top of
Longe hill the northside and the east and west ends buting against
the common the south side bounded by land laid out vnto Jachin
Rayner

To John Brocklebanke fiue Acres be it more or lesse lieing
vpon The Top of long hill buting against Common land on the
south and east and west ends the North side bounded by land of
Samuell Brocklebanke

To Samuell Brocklebanke eight Acres be it more or lese fiue
of which lieth on the north side of John Brocklebankes land on
long hill bounded on all parts else by the common the other three
Acres be it more or lese lieth against the south side and west end
of the land that he purchased of matthew Boyes that lieth not fare
from the west end of the towne and in the west end oxe pasture on
all parts else joyneing vnto the said oxe pasture land that lieth in
common

To William Scalles three Acres be it more or lese. adjoyning
vnto the north side of his owne land at the new plaine on all parts
else joyneing vnto the towne Common

To William Stickney eight Acres two of which belonged vnto
the Right of Samuell Stickney the which eight acres of land be it
more or lese lieth vpon a litle plaine on the east side of the brooke
that Runeth neere vnto the south east end of long hill not fare from
the said hill end and it is bounded by a small swampe that runeth
allong the north side of it into the foresaid brooke buting against
the brooke on the west end of it the east end buting against the
towne common The south side bounded by land laid out vnto
James barker

To James Barker seauen Acres Be it more or lese lieing on
the south side of William Stickneys land buting against the brooke
on the west end the east end buting against the towne common the
south side bounded by a small swampe

To Gorge Kilborne fiue acres be it more or lese lieing on the
south side of James Barker land the midle of the swampe deviding betwixt them on all part else bounded by the common

To James Dickinson seauen acres and one halfe be it more or
lese lieing part at the south end and at the west side of his land
that was laid out vnto his father thomas Dickinson in the plaine

commonly called Bradforth Street New plaine the south east and west parts of it buting against the towne common the north end bounded by land laid out to Richard Swan as the right of the gates that belonged to micaell Hobkinsons lot.

To Richard Swan as belonging to the gates of micaell Hobkinsons lot two acres and three quarters one acre and three quarters of it lieth on the northwest side of James dickinsons land the west end buting against the Common the east end against the new plaine the other acre lieth at the east end of the said plaine against the land laid out to John Trumble hugh smith william Jackson and Thomas pallmer on all part else bounded by oxe pasture land in common

To Jonathan Plats two acres be it more or lese lieing on the north side of the foresaid Richard swans land at the west end of the new plaine the east end buting against the said plaine land the best end buting against the towne common

To Abraham Jewet three acres be it more or lese lieing on the north side of Jonathan Plats his land buting as he doth on the plaine and common

To John Mighill three acres be it more or lese lieing on the north side of Abraham Jewetts land buting as afforesaid

To Jeremiah Elseworth seauen acres be it more or lese lieing on the north side of John Mighills land buting as afforesaid only the north side of it is bounded in the midle of a swampe that part it and land laid out to William Acie

To John Remington Junior two Acres of Land at the end of the towne be it more or less, bounded on the Northwest corner by a stumpe now standinge at the corner of the saide Land, and so from that stumpe alonge by the roadeway as it is fenced till it cometh to the corner of the fence, and so cross to the well, and so square from the well, to the side of Thomas Crosbeis Land.

The second Devission for the east end of the Towne was laid out as followeth

To Mosses Broadstreet one Acre and one quarter be it more or lese as it lieth bounded by Thomas Nelsons first devission that lieth on the west side of The mill Riuer on the nor side buting against the Riuer on the east the west end buting against a high way that Runeth allong on the east side of the hill

To Samuell Mighill two Acres lieing on the south side of Mosses Broadstreets land buting as afforesaid

To John Grant one acre of land lieing on the south side of Samuell Mighills land buting as afforesaid

To John Harris three Acres lieing on the south side of John Grants land buting as afforesid

To Ezekiell Northend fiue acres and one halfe be it more or lese lieing on the south side of John harris his land buting as afforesaid

To John Tod one Acre and one halfe be it more or lese lieing on the south side of Ezekiell Northends land buting as afforesaid

To William Law one acre and one halfe acre be it more or lese lieing on the south side of John Tods land buting as afforesaid

To Samuell Plats two Acres and one halfe be it more or lesse lieing on the south side of William Laws land buting as afforesaid

To Thomas Wood one Acre and one halfe acre be it more or lesse lieing on the south side of Samuell Plats his land buting as afforesaid

To Ezekiell Northend a peace of land by estemation sixe acres be it more or lese which was laid out vnto him in consideration of the badnes of his second devission of land and the badnes of the land that he purchased of seuerall men about his second devission beyond the mill Riuer ; lieing and being next to some meadow that the said Ezekiell purchased of mᵣ Phillip Nelson neere vnto the plaine commonly called Andever plaine wher the way goeth downe vnto nubery falls it lieth easterly on that way and is bounded by the foresaid meadow on the east and north the other part of it buting against the common and in some parts it Runes along in swamps downe to a litle Runell that goes downe his meadow into the brooke acording as trees ar marked

also Laid out vnto Ezekiell Northend one halfe acre of land one the south side of Thomas Woods land the east end buting on the mill Riuer the west end on the highway vnder the east side of the hill

Laid out on the south side of the abouesaid halfe acre vnto the said Ezekiell Northend as exchainging his Right in the first devission of dorrity Chapman sometimes Abbot after hir death to be hirs for euer to dispose on and he accepts of the pʳsent possesion of this second devission that belonged to hir for hir life ; as his full satisfaction the Right of the second devission being as the first to the right of Thomas abbots lot one acre and twenty Rod. acording to the gates they being two and one quarter the which acre and twenty Rod be it more or lese is bounded on the south by the first deuission of Edward Chapmans land as the right of his wife dorety part also of the Right of the said dorety as belonging vnto one purchased gate buting against the said land of Ezekiell Northends the east end buting against the mill Riuer the west end against the high way vnder the east side of the hill

Laid out vnto Edward Chapman at the east end of his first devission of land halfe an acre be it more or lese being his second devission of the right of his wife dorety vnto the purchased gate bounded on the east in the ege of the swampe on the north buting against Ezekiell Northends land the south end buting against Richard hollmes his first devission of land

To Richard Hollmes two acres and one halfe sixty Rod of which lieth in a swampe at the east end of his first devission of land the Rest two acres and twenty Rod lieth on the east side of the swampe that lieth on the east side of William Tenneys first devission of land buting against the said tenneys land on the west the north side bounded by a swampe on the towne common the east end also abuting against the towne Common

To Edward Hassen as his first devission of land three acres and one hundred Rod be it more or lese lieing on the south side of Richard hollmes his land the west end buting against william tenneys land the east end against the common

To Edward Sawyer one acre and a halfe lieing on the south side of edward hassens land the east end buting against the common the west end buting in the swampe acording vnto the seuerall marked trees in the swampe deuiding ther land on the west side of the swampe from theirs on the east side

To Richard Longhorne thre acres Sixty Rod of which lieth in the Swampe at the east end of Richard hollmes first devission the Rest lieth on the south side of Edward Sawyers land buting as afforesaid

To James Bayley foure acres Sixty Rod of which lieth in the Swampe at the east end of Richard hollmes his first deuision The Rest lieth on the south side of Richard longhorns land buting as afforesaid

To William Tenney three acres lieing on the south side of James bayley land buting as afforesaid

To Abell Langley three acres two of which lieth on the south side of William Tenneys land buting as afforesaid the south side bounded against the towne common the other acre lieth on the west side of vxor Smiths second devission of land aboue the mill hill

To Marke Prime two acres and one halfe Sixty Rod of which lieth in the Swampe amonge the vndevided land at the east end of Richard hollmes his first devission of land which land is when euer those proprietors thinke good to devide it to be equally devided vnto euery one his share as it may fall more or lese only Richard hollmes share is to lie against his owne land ; the said Marke hath also a way allowed him from his own first divission at the east end of James balleys land and Richard longhorns land to goe vnto the said 60 Rod of land the other two acres and twenty Rod be it more or lese lieth against the south ends of the first deuision of Charles browne Richard Swan and all the lots lieing betwene them the east end buting in the Swampe against the west end of James balleys land the west end buting against the   the south side bounded by land of edward hasen

To Edward Hasen three acres and one hundred Rod lieing on the south side of Mark Primes land the east end buting in the swampe against the west end of William tenneys and abell langleys second devission of land the south side bounded by the towne Common the west end buting against the land of

To Henory Royley two acres be it more or lese lieing on the west side of a high way betwéne simonds meadow that John Pearson posseseth and the said land the south side bounded neare vnto the common Roade to hauerell the west end buting against the rocke hill commonly called Simonds great Rocke the north side bouncd by land laid out vnto Andrew hiden

To Andrew Hiden one acre and one halfe lieing on the north side of henory Royleys land on the west side of simonds brooke bounded on the north by a highway that commeth downe on the south side of brooke that Runeth easterly in to simonds brooke the east end buting against the high way on the west side John Pearsons meadow the west end buting against the Common vpon the hill side

At a generall and Legall Towne meeting held the 30 of January 1662

we whose names are hereunder written dissented from the first order which doth give the prudentiall men there power

Philip Nellson
Jonathan Plats

Be it knowne vnto all men by These prsents that I Ezekiell Rogers of Ipswich in The County of Essex doe owne to haue

Receaued of the Towne and Church of Rowley the full Comple-
ment of one hundred and Sixty pound Bequeathed By m^r
Ezekiell Rogers of Rowley in his last will and Testament of which
Leagacy I doe discharge and acquite the Towne and Church of
Rowley from all dues vpon the account of the said leagacy in
wittnes where of I set to my hand and Sealle
the hand and sealle being
set vnto the same

Dated January 6th (1662)
Signed Sealled and Delliuered
In p^rsence of vs

Simon Tuttell   Sworne in Court held at Ipswich
John Whipple   The 31 of march 1663 by the wittneses
                  Simon Tutle and John Whipple
                    P   me   Robert Lord Clarke
Recorded amonge the Records for essex at Ipswich follio 129
                  P   me   Robert Lord Recorder

     The Towne Charge for the yeare 1663 amounts vnto
£24 – 04 – 03
     The rate put into the Constables hand for the defraying of the
abouesaid Charges amounts vnto £31 – 15 – 00
     The ouerplus to be disposed by order from the sellectmen

     giuen in by a bill of fines to the marshalls hand in August
1663 towards defray— of publicke charge 2 – 05 – 0 as may apere
in that bill fined acord— to towne order

     The Sellectmen considering the great care and trust that the
generall court hath laid on them as a duty to take care that damage
in corne may be pruented and vnrully catell be restrained doe hereby order and declare vnto the towne that if any man or men or any
other person or p^rsons doe let goe or sufer
published at a legall to goe any beast or beasts vpon the towne
warned towne common or any comon pasture or
meeting the 12th of p^rtickuler inclosure lieing against any
August 1663 corne feild without such shackles or
fetters as may restraine them from doe-
ing damage after such person or p^rsons haue had notice of the
vnrullienes of such beast or beasts by any two of the sellect men
that then if they be found on the common or any such inclosure

afore mentioned being against any corne feild He or they shall pay
for euery such beast ten shillings the one halfe to him that im-
pounds them and the other halfe to the use of the towne and it
shalbe in the pouer of any man that is and inhabitant of the towne
to impound any such beast or beasts that are found vpon the common or any such inclosure afore mentioned without such shackles
or fetters that may in and ordenary way restraine them

At a legall Towne meeting held the 8th of January 1663 were
chosen Towne oficers for the remaineing part of the same yeare
and part of the yeare 64
    In primis for Constable & marshall William Law
    for Sellect men Richard Swan Ezekiell Northend Samuell
Brocklebanke Abell Langley Jeremiah Elseworth
    Overseers at east end Richard Hollmes Samuel Plats
                at west end John Burbanke Leaonard Harriman
    for calling Towne meetings William Teney
    Ouerseers for Nubery fence John Jonson Thomas Nelson
    for pinders John Spoferd John Pallmer Samuell Stickney
    Pinder for west end William Jackson
    Pinders for the farme Mr Nelson and Henory Royley
    Judges of delinquients for not comeing to towne meetings
James Bayley Marke Prime James Barker William Stickney
    ouer seers for the fences and high wayes of our Neighbours at
merrimacke from Jonsons Creeke vpwards and downeward to
Nubery line Corperall John Gage Robert Hesseltine
    Goodman Kingsbury is ouerseer for ye towne of Rowley in
yt order about Cowper stufe

[NOTE.   The town orders in force before 1666 were arranged by
the town clerk at about that time in "Book No. 1" without dates ;
they were numbered from one to forty-two inclusive.   Where any
of these orders are found in the original record they appear herein
in the order they were made but the following orders are lost from
the original record and are inserted here from "Book No. 1" and
numbered as they appear therein.   Most of the town orders were
in force until after 1700.   G. B. B.]

17
    And to the end that perticuler mens fences may be knowne It
is ordered That all propriators that haue any land lying in any feild

more or les or any ox pasture shall proportion ther fence. According to ther land which lyeth ther in. and shall mark ther fence soe
proportioned. And enter the same into the Towne booke before the
Twentith of Aperil next. and in case the propriators, cannot agree
about ther fence : it shall be determined by three Indeferant men,
who shall be satisfied for ther labour. and if any be defectiue in
the performance of this order. such shall pay for euery defect fiue
shilings a hole and a stone is to bee at the foot of euery devision

18

wheras ther is yearly hurt done by Catle horses and sheep in
eating mens medowes and both eating and Treading men corne in
the spring and summer time in the north east feild and farme and
other common cornefeilds withing a mile and one half of the
towne : it is ordered that from the first of Aprill from time to time
it shall be lawfull for the pinder or pounders to impound them and
be paid for them as foloweth for sheep 4^d ahead for catle 4^d for
horses 8^d vntill the last of may : and after that time till the feild be
broken all horses shall be 2^s shilling ahead and catle 1^s ahead
and sheep 6^d pence ahead and if any man shall find any the
catle aforesaid in the feild it shall bee lawfull to impound them and
haue half the wages the pinder should haue and if the pinder or
Any other cannot bring vp such horses that may bee found in the
feild or farme. if he haue wittnes that such cattle or horses were
ther : and informe ther owners of them his wages shall be as due as
if he had impounded the same Catle or Horses

19

It is ordered that noe heardsman or any other man shall break
the foresaid northeast feild or farme. after or before harvist with
out libertie from the select men. or the maior part of them the
penaltie for euery such defect is 19 shilling 6^d : it is herby declared
that if any leaue or put ther oxen or horses in the night time or any
part of it : into the places abouesaid they shall be looked vpon as
breakers of this order. and soe liable to the aforesaid penaltie.

22

It is ordered if any man or man servant shall by his neglect in
opening or shutting the ox pasture gattes or Gapps. and let out or
leaue out any oxen soe as to disturbe the Cow heards. he shall pay
for euery such default That is proued against him one shilling six
pence : allsoe iff any person shall leaue open eyther gapp or gate in

land or medows That lie in common they shall for euery such default pay one shill six pence

24

It is ordered that noe Inhabitant or owner of any house or land in the Towne shall bring in any Tenant to Dwell thering. without the consent of the towne vnder The penaltie of 19 shillings the moneth euery month they continue in the towne or bounds of the towne without consent

It is like wise ordered That noe man shall sell any house or land more or less vnto any stranger before he ofer the same to the select Men at an Indeferant vallue vpon paine of ninteene shillings the moneth for euery percill of land soe disposed of contrary to this order

27

It is ordered That all hogs and pigs aboue eight weeks old shall be driuen duely into the woods as foloweth : vid Bradford street shall driue as far as long medow and wetherfeild street to mr Rogers shall driue ther hogs ouer Batchilars brooke at ther ox pasture end. and from goodman Wicams to Mr Philip Nelson ouer Batchilers Brooke : and the other Two streets ar to driue ouer at Batchilers Bridge and allsoe that all hogs are to be shut vp in some close place euery night and any Tyme of the day when They come home if the owner knowe of them. provided That if any person suficiently yoak and ring ther hogs and keep them soe According to order they may be exempted from this order of driueing and if any fail hearing for euery time soe Doeing he or they shall pay 4d ahoge half to the-Informer. and half to the Towne—and further it is ordered conserning such swine as are not driuen or yoked as afore said if they be found in any mans corne or medow such hogs shall be liable to pay duble dammage : (68 nulled)

37

It is furthur ordered that when the ouerseers shall giue notice to any person to whome it conserns that ther common gap or fence lies downe or not acording to order That such persons shall goe about repairing the same forthwith and in case they who haue this notice shall not soe doe. they shall be fyned doubl soe often as the ouerseers shall fynd it vndone

38

It is ordered that all Towne Streets shall bee made and maintained fower Rodd Widd and shall be made cleare of wood Carts or any other impedyment Three rodd widde that soe ther may be comfortable passage for catle To and fro before the Twentith of Apperil next and soe kept till the last of October vpon paine of euery such default fiue shillings but in case any beast receiue hurt by any neglect of this order the delinquent shall pay the dammage

40

It is ordered That if any man put any catl vpon any of our commons or any catle he found there aboue a yere old That ar not giuen in to pay as young cattle or cowes they shall be liable to pay two shillings six pence a head besidds the heardsman wage and if any cows or calus be found vpon the cowe comans vnles they be of ye catle giuen in to the heards which are to be driven vp againe The heards man or any other shall haue power To bring them vp : and to put them into the Places wher the youge Cattle are put and To bee driuen away as other younge Cattle are

41

It is allsoe agred that such as doe not exceed yr proportio of gats and yet improue at sertain tims ther intrest in whol or in part those persons shall giue to two of the select men the number of Catl they take off and the time when and if ye doe not fathfully obserue soe to doe they shall be delt with all as breakers of ye afor said order

42

It is ordered that no person in the towne shall fall lopp bark or girdl any tree on the north or norwest side of any hous or houslot in the towne with in one quarter of a mile vpon the peanalty of fiue shillings for euery tree soe faled loped or girdled contrayrye to this order

———————•———————

At a legall Towne meeting held 22th of January 1663 it was Agreed by the generall consent and voate of the towne that that meadow in Crane meadow and that meadow at the west end of Pentuckit Pond that is Recorded laid out vnto mr Ezekiell Rogers should hereby be declared that it was laid out as that Right that was due vnto Thomas Barkers lot

The select men considering of the great co ╪ ╪ of damage done by swine in meadow espesally for want of Ringing doe therefor order that all swine that are taken

Published at a in impropiated meadowes and pastures
legall meeting held that are fenced from great cattell and not
the 6 of Aprill Ringed they shall be liable to pay for the first
1664 time they are taken two pence ahead in way of poundage and the owner to haue notice by the party damnefied to take care sufficiently to ring his hoges and if they be taken a second time not Ringed then they are to pay to the party damnefied 1ˢ per head and soe from time to time soe often as they are found not sufficiently Ringed to pay one shilling for euery swine head taken doeing damage in any such affore said inclosed meadow

At a legall Towne meeting held the 11ᵗʰ of may 1664 it was granted ane voated that John Trumble should haue what land could conueniently be spared on the west side of the high way to Ipswich ouer against John pickards and on the south of Jonathan plats land soe as ther be sufficent high wayes acording vnto the intent of the towne the men appointed by the towne to lay it out vnto him are John pickard maxemillion Jewet and ʼezekiell Northend

At the same Towne meeting it was granted and voated that Beniamin Scot should haue what land could conveniently be spared betweene edward hasons and the end of mʳˢ Rogers land leaueing sufficient way to the clay pits the men appointed by the towne to lay it out vnto him áre Richard Swan

At a leagall Towne meeting of the inhabitants of the towne of Rowley Held the 13ᵗʰ of Aprill 1664 The towne considering vpon an expression in the will of mʳ Ezekiell Rogers that seemes to inwrape all the lands of mʳˢ Rogers that weare Thomas Barkers Throughout the bounds of Rowley to be to the church and towne of Rowley, which is thought to be either an error in writing of it or at least it appearing vnto the towne not to be any way his intention nor will for to giue away the afforesaid land that was Thomas Barkers (excepting only the halfe of the warehouse pasture) but to leaue it fully and freely to be vnto the will and despose of mʳˢ Rogers according vnto the will of hir former husband Thomas Barker; The Towne and Church doe therfor fully and freely for our sellues our heires and sucksessers for euer disclaime any Right of interest whereby we may expect any part in the afforesaid lands that weare the Right of Thomas Barker and foreuer acquit for our sellues our heires and sucksessers any such claim that soe it may Remaine to be free vnto the will and despose of the said m^rs Rogers with out Trouble from us the Towne and Church of Rowley our heires and sucksessers for euer And the Towne and Church doe agree and determine by ther owne act That the Sellect men shall haue full power in the name of the wholle Towne and Church for to make or to procure any such instrument to be made as that it may be left vpon Record in Court that soe all after Truble may be preuented; The originall copy of this was writen Read and voated at the meeting aboue expresed; The Reason why the exception of halfe the warehouse pasture made is because though the former husband of m^rs Rogers Thomas barker bought the wholle warehouse pasture yet he paid but for halfe of it the other halfe hir later husband m^r Ezekiell Rogers paid for This was wittnesed by Samuell Brocklebanke Ezekiell Northend Maxemillian Jewett William Acie John Pearson Jeremiah Elseworth

The fiue aboue named Testefied in Court held at Ipswich the fift day of May 1664 this writing aboue to be the act of the Towne of Rowley   P me Robert Lord Clarke

Recorded the 10th of may 1664 amonge the Records of lands for Esex at Ipswich in the Second booke folio 198 & 199
          P me Robert Lord Recorder

This is a copy of the act of the towne of Rowley To m^rs Rogers entered   by me Samuell Brocklebanke

Entered 1664

According vnto the grant of the Towne of Rowley vnto Robert Heseltine William Wild and John Heseltine there Land was laid out vnto them by the men appointed by the Towne for that end and it being neglected to be brought into Record acording vnto the order of the towne by the approbation of the select men acording vnto ther description of it is entered as it lieth bounded

In primis Laid out vnto John Heseltine for a lot to build on containeing ten Acres be it more or lese bounded by land that then lay in common vnto the towne but now laid out vnto them on the east side the west side bounded by land laid out vnto william wild one the north it buts against a high way that Runs along by

merrimacke Riuer the south end bounded by other land laid out
vnto the said John Heseltine and land laid vnto Robert Heseltine

To the said John Heseltine more one acre adioyneing vnto the
east side of the aboue mentioned ten acres

To the said John laid out more ten acres be it more or lese
bounded on the North vpon part of his first ten acres and part on
some land laid out vnto Robert hesseltine on the west it is bounded
by land also laid out vnto Robert heseltine and on the south end
buting against land laid out vnto Gorge hadley which was part of the
land granted by the towne vnto william wild bounded on the east
by Robert Heseltines pasture land

To the said John ther is laid out more foure acres and one
halfe be it more or lese bounded by the high way by the Riuer on
the north by land laid out vnto Robert hesseltine on the west and
by Robert Hasseltines pastor land on the south the east side bounded
by the pasture land of the said John Hesseltine

To the foresaid John Hesseltine is laid out more two hundred
acres of pasture land be it more or lese with in which is included
the Rest of his plowing or aurable land acording vnto the grant of
the towne and it lieth bounded by merimacke Riuer on the north
by land of his owne and by the pasture land of Robert heseltine
on the west by the pasture land of Gorge hadley on the south and
by land laid out vnto Thomas abbot on the east through which
pasture land ther is to be left a sufficient and conuenient high way

Item   Laid out vnto Robert Hesseltine ten Acres for a lot to
build on bounded on the east by land that was laid out to william
wild on the north it buts against the high way by merrimack Riuer
on the west its bounded by more land that was laid out to william
wild bounded on the south by some other land laid out vnto the
aid Robert

To the said Robert Hesseltine laid out more by estemation
one acre be it more or lese adjoyneing vnto the former ten acres
vpon the east and south adjoyneing the high way by the Riuer on
the north and bounded by a small Runet of water on the west

To the said Robert laid out more foure acres be it more or lese
bounded on the west by land laid out vnto John Hesseltine on the
north bounded by a high way by the Riuer on the south bounded
by other land laid out vnto the said John hesseltine on the east
bounded by the pasture land of the said Robert hesseltine

To the said Robert laid out more foure acres and one halfe be
it more or lese bounded by land of John hesseltine on the east by

the high way by the Riuer on the north on all parts else by the pasture land of the foresaid Robert hesseltine.

To the said Robert was laid out more ten acres be it more or lese bounded on the north by the south end of his first ten acres laid out to build on and vpon part of land he purchased of william wild by exchainge and vallueable consideration and on part of John hesseltines land that he purchased of william wild part of it by exchainge the rest for valluaeble consideration bounded on the west by land of gorge hadley which he purchased of william wild bounded on the east by land laid out vnto John Heseltine bounded on the south by land of Gorge hadley

To the said Robert was laid out more two hundred acres be it more or lese for pasture land within which is included the Rest of his plowing or aurable land according vnto the grant of the towne as it lieth bounded by the highway by the Riuer on the north bounded on the east by the pasture land of John heseltine bounded on the west part by land of John Heseltine and part by other land of the said Robert heseltines bounded on the south by the pasture land of Gorge hadley

According vnto the Grant of the Towne there
meadow was laid out vnto them as followeth

In primis Vnto John Hesseltine was laid out ten acres be it more or lese as it lieth bounded on the west by the land commonly called the village land which is laid out vnto John Jonson and Charles Browne being part of it with in there lines lieing on both sides the brooke that Runeth easterly Into the pond commonly called pentuckit pond the west end is bounded by marked trees on both sides of the brooke that face ouer to the vpland on both sides the meadow being very litle on the brooke at the west end, soe it is also bounded on both sids of the brooke as it cometh easterly by the vpland only on the south part of the south side it is bounded against some meadow laid out vnto m^{rs} mary Rogers as it may apeare by a marked tree on the westerly side of that glade of meadow and a stake on the easterly side bounded one the east by meadow laid out to william wild now in the possesion of Gorge Hadley and John Griffin griffins being on the south side of the brooke

To the said John laid out more fiue acres three of which be it more or lese lieth on the south side of the afforesaid brooke not

very fare from the brooke bounded by vpland laid out vnto mr^s
mary Rogers as the Right of Thomas Barker in the land commonly
called the village land ther being severall marked trees about it that
devide it from the vpland and at the south end haueing marked trees
or stackes to stope it at the end faceirg ouer one against another
and on the east side it is bounded by meadow laid out vnto Robert
heseltine; the other two acres be it more or lese lieth on both sides
of the brooke at the east end of Robert hesseltines twellue acres of
meadow that lieth one the forementioned brooke on the east its
bounded by meadow laid out vnto Gorge hadley the south and
north sides bounded by land lieing in common being of the three
thoussand acres belonging vnto the towne only on the south side of
the brooke it toucheth on some common meadow that lieth on the
south east of it

To the said John is laid out more two acres be it more or lese
lieing on the east side of Johnsons brooke not fare below where
ther highway goeth ouer vnto ther great meadow bounded by
vpland on the North and south the east end buts against the
swampe

To the said John is laid out more one acre be it more or lese
in the meadow commonly called the longe hill meadow bounded
on the east by a brooke bounded on the west by meadow laid out
vnto william wild now in the possesion of Beniamin Kimball the
south and north ends bounded by the vpland

To the said John hesseltine is laid out more two Acres be it
more or lese in the meadow commonly called the dead hill meadow
lieing toward the south east end bounded on the north west by
Robert hesseltines meadow

To Robert Heseltine was laid out Twellue acres be it more or
lese lieing toward the easterly end of ther meadow that lieth by
that brooke that Runeth into pentuckit pond it lieth where the line
goeth ouer it that parts m^{rs} Rogers land and the townes three
thoussand acres; being on both sids of the brooke buting on the
east on John hesseltines meadow the townes land and m^{rs} Rogers
land bounds it on the south and west ther being seuerall marked
trees and stakes that devide it only on a part of the west it is
bounded by meadow laid out vnto william wild now in the
possesion of Gorge hadley the meadow on the North side of the
Brooke is Bounded by vpland laid out to John Pickard his meadow
on the north side goeth higher vp the brooke westward then that on
the south side; vntill it come to a great Rocke that parts it and that

which was laid out vnto william wild that Rocke being the bounds betwixt them

To the said Robert is laid out more three acres be it more or lese lieing on the south siae of the forementioned Brooke being more westerly then the former ther being a percell of vpland betwen them it lieth a little distant from the Brooke bounded by m^rs Rogers vpland ther being seuerall marked trees and stackes that devide it from the vpland on the east and south only at the south end it croseth a peace of meadow from a stacke to a marked white oake tree that standeth on the westerly side of that point of meadow being the bounds betwene John hesseltins meadow and the said Roberts bounded on the west by John hesseltines meadow

To the said Robert is laid out more two acres be it more or lese lieing from Johnsons brooke southerly at the end of a swampe that issueth with a litle brooke that cometh out of this meadow Runeing into Jonsons brooke not fare below the pond the which meadow lieth in land laid out vnto John Pickard as part of land he had due in the land commonly called the village land; bounded by the said Pickards vpland on the north east and west bounded on the south by meadow laid out vnto william wild now in the possersion of John Griffin

To the abouesaid Robert is laid out more one acre be it more or lese bound on the east by meadow formerly laid out vnto william wild now in the possesion of Beniamin Kimball on all parts else bounded by the vpland

To the afforesaid Robert hesseltine is laid out more two acres be it more or lese in the meadow commonly called the dead hill meadow bounded on the south east by John heseltines meadow haueing a brooke Runing through it all parts else bounded by vpland laid out to John heseltine being his deuission of the land commonly called merrimacke land

officers of The Towne for the Remaineing part of the yeare 64 and 65 Chosen at a Legall Towne meeting 9th of January 1664

for counstables and towne marshalls Richard Swan and William Tenny

for moderator of towne meetings deacon Jewett

for selectmen Thomas Leauer Samuell Plats Thomas Nelson John Brocklebanke Leaonard Harriman

ouerseers for east end of the Towne Thomas Tenney John Pallmer for the west end John Burbanke John Boynton senior

ouerseers for Nubery fence John Jonson John Lambert

for pinders for east field and farme Mr Phillip Nelson John Spoferd Samuell Stickney Andrew Hiden

for calling Towne meetings William Tenney

Judges for to fine dellinquents for not coming to towne meeting Marke Prime James Bayley Samuell Brocklebanke James Barker

At a Legall towne meeting held the 9th of Jenuary Richard dowell of Newbury desiring to know how the grant formerly about ye diuision of plum Iland was vnderstood they generally by votte declared they vnder stood it to be ment of being deuided to the then being present householders when that grant was votted

The Select men for this yeare 1665

Have Agreed and Bargained with Charles Browne to keepe the young Catle Heard as foloweth that for his wages he shall haue two shillings & six pence by the day to be payed in Corne or that which is Equivalent: And also the same Select men are hereby ingaged to provid the said Charles a Cow for to giue him milke while he keeps the catle: & the said Charls is to keepe the Catle one weeke of the time and his two sons Beriah and John another week of the time and not more at once: & that the said herds men are to be going be that time the Sun is halfe an houre high on the Second day morning vpon the penalty of one shiling six pence.

At a leagall Towne meeting held Janevary the 20th day

It is ordered and agreed that noe towene act for the yere insueing shall be held and acounted avaled act of the towne that is not Concluded and voated by sunsett that day: (at least whil ye day light of That day serveth to record the same. ye last line & half unvoated)

At a leagall Towne meeting held the 27 of Janevary 1664

granted to Mr Samvel philip all that medowe not exeeding four acre this out of the new ox pasture nere the lyne—but not any withing the foresaid ox pasture

At a leagell Towne meetting held march ye 24 64 or 65

It was agreed & voated that Left Samuel Brocklbanke Richard Swan & Ezekiel Northend are impowered to consider materiall sufer-ings as any person or persons by highways ouer ther medowes soe as it may be madout to ye aboue said mens satisfaction and to lay out vnto those sufers recompence for such lots out of ye coman medow called hoge Iland marsh according to ye nature and degree of such mens sufering after ye best light of those 3 men abouesaid and allsoe y^t thes complaints be made to thes men aboue said withing one moneth after ye date hereof or else be voyd in poynt of releeff by medow

Levetenant brockelbank & ezekiell northend chosen to answer ye sute with gold & Andrewes

To John Pearson purchased of Ezekiell Jewett as the Right of faith his wife being part of the Right of gates of hir father francis Parrat and what he purchased of Thomas Remington part that be-longed to the said Thomas and part that the said Thomas purchased of John tenney which was the right of his wife mercy that was also part of the Right of hir father ffrancis Parrat sixe acres wanting eight Rod be it more or lese as it lieth part of it lieing on the North west side of the high way to Nubery the south end bounded by high way in to the Commons the north west side bounded by the Common land not far distant from the line That devideth betwene the Towne of Nubery and the towne of Rowley it being a tryangle peece the northly point of it buting against the high way to m^r Dumers farme The other part of it lieth one the east side of the mill Riuer the said Riuer being the westerly bounds of it the southerly end of it bounded by a brooke that comes out of pollipod meadow and falls into the mill Riuer that end being Twenty Rod or Ther about the easterly side bounded by the towne Common being forty Rod or there about the north end also bounded by the Towne Common being in bredth from the mill Riuer to a wallnut stumpe that is the north east corner of it Twenty Rod or there aboutt

To Thomas Burckbie one acre and a halfe be it more or lese lieing on the North side of Richard Hollmes his second devission of land ther deuiding bounds being about the middle of the swampe the west end of it bounded also in the swampe that parts William Tenneys first devission and it the east and north parts of it buting against the towne Common the high way in to Simonds feild goeing through it toward the northerly end of it being allowed for

To Richard Swan foure acres be it more or lese three acres of it lieing at the west end of marke primes second devission of land

and at the west end of edward hassens first devission of land the south side buting against the Common the north side bounded by land of Thomas leauer the west end buting against a litle peece of land laid out to faith Smith for the badnes of hir first deuission of land in the same feild

To Thomas Leauer two acres be it more or lese lying on the north side of Richard Swans land the east side bounded by a high way allowed for Richard Swan or any beyond as marke prime and edward hasen to come in to the high way ouer the lots the west side bounded in the Swampe by seuerall marked Trees bounding william acies land and at the north end of it joyning partly to the south end of his owne first devission of land and partly to the first deuission of Thomas Tenney and of John Scalles lands

To Thomas Tenney three acres be it more or lese lieing on the north side of Richard lightons land the north end bounded by Simonds Brooke the south end buting against a hill of Comon land

To John Scalles three acres be it more or lese lieing on the west side of Thomas Tenneys land the north west end buting against Simonds Brooke the south east end partly buting against the fence and partly against Common land within the fence

At a Leagall Towne meeting held the 6th of May 1665 it was agreed and voated that vpon condission of Mr Samuel Shepard staying and settleing among vs of the towne of Rowley that for his incuragment to setle it was granted that he should haue that peace of land betwene the high way and Mrs Rogers lot vpon the traineing place for a place to build vpon at the same meeting it was granted that he should haue twenty acres of meadow 7 or 8 acres of fresh meadow at the south east corner of the great plaine and the Remaineing part of the twenty to be made vp in the salt marsh caled hog Iland marsh at the same meeting it was also granted that he should haue eight acres of planting land 4 acres of it to lie at the north end of batcheler plaine the other 4 is to lie vpon the hill on the Right hand as we goe from the towne to the mill and is to joyne vnto the land of John haris and those lots that were the first deuission on the account of gates ther being a swampe betwene ther land and the land granted to Mr Shepard the which swamp is also granted vnto him that he may joyne his land with the feaild toward the mill only ther is to be left a sufficient way for them lots and

+   +   +   +   +   +   +   +   +   +

According vnto The Grant of the towne vnto m^r Samuell Sheppard for his Incouragment to Settling heare was

Laid out for a house lot or place to build vpon a peece of Land about two acres be it more or lese as it lieth bounded by land that was Mr Ezekiell Rogers our former pastor on the west and north west on all parts else bounded by the Common or high way

Laid out also vnto him foure acres for planting land together with land granted him for a pasture as it lieth bounded on the north west by land laid out vnto John Pallmer Mosses Broadstreet and others on the North: part bounded by land formerly laid out vnto m^r Thomas Nelson and part by the oxe pasture on all parts else buting against the towne common only the said Pallmer and the rest and John Person are to haue a high way through

Laid out also vnto the said Mr Samuell Sheppard eight acres of fresh meadow be it more or lese as it lieth bounded by the towne common being neere vnto the southerly corner of the great plaine formerly called the Rie feild

Laid out also vnto him twelue acres of salt marsh be it more or lese at it lieth in the marsh commonly called hogg Iland marsh bounded on the north west by marsh laid out vnto m^r Anthony Crosbie now in the possesion of Thomas Leauer the southerly end bounded by marsh laid out vnto Ezekiell Northend and marsh laid out vnto Richard Hollmes. bounded on the East, and South East upon the great creeke that doth part hog Iland marsh, and Nellsons Iland marsh.

Janvary the 9 1665 for ye yeare 1665 & 1666

Thomas Teny & John Palmer ar chosen Constables

Ezekill Northend James Bally John Dresser Lenord haryman Thomas Leauer

ouerseers at our end Abell langley John Grant

for ye other end John Spoferd & James Dickinson

for merymake Joseph Pike Len Gage

Pinders for our end henery ryley Samuel Stickney Andrew hiden Anthony Austin

Judges of Delinquents :

      for our End   William Asee : Edward Hazon

      for Bradforth streete end : James Barker :

                    Jonathan Plats :

at leagall meeting held Janevary yᵉ 26 65

It was agreed & voated that Richard Swan ezekil northend Left Sam brocelbanke mark pryme & william teny are impowerd by the towne to set out acording to yʳ best light yᵉ bounds of yᵗ acre of medow or swamp land Desynd & granted by the towne for the maintainance of the bridge ner Sachell medow between this & yᵉ 24 of march next folowing

febury yᵉ 14 65 agreed a month time mor giuen to mak Com

+ + + +

At a leagel towne meeting held febuary yᵉ 14 1665

It was voated after twice propounding that John Tod shall haue yᵗ Iland which lieth in his marsh bought of Mʳ Edward Carlton at such a price as the select men then in beeing did agree with him for which was twenty shillings

Agreed at ye same Towne meeting yᵗ left brocklbanke Ezekiel Northend John Pickard richard Swan ezekiel Mighell or any thre of them are   +   +   +   +   +   +   +
+   +   +   +   +   +   +   +   +

Deliuerd to the Constable Thomas teny of Rowley for defraying yᵉ Charges of yᵉ Country County & Colidy for yᵉ year 1665 which is   65 – 10 – 0
I say deliuerd to them a rait Containing   67 – 2 – 3

A bill of yᵉ Charges of yᵉ towne in yᵉ yeer 1665

Imprimis for Deacon Jewits for his deputieship at yᵉ seuerall generall Courts

fifty Day 1. 6 by Day...........................	3 –15 – 0
for his diat to be paid at boston.................	2 –10 – 0
for horse pasture feray & yᵉ petition.............	0 –18 – 6
for his horse hire..............................	0 –12 – 0
and carying the pay for........................	0 – 6 – 0

Left Brocklbank for tendings at seuerall Courts Ipswich 4

days..	0 – 8 – 0
time 3 days and charges in part mony at Salem Court.......................................	0 –12 – 0
boston Court 4 days & one day with voats to Salem	0 –15 – 6
treating with gold at Ipswich & meeting about newbury lyn................................	0 – 3 – 6

for laying out land at Springe.................. 0 – 6 –0
To the generall Court for a petition............. 2 –10 – 0

John pickerd for meeting about newbury lyne.......... 0 – 2 – 0
    Ipswich Court tending about gold 2 Days........ 0 – 4 – 0
    for tending ye towns busynes with Mr Crosbe as
      aturney & wittnes 4 days.................... 0 –16 – 0
    for tending four Days at boston with 1s for a meal
      ye left had............................... 0 –16 – 0
    more about boston voage horse ferriag and mony 0 – 4 – 9
    for goeinto ye viliag to treat with ye viligers a day 0 – 4 – 0
To John Todd as a finall end of all accounts between
    him and ye towne.......................... 2 – 8 – 0
Accounted with ye Constabls of ye yeere Rich Swan
    & will teny for balancing of both raits and loss of
    corn due to them.......................... 1 – 0 – 0

to Rich Swan in perticuler for tending Ipswich Courts 5
    Days..................................... 0 –10 – 0
    for 3 tyms goeing to gold.................. 0 – 6 – 0
    for 3 days at Salem Court in chargs time & mony 0 –12 – 0
    for laying out land at Springe.............. 0 – 6 – 0
Jeremiah Elsworth Jury........................ 0 – 1 – 0
to Thomas Stickney for killing a wolf............... 2 –10 – 0
to Thomas nellson for a select man warning meeting & a
    hors to Salem............................. 1 – 4 – 6
to Lenord harryman for same service burning marsh &
    goein to golds............................ 1 – 5 – 4
to John Brocklbank for selectman tending Ipswich Court
    goeing day to golds....................... 1 –10 – 0
to Samvell plats as select man and goeing to Court...... 1 – 3 – 0
Exekiel northend for running ye lyn about 3000d acrs &
    to newbury & laying out land.............. 0 –12 – 0
James Bally for Juryman....................... 0 – 8 – 0
Thomas Leauer for goeing to Salem once............. 0 – 3 – 6
    for writings and warneings towne meeting....... 0 – 2 – 6
    and for his service as one of ye select men........ 1 – 0 – 0
Thomas teny for the worke of an ouerseer............ 1 – 1 – 0
John Palmer for the like worke..................... 1 – 1 – 0
Jonathan plats a day at Court.................... 0 – 1 – 6
George Kilburne for burneing woods................. 0 – 4 – 0
Charls Browne for burning younge Cattle walkes....... 0 – 5 – 0

Corperall John Gage for a Jury man 4 days............. o – 4 – o
and robert hasseltine for the same service .... o – 4 – o
Jeremiah Elsworth one day at Court one day........... o – 2 – o
Edward hasen a Day Jury man....................... o – 1 – o
William Acy for a Jury man......................... o – 1 – o
     and one Day at Court about golds busynes .... o – 2 – o
samvel plats burying a Horse....................... o – 1 – 2
and Andrew Hidden for y same worke............... o – 1 – 4
Mr Philip Nellson for goe with brok or pickerd to ye
     viligers .... o – 2 – 6
Ezekiell mighell for helpeing rune y lyne About ye 3000
     acrs .... o – 4 – o
William Teny for goeing to golds one Day............. o – 2 – o
James Barker senior Jury man one day................ o – 1 – o
John boynton for vewing fence 6 day and burning marsh
     and other worke........................... 15 – o
John Burbank for ouer seeing fence & other worke..... o –15 – o
     for writings to goodman lord of Ipswich......... o –10 – o
William Boynton for laders about meeting house and
     tending about   +   +   +........... o – 3 – o
     and sucoring windowes and the bell wheel..... o – 2 – o
William Jackson Jury man one day .... o – 1 – o
John Dreser Jury man 1 Day....................... o – 1 – o
William Teny for his ofice as marshall out of ye fynes ... o – 2 – 6
     & for Calling towne meetings .... o   3   o
John Lambert for Veiwing nubury fence............. o   1 – o
and John Johnson for ye same worke................. o   1 – o
To John power of newburry for looking to ye the gate
     between ym & vs ys yere .... o – 5 – o
     for wittnes aboute his case whering the towne
     pays him for all his pay behind for ye gat........
Mr Nellson and his man........................... o – 3 – o
James Dickinson .... o – 1 – 6
Henery Reiley .... o – 2 – o
William Teny.................................... o – 1 – 6
Tho: Nellson man................................ o – 1 – 6
Samuel Stickney................................. o – 1 – 6
Thomas Leauer .... o – 1 – 6
John Pickard.................................... o   1   6
Richard Longhorne .... o   3   o
Gilbert Willford and his mate for foxes.............. o   5   o
                                              1   16   6

Debts oweing to yᵉ towne

Mʳ Anthony Crosbe bill of costs	2 –16 – 0
for the Rent of hogg Iland............................	2 – 0 – 0
John trumble for hay cuting..........................	0 – 1 – 8
William Jackson for yᵉ same..........................	0 – 1 – 8
Petter Cowper for yᵉ same 4ˡᵈ........................	0 – 2 – 8
John burbanke for 3 load.............................	0 – 2 – 0
Richard Clarke 2 load................................	0 – 1 – 6

fines for want gats

Peter Cowper 3......................................	0 – 5 – 3
Jachin Rainer for want of one gat....................	0 – 1 – 6
James Dickinson one & half..........................	0 – 2 – 6
Thomas Teny for Delinquence in yᵉ ouer seers work....	0 – 3 – 0
John Pallmer for yᵉ same.............................	0 – 3 – 0
Daniell Wicome for land of yᵉ towne..................	1 – 0 – 0
for hey at merrimak Ezekiel Northend under takes to pay	0 –10 – 0
John Todd for his Iland bought of yᵉ towne...........	1 – 0 – 0
Court charges recouered of goodman Andrewes.........	0 –11 – 4
William Teny of old acounts.........................	0 –13 –
Will Boynton for fines...............................	0 – 0 – 6
John Scalls fines....................................	0 – 1 – 4
Vxor wicome	0 – 0 – 4
James Dickinson	0 – 0 – 4
Jer Elsworth..	0 – 0 – 4
Peter Cowper..	0 – 0 – 4
vxor mighill..	0 – 1 – 0
Will Jackson..	0 – 0 – 4
Gorg kilburn..	0 – 0 – 4
Jachin Rainer.......................................	0 – 0 – 4
John Spoferd..	0 – 0 – 4
Robt Shillito & John Simons.........................	0 – 0 – 4
Daniel Wycome.......................................	0 – 0 – 4
Will Boynton	0 – 0 – 4
Nicolas Browne for falling a tree	0 – 2 – 6

Left brockelbank Ezekiel northend & ezkiel mighel chosen to Renew the bounds of our 3000ᵈ acrs at young catl pasture

Received of Constables for the yeare 1664 the sum of ffifty eight pounds six shillings and a half penny in full of there Rate for

that yeare being according to my warant by vertue of generall
Courts order   58 – 6 – 0 =
24   3   66   by me Richard Rusel Treasurer

Received of the Constables of Rowley in full of there rates for
the yeare 1665 the sum of fifty six pounds thirteen shilling and half
penny being according to my warrant by vertue of the generall
Courts order   56 – 13 – 0 =
the 24 :   3   66   by me Richard Rusell Treasurer

Laid out vnto Samuell Brocklebanke a percell of land that
should haue bene laid out before vnto that Right of Captaine
Sebastim Brighams land that he purchased of William hobson to
make vp his share of lands equall vnto the Rest of the purchasers
acording vnto proportion And it lieth on the east side of the Pen
Brooke that is said to be his east bounds lieing against the Rest of
his land the north end bounding against Common land Runing on
a streight line from the brooke or corner of his land on the west side
of the brooke to the north west corner of the feild that was fenced
in by thomas mighill now in the posesion of John Brocklebankes
heires that feild and land that was sould vnto John Brocklebanke
by the order of the towne being the east and south east bounds of it
till it joyne vnto the brooke againe against the Rest of his other
land
Laid out vnto John dresser Senior one acre and one halfe of
vpland be it more or lese in the feild commonly called Bacheler
feild bounded on the east side by land of Richard Clarke the south
end and west side bounded by land now laid out vnto John Boynton
The north end buting against the west end oxpasture : This land
being neglected to be entered when it was laid out is now by order
of the Select men entered this eight of January 1666

                    The Select men   Thomas Leauer
                                           Ezekiell Northend
                                           Leaonard Harriman

            a generall towne meeting Janvary ye ninth 1666
        Thomas teny & John Palmer chosen for Constables this folow-
ing yeare being 1667
        Ezkell Northen   John Tod   John Person   William Tenny

Richard Clarke Chosen 5 men this year

John Lamberd John Johnson ouerseers for East end

James Dickisson John Spawford ouerseers for west end

James Baley Hennery Ryley ouerseers for nubery fence

Thomas Tenny & John Palmer are to be marshals fo ye yeare following

Thomas Wood and Samvell Stickney are chosen for pinders for ye yeare ensuing

Thomas Tenny is chosen for calling towne meetting for ye yeare ensuing

William asa & Edward hasen James Barker and Jonathan Plats are chosen for Judges for ye yeare ensuing.

Deacon Jewit and John Dresser senier chosen to seale leathr for ye yeare ensuing

Beniamin Gage & Joseph Pike are chosen for ouerseers for ye yeare ensuing

At a legal towne meeting held ye fifttenth day of ye Eleaventh month 1666 It was agreed by voat that ye common marsh at Hog Iland should be devided according to gates

At a legall towne meeting held the 14th of ffebruary 1666 it was agreed and voted that Deacon Brocklebanke, Ezekiel Northen, John Pickerd, Thomas Lever, Lenerd Harriman, are Chosen to lay out ye Common marsh at hog Iland and to proportiō it to every man according to gates

43

Vpon consideratiō of the great spoyle of wood in ye Commons for fire and other wayse; It is ordered that if any man Inhabitant servant or soioyner shal fall or lop any tree smal or great within a mile and a halfe of the towne vpon ye Commons, except ye said person falling or loping ye said tree shall cary it away or set it vp; ye whole tree body and top within six dayes after he have fallen or loped it, he shal be liable to pay ten shillings for any part of ye tree yt is not taken away or set up as is aboue specified halfe to ye informer; and halfe to ye towne, this order doth not intend ye taking away or seting up of ye brush wch is not worth cariing home, ye order yt is maid covering a quarter of a mile of ye north & nor-west side of ye towne is not hereby at al infringed by this order

Thomas Teny Thōas Leuer John Boarbanke John Boynton are chosen to se to yᵉ executiō of this order dated 14ᵗʰ ffebruary 1666

44

The beter pretectiō of timber for posts and rales and bulding It is ordered and this day declared, that if any person or persons shall get any of the aboue mentioned stufe or timber, and dispose therof out of the towne they shall forfit to the towne by way of fine for every hundred of railes after the rate of ten shillings the hundred and for every post, for fenceing six pence a post and for every pece of timber too shilling a pece whether greate or small ruffe or hewen

45

It is ordered that all those that haue not paid in there pay for purchasing of powder for the towne stocke shall pay ether in good merchanable wheat or barley or other pay at money priced

46

It is ordered that no person or persons whatsoever shall mow any grasse upon any common meddow, belonginge to the Towne of Rowley, or any part of the saide Towne without the consent of the Select men, or the maior part of them, not hauinge hired the same of them upon the penalty of four shillings the loade, to the use of the Towne, and two shillings beside the four shillings to any person that shall inform thereof

The publik Charges of the Towne of Rowley for the year 1666
To Richard swan his Deputie ship & expenses there-
      abouts for his time at yᵉ Court fortie fiue days... 3 – 7 – 6
      for his Diate to be paid in corn which is to be
         made at Boston and is provided for in the bill of
         yᵉ Country Rait therfore not Counted hear
         saueing the carrying and feriag which is....... 0 – 5 – 3
      for his horse hire and keeping ther......... .... 1 –10 – 0
      for his voage to Salem....................... 0 – 4 – 0
      for Runinge the line between newbury and vs and
         to Andever.............................. 0 –10 – 0

Toward a sertan debt of 42 shill was to be paid to
the treasurer and its order to be paid out of
Country bill & provisiō is laid in for that endinge
fore said bill................................

To Richard longhorne for the towne use.............. o –10 – o
To John Johnson for viewing newbery fence........... o – 3 – o
        To him for worke about the meeting house....... o – 3 – o
To Mr Philip Nelson for viewing the aboue fence....... o – 3 – o
To James Dickinson as ouerseer viewing Chimneys..... o – 2 – o
     for viewing fences............................. o – 4 – 6
     four times at ye new plaine viewing fences....... o – 4 – o
To John Spoferd for the same worke of viewing fence... o – 8 – 6
     for viewing chimneyes fiue times................ o – 3 – 4
To Joseph Pikke for gathering estats at merymak & bring in o – 3 – 6
To Samuel Wooster for the same worke bringing + + o – 2 – o
to Jeremiah Elsworth for a day at Ipswich Court........ o – 1 – o
to Richard Holmes four dayes at Court as Jury man..... o – 4 – o
To William Acie for a day at Court abouesaid.......... o – 1 – o
Robt heseltine for one Day as Juryman................ o – 1 – o
James barker for the same worke..................... o – 1 – o
To William Teny for ye same worke................... o – 1 – o
     for veiwing fence ocationally .... o – 2 – o
     for service at ye Court four dayes................ o – 4 – o
To John Pickerd Runeing the line between vs and
     Ipswich and Topsfield........................ o – 3 – o
     and one Day at mill About ye Contraverse of ye
     line betweē ye towne and newbury............ o – 2 – o '
To John dreser Junier for runeing ye line between vs and
     Ipswich and topsfeild and the towne.......... o – 3 – o
to John Acy for ye same service...................... o – 3 – o
To Samuel plats for a Juryman four days.............. o – 4 – o
John Scails for a Juryman Three dayes................ o – 3 – o
John pearson for a voage to Salem................... o – 3 – 6
     to thre days at Court......................... o – 3 – o
     and lay ye Country rait....................... o – 2 – o
To John Grant as ouerseer for the Coman gate......... o – 8 – o
     for viewing of the Coman fences................ o –11– o
To Abell Langley viewing fences..................... o –11– o
To Left Samuel Brocklbanke for goein twis to meet
     Nubury men at ye mill About ye line then in
     Contraversee................................ o – 4 – o

geythering ye last pay........................... o – I – o

for burneing the young Catle walks............. o – o5– o

To Ezekiel northend for helping rune newbery line and
    the line between andever and the towne & other
    things.. o –I3 – o

    layd into the hand of ezekell northend about burn-
    ings of the Comans............................ o – 5 – o

To John Boynton for burneing the Cowcomans at ye west
    end.. o – 5 – o

for two foxes to Robt hesseltine.................. o – 5 – o

To Beriah Brown for one fox...................... o – 2 – 6

To John Hopkinson for three blind foxes............. o

To Goodman poore of ye neck for looking to ye gate we
    Call newburry gate............................. o – 5 – o

The select men James Bally....................... o –I2 – o

Ezekiel Northend................................ o.–I2 – 4

To John Dreser senior........................... o –I2 – o

To Lenord Harryman............................ o –I2 – o

To Tho Leauer................................. o –I2 – o

    and for writings for the townes vse.............. o – 4 – o

John spoferd for somthing doeing about ye graues fence.. o – I – o

To Mistres Rogers for a board improued about ye meet-
    ing hous....................................... o – 2 – o

To John Boynton and Lenord harryman for burning hoge
    Iland marsh................................... o – 4 – o

To andrew hedden.............................. o – 5 – o

To Charls Browne.............................. o – 4 – o

    and to him.................................... o – 3 – 6

To daniel Wicome for a hundred nails for meeting hous o – I – 6

Debts and fyns owing to the towne by those persons vnder
    writen for hey at Polipod Mark pryme........ o – o – 8

        Edward Sawier .... o – o – 4

        John Harris .... o – I – 3

        John Scails .... o – o – 8

        Richard Lonhorne .... o – o – 4

for hey in Cowcomans Thomas Palmer a load......... o – I – o

        John Trumbl a load................. o – I – o

        William Jackson.................... o – I – o

        John Burbanke..................... o – I – o

        Jonathan hopkinson................. o – I – 8

        peter Cowper about 4 load........... o – 2 – 8

Richard Clarke about such quantie...... o – 2 – 8
Thomas leauer about a load & half...... o – 1 – o
John pearson for about 3 load......... o – 1 – 8
John Acy........................... o – o – 8
Ezekiel Jewit....................... o – o – 8
o –18 – 3

Fines Comein to the towne vse

in polipod lots 2 lenths....................... o – 1 – 4
John Stickney for one lenth................... o – o – 8
Jachin Reyner a lenth........................ o – o – 8
William Scails a lenth........................ o – o – 8
George Kilburne a lenth...................... o – o – 8
Richard Swan at new plaine 4 lenths.......... o – 2 – 8
Deacon Jewit a lenth......................... o – o – 8
William Jackson a lenth...................... o – o – 8
Petter Cowper 2 lenths....................... o – 1 – 4
Richard clark a lenth......................... o – o – 8
John Dresser seni and Rich Clark }
one lenth between them   } .... o – o – 8
10 – 8

The towne Rate for yᵉ yeare 1666................ 23–18–11
    fines coming to yᵉ towne..................... o–10– 8
    other debts due to yᵉ towne.................. o–18– 3
25– 7–10

The County Rate for the yeare 1666 is in all 75 – 5 – 6

vpon The Complaint of Thomas Tenny Thomas Leaver John Scales and others, the Select men haue apoynted Samuell Brokelbanke Ezekiel Northen and John Person Senior, to lay out the high waies in that feild by Symons that hath yᵉ woulfe pen in it march 22 66 1667

John Tod
William Tenny
Richard clarke

At a legall towne meeting held the 10 of Aprill 1667 it was agreed and voted that andrew Headen should haue halfe an acer of

meddow laid out to him vpon that river nere ye old calfe pen by y^e
layers out of ye land y^t was laid for gates, for want of measure
of a peçe of land that was laid out to him neare ye mill for gates
they are not to exceed to lay out aboue halfe an acer to him for it

At a legall towne meeting held the 23th of Aprill 1667 it was
granted and voted that Mr Samvell Shipard should haue for inheritance foure gates vpon the cow Commans and too oxe gates in
Bradford street oxe paster making fence for them as they doe

Receiued of the Constables of Rowley in full of there Towne
proportion to the Cuntry Rate the somme of fiftie one pounds six
shillings fiue pence for the yeare : 1667 : beinge accordinge to my
warrant, by uertue of the Generall Courts order I say per me
30 (2mo) 67   Richard Russell Treasurer.

May 16 1667

Receiued of James Baly and Sammuell Plats Constables of
Rowley the full of there County Rate six pounds eight shillings
four pence I say receiued by me
                              Robert Paine Treasurer.

At a legall towne meeting held the 20th of May 1667 it was agreed
and voted for ye laying out of hog Iland vpland and mars according
to gates at the discreetion of ye men chosen to lay it out; that Ezekiell Jewit should begin and John Dresser Junier next Abraham Jewit
next John Trumball next Jonathan Plats next, Richard Clarke next
and downe bradford street to George Killborns ; Jackin Rainer next.
James barker next. Jo Stickney. vxor Wickam. William Scales next
John pickerd next vxor Broklebanke next Williā Boynton next
Deacon Brokelbank next John Dreser Senior next vxor Mickell
next Daniel Wickam next vxor Hobson next Mr Rogers next M^r
Shipard next Thomas Nelson next Edward Hasen next John Person
next Richard Lighton next Ezekiell Northern next Samvell Stickney
next Thomas Wood next Mr Philips next Henry Rila next William
Asa next Edward Chapman next John Scales next Richard Holmes
next Thomas Tenny next Edward Sawer next Thomas Lever next
Richard Longhorne Richard Swan next James Baley next Thomas
Burkby next Williā Tenny next Abell lonley goodwife Tenny next
marke Prime goody law next John Johnson next Thomas Riminton
next John Lambert next Charles Broone next Andrew Headen

next Samvell Plats next Williā law next John Tod next John Palmer next John Haris next John Grant next Nehemiah Jewit next Samvel mickell last

At A Leagall Towne meeting held the fifteenth day of the Eleventh mounth one Thoussand six hundred sixty six it was Agreed by voat that The Common marsh at hog Iland should be Devided according to Gates

At a Leagall Towne meeting held the fourteenth of february one Thoussand six hundred and sixty six it was agreed and voated That Samuell Brocklebanke Ezekiell Northend John Pickard Thomas Leauer Leaonard Harriman are Chossen To lay out the Common marsh at Hogg Iland and to proportion it to euery man according To gates: Begining as the Towne Agreed,

According vnto the order of the towne by the men Appointed to lay out this Hog Iland marsh it was Laid out as followeth

In primis Laid out vnto Ezekiell Jewett for foure gates Joyneing vnto the Riuer one the southerly side being in length two and Thirty Rod the north west end buting against a creeke the south east end bounded by a streight line that parts them and ther neighbours that haue ther proportions in the next devission

To John Dresser Junior for three gates a percell of marsh lieing on the north east side of Ezekiell Jewetts marsh buting as afforesaid

To Abraham Jewett for three gates a persell of marsh lieing on the north east side of John Dressers march buting as afforesaid

To John Trumble for two gates a percell of marsh lieing on the north east side of Abraham Jewetts marsh buting as afforesaid

To Jonathan Plats for two gates a persell of marsh lieing on the north east side of John Trumbles marsh buting on the creeke at the north west end the creeke being his bounds on the north east side allong part of his lot till he is stoped by a stake his south east end buteth as the Rest of his neighbours doth it being but two Rod wide at that end

To Richard Clarke for three gates a persell of marsh lieing on the north east side of Jonathan Plats marsh toward the north west end the creeke bounds betwixt Jonathan and him on the southerly side buting on a creeke on the north west end the south east end buting as afforesaid

To Nickolas Jackson for fiue gates a persell of marsh lieing on the north east side of Richard Clarkes marsh buting as afforesaid

To Peter Couper for fiue gates a persell of marsh lieing on the North east side of Nickolas Jacksons marsh buting as afforesaid

To John Burbanke for six gates a persell of marsh lieing on the North east side of Peter Coupers marsh the south east end buting as Peter Coupers doth the north west end extending it selfe longer than the Rest of his neighbours being bounded by a creeke on the west the north east part of it bounded by marsh laid out in consideration of high ways ouer m^r Ezekiell Rogers twenty acres of marsh in the farme neere to Sandy bridge

To Thomas Pallmer for fiue gates a percell of marsh lieing on the north east side of John Burbankes marsh buting on a creeke on the north west end the south east end bounded by the devission line that parts them and ther neighbours on the next devission beyond toward the south east

To William Jackson for foure gates a persell of marsh lieing on the north east side of Thomas Pallmers marsh buting as aforesaid

To Jeremiah Elsworth for seauen gates as the Right of Hugh Smith and his owne a persell of marsh lieing on the north east side of William Jacksons marsh buting as afforesaid

To Jonathan hopkinson for two gates and three quarters as the Right of his father hopkinsons a persell of marsh lieing on the north east side of Jeremiah Elsworths marsh buting as afforesaid

To James Dickinson for eight gates one halfe gate of thes was laid out in this devission of marsh and only the benfit of halfe a gate Right and it was accepted as full satisfaction for the apprehention of former injury done them in not haueing gate land at prospect hill this persell of marsh lieth in a neeke incompased with a creeke only at the goeing into it it joyneth vnto Jonathan Hopkinsons marsh

To John Boynton for foure gates a persell of marsh lying on the North east side of Jonathan Hopkinsons marsh buting at the south east end one the devission line the north west end buting against a creeke that parts James Dickinsons marsh and his

Vpon The Next deuission

To Maxemillion Jewett for seauen gates a percell of marsh bounded by the Riuer on the southerly side the north west end buting against the devission line that parts this devission and the former deuission being in length about 32 Rods the south east end buting against another streight devideing line that parts them and the next devission only this lot extends with a corner by reasson of a creeke, longer next to the riuer and soe toward the easterly side takes that line on the east of the creeke

To Leaonard Harriman for fiue gates and one halfe (which halfe he had of Ezekiell Northend by exchange) a parcell of marsh part of which lieth on the north east side of Maxemillion Jewetts marsh buting as his doth the rest lyeth

To George Kilburne for fiue Gaets a percel of Marsh Lying on the Noreast side of Leonard Harryman Butting as aforesaid

To Jachin Reyner for fiue Gates A percel of Marsh Lying on the Noreast side of George Kilburne: Buting as aforesaid

To James Barker seniour for seuen Gates A percel of marsh Lying on the Noreast side of Jachin Reyner Butting as aforesaid

To John Stickney for six Gates A percell of Marsh. Lieing on the Noreast side of James Barker aforesaid and Butting as aforesaid

To Ann Wickam widdow for foure gates a persell of marsh lieing the wholle length of John Stickneys marsh being on the northeast of him and soe streching a streight line from his easterly corner to the Iland the northwest side bounded by the line of the first devission along to the Iland being on the Iland about four Rod wide

To John Pickard for seauen gates a percell of marsh lieing on the North east side of John Boyntons marsh and alonge by the creeke against James dickinsons marsh till he come to a stake or bound that parts him and the marsh of Sara Brocklebanke (alias) Adams being at the north west end about three Rod wide and soe streching a streight line by the nearest tree on the southerly corner of pine Iland vnto the other Iland to a litle tree ther marked buting with his south east end against the north west side of Ann Wickams marsh

To William Scalles for three gates a percell of marsh in a Necke of marsh extending it selfe toward the towne bounded by a great creeke that cometh corcuterly about it only on the easterly side its bounded by William Boyntons marsh

To William boynton for foure gates a persell of marsh lieing in the same necke on the easterly side of William Scalles marsh buting on a great creeke at both ends

To Sara Brocklebanke: or, Adams: for fiue gates a percell of marsh lieing on the easterly side of William Boyntons marsh buting at both ends on the creeke only at the south east end it buts in part against John Pickards marsh

To Samuell Brocklebanke for eight gates a percell of marsh lying on the north east side of Sara Brocklebanks and John Pickards marsh the northwest end buting against the great creeke takeing in the pine Iland and soe runing vp on the other Iland till it joyne on The bounds of that marsh that lieth on the southeast side of that Iland

To John Dresser Senior for foure gates a percell of marsh lieing on the Northeast side of Samuell brocklebankes marsh the south east end comeing betwen the Ilands on the midle part of it and joyneing vpon the ends of the marsh that is laid out on the southerly side of the Ilands as they are parted by deviding bounds the north west end next to Samuell Brocklebanke stoping at a creeke that leads it downe to the great broad creeke and then it· buts against that great creeke The north east corner also stoping at a small creeke that leads it to the great one

To Ann Mighill widdow for nine gates and one halfe a persell of marsh lieing on the Northeast side of John Dresers marsh the south east end buting against the Iland the north west end bounded by the afforesaid great creeke feching in a corner that extends north east and soe comeing about by a coue of water that comes toward the Iland and alonge on the westerly side of a creeke to a bound that stands on the southerly side of that creeke that parts them and the marsh of daniell wickam

To Daniell Wickam for two gates a percell of marsh lieing on the northeast of Ann Mighills marsh buting against the Iland and against a creeke on the other side of it the creeke is that creeke that is next to the Iland it being but a narrow peece

To Edward Sawier for three Gates A percell of marsh lieing .on the noreast side of Daniell Wickam extending ouer that Creek which bound the afore said Wickam to another creek butting vpon An Mighell

To Ann Hobson widdow for twenty Nine gates part where of lieth at the north east end of the Iland bounded by Ezekiell northends marsh on the south east the north east and north west parts of it buting against a great creeke and the Riuer the south end buting on the Iland the south west side bounded by Edward Sawyers marsh Through this marsh There is to be allowed from Time to time and at all Times a free passage and high way for the Indians to ther fishing place

The other part of hir marsh lieth by the Riuer that cometh downe to the ware house the Riuer being the south bounds the north west end buteth against the deviding line at the south east end of maxemillion Jewets Leanard Harrimans and other of ther neighbours marsh the east side of it bounded by marsh laid out vnto m^rs mary Rogers the easterly corner is bounded by a creeke that stopes hir wher she turneth by that creeke downe southerly to the Riuer

To m^rs mary Rogers as the right of Thomas Barker for twenty gates and one halfe gate a persell of marsh lying on the north east side of An Hobsons marsh the southerly end of it extending beyond an Hobsons on the south east side of the creake that stopes hir and buts on the south east on another great creeke the which creeke compaseth a neecke of marsh that is hirs also haueing a very narrow passage into it of from the rest of hir marsh and soe alonge by the great creake untill it joyne to m^r Shepards marsh and from the south east corner of m^r Shepards marsh alonge that line bounded by the said m^r Samuell shepards marsh and marsh laid out as the Right of Thomas Nelson vntill it come to the easterly corner of John Stickneys marsh

To Mr Samuel Shepheard for six Gates a percill of marsh lieing on the north east of part of Mistris Rogers marsh and butting on thomas Nelson marsh at ye norwest end & on part of Edward hazen marsh & on the south east end buting vpon a great Creeke

To John Pearson seniour for seuen Gattes a persell of marsh lying on the northeast side of Mr Shepherd his east end buting against a great Creek his north east side comeing alonge by a smaler creek till it come to stak and stopeth

To Thomas Nelson for eight gates and one quarter a percell of marsh lieing on the easterly side of Ann Wickams marsh the south-east end buting against m^r Samuell Shepards marsh the north west end vpon the Iland buting part against John pickard part against Samuell Brocklebanks land and a litle against John dresers marsh

To Edward Hazen for six Gates and one quarter a percell of marsh lying on the north east side of Thomas Nelsons marsh the south east end buting part on m^r Samuell Shepards marsh and part on John pearsons marsh the North west end buting part on John dressers marsh and part against the Iland

To Mr Phillip Nelson for Nine Gates and one quarter a percell of marsh lieing on the north east of Edward Hazens marsh and of John pearsons marsh the north west end buting against the Iland

Memorandum This Iland against which Mr Phillip nelson Ann Mighill Ezekiell Northend and seuerall others doe butt it is not laid out as the rest of hog Ilands are but according vnto the agrement of the of the towne it is Reserued for the indians to plant and improue as they may haue ocassion from time to time and at all times the proprietors of marsh that lye buting against it are only to improue soe much against ther seuerall propretyes as is conuenient to set vp ther hay in to stackes

To Ezekiell Nothend for ten gates and one halfe a percell of marsh lieing at the east end of the Iland on the southeast side of Ann Hobsons marsh one end buting against the Iland the other end against the Riuer

To Samuell Stickney for two gates a percell of marsh lieing on the southest side of Exekiell northends marsh the westerly end buting against the Iland it being scarse one Rod wide at the Iland the other end buting against the riuer Runing to the extent of ther lines

To Thomas Wood for four gates a percell of marsh lieing one the southerly side of Samuell Stickneys marsh buting as afforesaid only at the end at Iland its about two Rod wide one of these four he had of the Right of Moses Broadstreet gats

To Mr Samuel Phillips for nine Gates a percill of marsh lying on the southealy side of thomas wood marsh about four rod wide at the Iland and butting at the lower end at Nubery rever extending vpon a streight lyn one both sides

To William Acy for eight Gattes a percill of marsh lieing again part of Mr Samuel Phillips marsh on the southerly side beeing at ye Iland about three rods & lying northerly alonge by the side of mr philip nelson & wide at lower end

To John scails for seuen Gates A percil of marsh lying against the other part of the southerly side of Mr Samuel Phillips his north west end butting part of the south east of William Acys marsh and his southerly side bounded by marsh laid out to henery Ryley come a litle vpon the Iland and vpon a stright lyn downe to the reuer on that side next Thomas teny marsh

To Thomas Teny for six Gates a percill of marsh and vpland vpon the Iland lying on the south east side of John scailes butting at ye riuer with his marsh and vpon the southerly side on Thomas Burkbee marsh and vpland

To Henory Royley for foure Gates lying on the southerly side of John Scalles a percell of marsh buting on the north west end on part of the south east end of William Acies marsh the south east end on the Iland

To Edward Chapman for three gates and one quarer a percell of marsh as belonging vnto his wife sometimes Dorrety Abbot lying on the southerly side of henory Royleys marsh the north west end bounded by a creeke that parts it and the marsh of m^r phillip Nelson that creeke being the bounds of it till it comes to a bound that parts it and Richard hollmes marsh the southeast end buting on the Iland against the north west end of Thomas Burkbies and James baleys lands

To Richard Hollmes for fiue gates a percell of marsh lying with the north east end against the southerly side of Edward Chapmans marsh the north west side and south west end bounded by a Creeke

To Richard Lighton for two gates a percell of marsh lying on the south east side of Richard Hollmes his marsh the south west end buting against a creeke the north east end buting on the Iland about one Rode wide there

To Thomas Leauer for sixe gates a percell of marsh part of it lying on the south east side of Richard Lightons marsh the south west end buting against a creeke the which creeke is the south east bounds till it comes to a bound that parts Richard longhorns marsh and it, the north east end extending on the Iland and buting on the land of James Bayley the other part of it is two Small Thach bankes that lieth at the mouth of the creeke at the south east end of An Hobsons marsh by our Riuer and against the southerly corner of m^{rs} Rogers marsh

To Richard longhorn for six Gates two of which is of the Right of samuel mighills a percell of marsh lying on the easterly side of Thomas Leauers marsh the southerly end bounded by a great creeke the northerly end comeing on the vpland wher with a point it buts against Thomas Leauers and James bayleys lands

To Richard Swan for ten gates a percell of marsh lying on the easterly side of of Richard Longhorns marsh the south east side bounded by William Tenneys marsh the north east side bounded by marsh of James Bayley the north west point bounded by the said James and Richard longhorn on the vpland

To James Bayley for eight Gates a percell of marsh lying on the North east of Richard Swans marsh the north west end buting against Edward Chapmans land the southest end buting against the Riuer his lines on both sides Runing vnto the Riuer at ther extent

To Thomas Burkebie for Three Gates a percell of marsh and vpland lying on the north east of James Bayleys marsh his easterly end buting against the Riuer his north east side bounded by the land of Thomas Tenney his westerly end bounded by land of henory Royley

To William Tenney for sixe gates a percell of marsh the north-east end buting against part of the south west side of James bayleys land the south west end buting on a great Creeke the north west side bounded by the southeast side of Richard swans marsh

To Mary Parrat and Merthy Parrat for sixe gates as part of the Right of the gates of ther father francis parrat a percell of marsh lying on the easterly side of William Tenneys marsh the north east end buting against Nubery Riuer the south west end buting part against a great Creeke and part against an open way that goeth in to that point of marsh wher John lamberts marsh and thers meet together at a bound in the narrow place of entery

To Abell Langley for sixe gates a percell of marsh lying on the easterly side of francis parrats childeren afforesaid the north east end buting against the Riuer the south west end buting against a crooked creeke that goeth with many points in and out which creeke part them on the north east side and charles browne on the north west side of it

To faith Law sometime the wife of John smith for six gates A percill of marsh lyeing on the easterly side of Abell Langley butting at both ends as aforesaid

To Marke Pryme for fiue Gates A percil of marsh lying on the easterly side of the marsh of faith the wife of william law butting at both ends as aforesaid

To John Johnson for fiue Gattes a percil of marsh lyeing in a poynt of marsh which lieth at or vpon the south west end of seuerall of the aforesaid lotts bounded by a greet at both ends and one side

To Thomas Remington for four gattes two of which was the Right of ffrancis parrats a percell of marsh lieing on the north east sid of John Jonsons marsh his northerly end buting against a great creeke his southerly end buting against the Riuer

To John Lambert for eight Gates a percell of marsh lieing on the north east side of Thomas Remingtons marsh buting as afforesaid only at his north east corner he is stoped by francis parrats childerens marsh at the entery in to that point of marsh and against the crooked creeke that parts Charles browne and the rest that lye on the other side against him

To Charles browne for Three Gates lying on the easterly side of John Lamberts marsh a percell of marsh on all parts else incom-pased with a creeke

To Andrew Hiden for Two Gates a percell of marsh lying on the easterly side of Marke Primes marsh the on end buting against

the Riuer   The other end against a creeke that is short of that
creeke wher the said Marke ends

To Samuell Plats for fiue gates and one halfe one and a halfe
of them of the Right of mosses Broadstreet a percell of marsh
lieing on the easterly side of andrew hidens marsh about two Rods
at the end to nubery Riuer and Runing southerly wider vntill it
cleare the bound betwene the afforesaid Andrew and it and then
it extends it self along by the creeke toward the north west against
the end of andrew hidens marsh and soe is encompased with
creekes small and great vntill it come to a bound betwene the marsh
of william Law and it

To William Law for Three Gates a percell of marsh lieing on
the easterly side of Samuell Plats his marsh the northerly end
buting against Nubery Riuer the southerly end buting against a
creeke that parts Samuell Plats marsh and it

To John Tod for fiue Gates the priuelige of one of these he
had out of the Right of Edward Hasens gates a percell of marsh
lieing on the easterly side of william lawes marsh the northerly end
buting against the Riuer the southerly end at that side next to John
Pallmers marsh buting against a great creeke

To John Pallmer for seauen Gates a percell of marsh lieing on
the earterly side of John tods marsh the one end buting against
newbery Riuer the other end buting on the great creeke that John
tod buts on

To John Harris for Sixe gates a percell of marsh lying on the
south east side of John Pallmers marsh the easterly end buting
against newbery Riuer the westerly end buting against a creeke

To John Grant for two Gates a percell of marsh lieing on the
south side of John harris his marsh southerly end buting against the
great Riuer turneing the point the north west end buting against
Samuell Mighills marsh

To Nehemiah Jewet for two gates a percell of marsh lieing on
the south west side of John grants marsh it being .a point at the
southerly end to the great Riuer and soe alonge by the Riuer to a
bound that parts it and Samuell Mighill the north west end buting
against the said Samuells marsh

To Samuell Mighill for foure Gates a percell of marsh lieing
against the north west ends of Nehemiah Jewetts and John grants
marsh on all parts else bounded by creeke and Riuer

Memorandum it is Agreed befor the deviding of the affore
expresed Hog Iland marsh that ther is to be and it is soe laid out

that ther shalbe at all times a conuenient foot way for one proprietor to pas ouer another to ther owne propriety and a conuenient way ouer one another time for euery proprietor to fech
away ther hay without any dissturbance of one another or any
claime by all or any on for any damage that may be done by any
such highwayes

Whereas Ther was a great complaint made vnto the towne
by seuerall of damage done them by high wayes that ther neighboures had necessety of for conuaying of ther hay and corne ouer
the land and meadow one of another it was Agreed by the towne
that such as suffered dammage in that kind should make there
complaints vnto such men as the Towne appointed for that end
(viz) Richard Swan Ezekiell northend Samuell Brocklebanke
James bayley that soe they might haue allowance in land for highwayes ouer land and meadow for highwayes ouer meadow and
acording vnto the Agrement of the towne such as wanted Releife
in that kind were attended vnto and by the abouesaid men ther was
    Laid out vnto Jonathan Plats for a way ouer meadow he
bought of m^r Anhony crosbie to the marsh called m^r carltons marsh
and for a way to m^r Nelsons Iland ouer marsh formerly laid out
vnto Leiftennant John Remington now his by purchase a certaine
percell of marsh in the marsh comonly called hog Iland marsh lieing
at the southerlyest corner of that marsh encompased with a great
creeke on the south east and north west the north east side of
it bounded by a litle peece laid out vnto Richard Clarke on the same
acount of highwayes the which small percell of about foure rod be
it more or lese together with foure Rod laid out on the same account
of highway to Joseph Chaplin the abouesaid Jonathan hath
purchased and acording to ther order and agrement appointed it to
be Recorded vnto him soe that now his northerly bounds is on marsh
laid out vnto John Pickard vpon the abouesaid account of highwayes
    To John Pickard a percell of marsh lieing on the northeast of
the foresaid Jonathan Plats his marsh the northeast side bounded by
marsh laid out to James dickinson
    To James Dickinson a litle percell of marsh on the foresaid
account Lieing on the north east of John Pickards marsh bounded
elsewhere by marsh of his owne that was formerly laid out to his
father Thomas dickinson
    To Petter Cowper a peece of marsh lieing on the south east of
the said James dickinsons marsh that was formerly laid out vnto his

father Thomas dickinson the south side bounded by a great creeke both ends buting against creekes haueing allowance for the high way that lieth in it and for those that lie beyond him as they need

To James Barker Senior a peece of marsh lieing on the south east of petter Cowpers marsh both ends butting against creekes

To William Jackson a peece of marsh lieing on the south east of James Barkers marsh buting as afforesaid

To Jeremiah Elseworth a peece lieing on the south east of william Jacksons marsh buting as afforesaid

To Jonathan Hobkinson a peece of marsh lieing on the south east side of the creeke that bounds Jeremiah Elseworth and him butting on the creeke on the south and on the north on ezekiell Northends marsh

To John Boynton a peece of marsh lieing on the south east of Jonathan Hobkinson marsh buting as the said Jonathans doth on all parts else incompased with creekes

To William Boynton a litle peece of marsh bounded by Ezekiell northends marsh and part on a creeke on the north east the south west side bounded by a creeke

To James dickinson and his mother Whiple a peece on the south east of William Boyntons marsh the south east side bounded by a pondy creeke the west side by a creeke the south end by marsh of deacon Maxemillion Jewetts

To Maxemillion Jewett a peece of marsh on the south of James dickinsons and his mother Whiples marsh the north west and south parts of it bounded by a creeke the north east by a pond

To Leaonard Harriman a peece of marsh on the south east of maxemillion Jewetts marsh and the creeke that parts him and James dickinson and his mothers marsh on all parts else encompased with creekes

To Samuel Plats a point of marsh on the south east side of the creeke that is on the south east side of John boyntons marsh bounded Round by the creeke only on the south where it is bounded by John dressers marsh

To John dreser Senior a litle peece on the south of Samuell Plats his marsh buting on the north on daniell wickams marsh

To Danniell Wickam a percell of marsh lieing on the south east of Samuell Plats and John dressers marsh both ends buting against creekes

To Nehemiah Jewett a peece on the south east of daniell wickams marsh buting as afforesaid on the creekes

To John Harris a peece of marsh on the south east of nehemiah Jewetts marsh butting as afforesaid

To John Pallmer a peece on the south east of John Harris his marsh butting as afforesaid

To Samuell Mighill a peece lieing on the south east of John pallmers marsh the south west end buting as he doth the north east end buting against m^rs mary Rogers marsh

To Ann Hobson a percell of marsh lieing on the south east of Samuell Mighills marsh on all parts else encompased with creekes

To Ezekiell Mighill or his mother Ann Mighill a peece of marsh lieing on the south side of the creeke that parts Ann hobsons marsh and it the north end buting against the south side of Samuell Mighills marsh and on a creeke that parts them on all parts else incompased with a litle creeke that parts Samuell Brocklebankes marsh and it

To Samuell Brocklebanke a peece of marsh lieing on the South of the afforesaid creeke the south east end buting against the Riuer and by a great creeke the north west end buting against a great creeke

To Henory Royley a peece of marsh lieing alonge on the southeast of a great creeke the north east end buting against Samuell Brocklebankes marsh the south east corner buting against the great Riuer

To Seuerall of the proprietors of Satchwell meadow that made claime for dammage done them by high wayes ouer ther meadow both in sumer and winter was laid out a peece of marsh lieing on the south east of henory Royleys marsh ther north east bounds buting against Samuell Brocklebankes marsh bounded by the Riuer in the south east

To m^rs mary Rogers as the Right of Thomas barker a peece of marsh lieing against the north east end of Samuell mighills marsh and part of John pallmers marsh The north part of it bounded by a creeke that parts it and Leaonard Harrimans marsh the south east part of it bounded by seuerall lots that buts against it

To m^rs mary Rogers for the land or marsh she hath for hir life and after hir decease is to the Towne fulfilling the condision was laid out a peece of marsh on the north east side of that marsh that was laid out to hir as the Right of Thomas barker the North west bounded by the creeke that parts Leaonard Harrimans marsh and it the northeast end buting against John Jonsons marsh the southeast side bounded by seuerall men that buts against it

To Ezekiell Jewet a peece of marsh lieing on the north east side of the creeke that parts him and ann hobsons marsh his north west end butting against m^rs mary Rogers marsh his south east end buting against a great creeke

To Richard Longhorne a peece of marsh lieing on the north east of Ezekiell Jewets marsh buting as afforesaid

To Ezekiell Northend a peece of marsh lieing on the north east of Richard longhorns marsh buting as afforesaid

To Thomas Nelson a peece of marsh lieing in the north east of Ezekiell Northends marsh buting as afforesaid

To Thomas Burkbie a peece of marsh lieing on the north east of Thomas Nelsons marsh his north west end buting against m^rs Rogers hir towne marsh his south east end against a creeke

To Abell Langley a peece of marsh lieing on the north east of Thomas burkbies marsh abutting as he doth

To John Acie a peece of marsh lieing on the north east of Abell Langleyes marsh buting on the foresaid m^rs Rogers towne marsh with the northwest end on all parts else encompased with creekes :

To Dorrety Chapman (allias) Abbot laid out a peece of marsh on the south east of Ezekiell northends marsh that was formerly laid out to thomas nelson now the said Ezekells by purchase the south of it bounded by marsh laid out to william Law the north corner being a stake by a creeke that was set for a bound of marsh laid out for m^r Anthony Crosbie it being a tryangle peece

To Ezekiell Northend a peece of marsh lieing on the north east of dorrety Chapmans (allias) Abbots marsh the north west side bounded part on marsh laid out to m^r Crosbie and part on marsh laid out to m^r Samuell shepard

To Richard Hollmes a peece of marsh lieing on the north east of Ezekiell Northends marsh the north west side partly by m^r Shepards marsh and partly by a creeke that comes about the north east end

To James Bayley a peece of marsh lieing on the south east side of Richard Hollmes his marsh his east end buting against a creeke his west end buting against Ezekiell Northends marsh

To Marke Prime a peece of marsh on the south of James Baleys marsh his west end buting against the south east side of Ezekiell Northends marsh his east end on the creeke

To ffaith Law (allias) Smith a peece of marsh lieing on the south of marke Primes marsh buting on Ezekiell northends marsh and the creeke as the said primes doth

To William Law a peece of marsh a litle tryangle peece haveing the high way in it lieing on the south of dorety Chapman formerly abbot and on south of ffaith his wife formerly Smith the

the south side of it buting part against a creeke and part against
James Dickinsons and his mother whiples marsh

To Abell Langley a litle peece of marsh lieing on the south
east of william Lawes marsh buting on a creeke on the south the
north east end buting against ffaith Laws (allias) Smiths marsh

To John Jonson a peece of marsh lieing on the south east of
Abell Langleys marsh the north east side bounded by ffaith Lawes
marsh the south east bounded by m^rs Rogers Towne marsh

The high way to hog Iland is to be free wher it ussually was
Troden and all the seuerall percells of marsh aboue writen called
highway marsh is to let each other as they lie beyond one and other
to haue free passage both Sumer and winter and at all times for the
improuement of ther seuerall persells both to get and fech away
ther hay as they may haue occation without any disturbance

It was agreed and voated at a generall and leagall towne
meeting That m^r Joseph Jewett should have a Thoussand Acres of
land in the Necke Beyond the heseltines and he is to haue forty
acres of meadow as conueniently as can be in the townes land which
forty acres is to be for part of the Thoussand in the Necke in
exchainge of three Thoussand acres of land which is to be laid out
as conveniently as can be for The towne of Rowley in the village
land about the bald hills

According vnto the grant of the towne ther in laid out vnto m^r
Joseph Jewett Nine hundred and Sixty acres of vpland in that
Necke of land beyond the hesseltines bounded by a Runell of watter
that falls into merrimacke Riuer at the east end and soe from the
River it Runeth a westerly line vnto a white oake Tree not very
fare distant from the line betwene Andever and the towne of Rowley
and soe from that white oake streigh to the Riuer wher it turneth
the Rest of the bounds is by merrimacke River ther is laid out also
vnto m^r Joseph Jewett forty acres of meadow in three persells one
prsell in a meadow they call the longe meadow lying for twenty six
acres lying in the village land incompased by vpland laid out to the
Right of m^r Thomas Nelson an other persell lying for fiue acres a
certaine way distant from the long medow toward the south east
ward bounding a litle pond in or by it it also being bounded by the
afforesaid vpland of m^r nelson the other persell lyeth distant from
this more southerly lying for Nine acres and it is bounded partly by
the afforesaid land and partly by land laid out to John dreser and
Joseph Chaplin

Received of the Constable for the yere 66 in full the Countrey rate with adisions according to Court order the sum of sixty nine pounds fiffteene shillings and eleaven pence I say received as by my warrant this 10 of June 1667   69 – 15 – 11

Received by discompt for John pickard 42ˢ for deputies diet 4 or 5 yeres past

by me Richard Rusel treasurer

The Country and County charges with the Colidy proportion comes too in all in the year 1667..........57 –14 – 9
to Richard Swan deputy for his diet horse meet & ferage 3 – 4 – 6
for the five men worke............................... 2 –10 – 0
$$\overline{63 – 9 – 3}$$
The Contry rate for yᵉ yere 1667 comes too in al.......64 –13 – 4
remaining over to yᵉ towne........................... 1 – 4 – 1

A Bill of the Charges of the Towne of Rowley
for the yeare 1667 :

Richard Swan for Deputyship....................... 3 – 9 – 6
  for lainge out land and goinge to Salem & house hire 0 –13 – 0
John Poore senior for the gate keepinge in repaire...... 0 – 5 – 0
Leutenant Brocklebanke for lainge out land and other
  worke.. 0 –15 – 6
Ezekiell Northen for lainge out land and other worke... 0 –17 – 6
  more for his fiueman ship and other worke....... 0 –16 – 6
James Barker sen: for Juriman..................... 0 – 3 – 0
Robert Hazeltine for Juriman...................... 0 – 3 – 0
William Tenny for fiueman ship and other worke....... 1 – 2 – 6
John Tod for fiue manship and other worke........... 0 –18 – 0
James Dickinson for ouerseinge fences.............. 0 –13 – 0
John Spofford for the same worke................... 0 –13 – 0
John Spofford for a wolfe........................ 2 –10 – 0
John Johnson for ouerseinge fences and chimnyes...... 0 –12 – 0
Vxor Lambert for the same worke................... 0 –11 – 8
John Dreser senior for nails to the metinge house....... 0 – 0 – 4
John Bointon for burninge hog Iland and other worke... 0 – 3 – 6
Leonard Heriman for the same worke............... 0 – 2 – 6
John Scales for ueiwinge fences.................... 0 – 5 – 0
Edward Hazon for the same worke................. 0 – 3 – 0

James Baly for·seruinge of the Jury at Ipsw : . . . . o –10 – o
Sammuell Plats for the same worke. . . . . o – 6 – o
James Baly and Henry Riley for uewing fences. . . . . o – 4 – o
John Pickard for helpinge about cuntry rate and goinge
    to Salem. . . . . o – 7 – 6
John Pearson for fiue manship and other worke. . . . . o –14 – 6
Richard Clarke for fiue manship. . . . . o –10 – o
John Tenny for takinge in estates and other worke. . . . . . o – 6 – o
Richard Longhorne. . . . . o –15 – 6
Beniamin Gage for uewinge fences. . . . . o – 2 – o
William Tenny for nails and paper . . . . o – 2 – 6
Daniell Wicom for worke at metinge house and other
    things. . . . . o – 9 – o
John Person for worke to the Towne. . . . . o – 8 – o
Henry Riley for 4 Boults to the meetinge house. . . . . o –12 – 6
John Person. . . . . o – 3 – 4
Andrew Hidden. . . . . o – 4 – 8
John Spoford. . . . . o – 1 – o
Abraham Jewet for four dayes Juriman at Ipswitch. . . . . o – 4 – o

                The Totall somme is. . . . . .20 –11 – o

Debts due to the Towne, for medow

Inprimis John Gage for medow. . . . . o –12 – o
Joseph Pike. . . . . o – 6 – o
Robert Hezeltine. . . . . o – 4 – o
John Tenny. . . . . o – 3 – o
Thomas Hardee Junior. . . . . o – 3 +
John Hardee. . . . . o – 3-+
John Dreser senior hay 1 loade. . . . . o – 1-+
John Trumble 1 loade. . . . . o – 1-+

                              1 –13-+

William Jackson 1 loade. . . . . o – 1 – o
John Burbanke and uxor Cooper 3 loads. . . . . o – 3 – o
John Bointon 1 loade. . . . . o – o – 8
Jonathan Hopkinson 2 loade. . . . . o – 1 – 4
John Tod two loade. . . . . o – 2 – o
James Baly 3 loade. . . . . o – 3 – o
Edward Sawyer ·1· loade. . . . . o – 1 – o
Thomas Burkbee ·1· loade. . . . . o – 1 – o

Peter Cooper ·2· loade.............................. o – 1 – 4
Thomas Pallmor 3 loade............................. o – 2 – 8
Samuell Plats 1 loade............................... o – 1 – o
                                                    _____
                                                    o –18 – o
                                                    1 –13 – o
                                                    2 – 1 – o

for fines and other things

Inprimis Richard Holms............................ o – 1 – 6
Thomas Wood...................................... o – o – 8
Samuell Plats..................................... o – 2 – o
John Tod .... o – 2 – 9
Vxor Hobsen...................................... o – 1 – 6
Thomas Leuer the last of his purchas money.......... 1 –10 – o
More due to the Towne by the two oalde constables..... o –13 – o
Item charles Broune for hay .... o – 1 – o
John Harris for 1 loade of hay...................... o – 1 – o
John Scales for 1 loade of hay...................... o – 1 – o
                                                    _____
                                                    2 –14 – 5

Defectiue fence comeinge to the Towne

Mr Crosbee.. o – 5 – o
Richard Holms.................................... o – 1 – 4
John Spoforth.................................... o – 1 – 4
Samuell Mighill................................... o – 1 – o
Joh Harris John Tod John Pallmor and Richard Holms o – o – 8
Richard Holms.................................... o – 2 – o
John Asee.. o – o – 8
Simon Chapman................................... o – 2 – o
Edward Sawyer.................................... o – o – 4
Sammuell Mighill................................. o – 1 – 4
Marke Prime .... o – 1 – 8
Thomas Tenny..................................... o – o – 8
John Harris...................................... o – o – 8
John Scales...................................... o – o – 8
Richard Holms.................................... o – o – 8
Jeremiah Elsworth................................ o – 1 – 4
Jeremiah Elsworth................................ o – o – 8
Peter Cooper..................................... o – o – 8
Daniell Wicom.................................... o – 1 – o
Barzilla Barker................................... o – o – 4
Thomas Pallmor.................................. o – o – 4

Nicholas Jackson	0 – 1 – 4
Daniell Wicom	0 – 0 – 8
Peter Cooper	0 – 0 – 8
William Scales	0 – 0 – 4
John Scales	0 – 1 – 4
John Simmons	0 – 2 – 8
Ezekiell Mighill	0 – 1 – 8
William Bointon	0 – 1 – 0
Richard Holms	0 – 0 – 8
Sammuell Sticknee	0 – 0 – 8
William Law	0 – 0 – 8
Thomas Tenny	0 – 0 – 4
Charles Browne	0 – 0 – 4
Simon Chapman	0 – 0 – 8
Richard Holms	0 – 0 – 8
	1 –17 – 4
John Harris	0 – 1 – 4
Thomas Tenny	0 – 0 – 4
Deacon Jewett	0 – 0 – 4
Leonard Herriman	0 – 0 – 4
Jeremiah Elsworth	0 – 3 – 4
Peter Cooper and John burbanke	0 – 0 – 4
Jeremiah Elsworth	0 – 1 – 0
John Scales	0 – 1 – 4
Robert Shillito	0 – 0 – 8
William Bointon	0 – 1 – 4
Richard Longhorne	0 – 0 – 4
Thomas Leauer	0 – 0 – 8
John Asee	0 – 0 – 4
Charles Browne	0 – 0 – 4
Sammuell Mighill	0 – 0 – 4
Richard Holms	0 – 0 – 8
John Spofforth	0 – 1 – 4
Thomas Leaver	0 – 0 – 4
John Harris	0 – 0 – 8
John Harris John Tod John Pallmor Richard Holms	0 – 0 – 8
	0 –16 – 0
	1 –17 – 4
	2 –13 – 4
	2 –14 – 5
	5 – 7 – 9

It is agreed by the select men that the pay that was dewe to those that layed out hog Iland marsh shall be added to euery mans Towne rate and to pay 4^d a gate for the lainge out of it and the recordinge of it.

John Pickard for his time of laynge out of it........... 1 – 0 – 0
Ezekiell Northend................................. 1 – 2 – 0
Leonard Heriman.................................. 1 – 2 – 0
Thomas Leauer.................................... 1 – 2 – 0
and to him for recording of it................... 0 –10 – 0

The rest of the gate money to Leftenant Brocklebanks for his time and recording of it

The Cuntry Rate for the yeare 1667 is the somme of

At a generall and a legall towne meetinge held the 28 day of february: 1667 : it was agreed and uoted that there should be a small farme laide out upon the thre thousand Acers of Land that was exchanged for the land at the necke and the rent of the saide farme it is agreed that it shall for euer for the use of the ministry or the townes use.

of The Negetive vote Samuell Brocklebanke that in time conuenient will giue Reason

At the same Towne meetinge the Towne did make choice of John Pickard John Pearson, and Ezekiell Northen to be added to the select men to make a bargon with any who should appeare to take the saide farme. prouided that they let not aboue thirty Acers of meddow, or halfe of the meddow belonginge to the thre Thousand Acers, prouided allso that they put the towne to no charges, prouided allso that they lay not out aboue thre score Acers of upland to the saide farme.

At the same towne meetinge John Pickard John Pearson and Ezekiell Northen were chosen for to lay out the saide farme.

April 16th: 1668:

Where as the Towne of Rowley hath not that common good and benefit and good that it might have by the brook and water courses that doe run through the said towne or any part of the Towne, and it hath not bene so beneficiall as other wayes it might be to the propriators of the Towne, it is therefore ordered that all the brooks about the Towne shall after the publication hereof sometime, at or before the twentyth day of June next followinge be kept

cleare of all wood or any other incumbrances whatsoever, that may
hinder the passage of water, and the saide brooks or water courses
shall be made thre foot wide, and two foot in depth and continnually soe kept, from time to time, In Bradforth streete begininge at
Jonathan Jacksons land, and downward and soe from Jachin
Ranors Downeward untill the brooks doe meete, and soe from
thence downeward untill the brooke doth enter into Satchwells
meddow, and from Edward Hazons bridge in his swampe downeward untill that runlet or water course doe enter into the brooke
that passeth through the towne, and this water course is to be made
two foot wide, and two foot deepe, and continnually so kept, and
where brooks doe crosse the streets they are to be made cleare and
kept cleare by common day works according to this order, and
whosoever shall faile for to make cleare and keepe cleare the brooke
that passeth through there or his land accordinge to this order he
shall pay twelue pence a rod for each Rod not done accordinge to
the saide order and the saide fiue to be imposed for euery month
untill it be done, neither shall any make stopage of the saide brooke
beinge thus done. for the ratinge of hempe or flax under the penalty
of fiue shillings. Red 73. 74 78 79 81 82 83 88 90 91
92 93 97 99 700 1701

According vnto A grant of the towne for the deviding of a
certaine Tract of land intended for a village and to be proportioned
according vnto purchase by such men as the Towne chose for that
end or the maior part of them and is now commonly called Rowley
Village land after the grant and before the devission seuerall selling
ther Rights therin it was laid out vnto the purchasers and therfor
now entered in ther Names as it was giuen in by the surviuers of
those that were apointed to devide (viz) John Pickard Ezekiell
Northend

Inprimis Laid out vnto Zakeious Gould three Thoussand and
Two hundred acres three hundred Acres of it was a farme that m^r
William Paine had of the towne of Rowley the Rest we laid it out
as village land and it is bounded as followeth on the south by
Ipswich Riuer on the west by Rowley line that Runeth from
Ipswich Riuer to the eight mille tree one the east and north side
bounded by a brooke comonly called the fishing brooke and by abell
Langleys land John Lamberts land Leift John Remingtons land
and by land belonging to Topsfeild all this Land with in these bounds

aboue named is Goodman Goulds excepting fiue hundred and fifty Acres Granted to m^r John Endicoate: The land Gould had as village land was 1000 Acres that he bought of m^r Rogers and 200 that he saith he bought of Mathew Boys the Rest was laid out to him by m^r Jewetts order

Laid out vnto the Towne of Rowley that was sould vnto m^r Joseph Jewet by the said Zacheous Gould three Thousand Acres of land which the said m^r Jewett bought for them who Imployed him for which he paid fourscore and ten pounds and Receaued of the towne by argeement for full satisfaction Nine hundred and Sixty Acres of land in the Necke of land by merrimacke and forty acres of meadow that lieth within m^r Nelsons village land this three Thousand Acres which is laid out for the Towne is bounded on the west by m^rs Rogers village land and by land laid out to John Pickard the north end bounded by a line that parts the village land and mearrimacke land the east side bounded by a line that parts the Townes land and village Land the south end bounded by a pond called the Elders pond or baldpat pond and by seuerall small lots belonging to sertaine men of the towne that lie in generall at p^rsent not devided

Laid out vnto Leiftennant John Remington fourscore acres bounded on the east by Topsfield Line on the west by Goodman Goulds Land vpon the North by Samuell Brocklebankes Land and the other end vpon John Lamberts Land of the meadow that is within this lot he is to have but eight Acres whereof that meadow close by topsfeild Line is part of the eight the Remainder of the eight is parted from Samuell Brocklebankes meadow by bounds at the southeast and northwest ends as it lieth in that meadow called Craine meadow the Rest of his two hundred acres Being sixescore Lyeth northerly from the northmost corner of the afforesaid four score haueing a way in to it at that north most corner and soe haueing a certaine bredth against the Northerly side of John Lamberts Land against which it butteth as also bounded by the said Lamberts Land on the north west bounded on the south east by Samuell Brocklebanks Land the North end butting against Backers meadow by Pye Brooke only in this sixescore ther Lyeth a percell of meadow Laid out vnto Abell Langley

Laid out vnto John Lambert fourscore Acres of Land be it more or lese Bounded on the west by Goodman Goulds land on the south by Leiftenant Remingtons Land on the north by Abell Langleys land the Remainder of his two hundred being sixscore lieth

against part of the easterly side of this fourscore and against part of
the easterly side of Abell Langleys fourscore together with which
sixescore Acres ther is aded sixty seauen acres that was the Right
of William Boyntons acre and halfe lot the which Robert Andrewes
bought as well as John Lamberts and soe had it all Laid together
and the whole is bounded by the Land of Leiftennant John Remingtons that Robert Smith hath in posesion : on the southeast the
Northwest side bounded by abell Langleys sixscore acres the north
end buting against Backers meadow by pye Brooke haueing one
quarter part of the bredth ther betwixt Ezekiell Northends land and
topsfield Line all the meadow that belongeth to the said andrews
that he purchased of Lambert and Boynton Lyeth within these
bounds : excepting a Litle percell of about three acres that lieth ta
the turne of the fishing Brooke thats compased with land that is
commonly called Wades Necke of Land

Laid out vnto Abell Langley fourscore Acres of Land be it
more or lese Bounded on the south east by John Lamberts land and
goodman goulds land and on the south west by a Brooke commonly
called the fishing brooke the Rest of his two hundred being sixscore
lieth from the north east of this land and is bounded on the south
east by John Lamberts and William Boyntons Land the northwest
side bounded by land laid out vnto dorman and the Rest of Topsfeild men. and by land laid out vnto Ezekiell Northend the north
end buteth against Backers meadow by pie Brooke haueing in
bredth ther one quarter part betweene ezekiell northends Land and
Topsfeild line The meadow belonging vnto Abell Langley Lyeth
part in Leiftennant Remingtons sixscore acres of land and part in
ezekiell Northends land at the Northeast end of the ceder swampe

Laid out vnto Samuell Brocklebanke two hundred acres be it
more or lese bounded on the south east by Topsfeild Line on the
south west and north west by Leiftennant John Remingtons land
now in the possesion of Robert Smith the northerly end buting
against Backers meadow by pie Brooke being at that end one
quarter part of the Bredth betwene the said topsfeild line and
Ezekiell Northend land all this land is his excepting a percell of
meadow by the said topsfeild Line that was formerly Laid out vnto
m^r Backer the meadow belonging vnto this land Lieth within the
bounds of the said land

Laid out vnto Ezekiell Northend three hundred Acres be it
more or lese as it lieth in two parcells that on the plaine commonly
called the village plaine is bounded by the line that devideth the

towne land from the village land from the highway that goeth ouer
the swampe on to the plaine downe southerly to pie brooke and then
the brooke to be its bounds till it come to abell Langleys land bounded
on the south by abell Langleys Land to the pine swampe the southwest part of it is bounded by the Land of Thomas Dorman William
ffoster and the Rest that were together the Northwest part of it is
bounded by Thomas Dickinsons Land : and the highway allong the
plaine is its northeast bounds only in this land ther is fiue acres of
meadow three at the east end of the meadow belonging vnto this
three hundred acres being devided from the said meadow of
northends by bounds on both sides of the brooke the other two acres
at the west end being divided where the vpland cometh Neere the
Brooke the Rest of the land of Ezekiell Northend Lieth in a three
square peece bounded on the northeast by the line betwene the
towne and the village land the north west end butting against a pond
commonly called Elders pond and against some meadow laid out vnto
elder Rainer the north west corner being a white oake, that is
grained neere the pond the south west side bounded by land laid out
to John Pickard to a Read oake tree that is in the line betwene the
towne Land and the village land ouer against the village plaine this
was the halfe Right of the two acre lots (viz) Joseph Jewett John
harris Thomas harris

Laid out vnto Thomas Dickinson two hundred acres of Land
be it more or lese vpon the northeast abuting on Ezekiell Northends
land the northeast corner being a marked tree which is neere a litle
Rocky hill by the high way to Andeuer that lyeth ouer the great
plaine which high way bounds the said Land on the North vpon
the west and North west its bounded by John pickards vpland and
meadow the south side buting vpon Topsfeild mens land thats not
devided in p{r}ticuler vntill it meete with Ezekiell Northends Land
this was the Right of his owne two acre lot

Laid out vnto John Pickard foure hundred acres be it more or
lese bounded vpon the North side by Rowley line and by Ezekiell
Northends land and the pond commonly called the Elders pond
bounded on the west with a high way six Rod wide Running from
the head of the Elders pond to Andever high way vntill it come to
a Run of water nigh vnto pye Brooke meadow also ther is vpland
and meadow that is on the other side of the path the vpland Runing
from the highway allonge by Thomas Dickinsons Land to the
brooke all the meadow is John pickards that is on both sides of the
brooke also a small percell of meadow northwest from the pine

swampe Runing allong by the minesters farme : also more
four hundred acres, Joyneing vpon the east and northest of the
foresaid four hundred acres and vpon a pond vpon the north west
Joyneing vpon Thomas dickinsons land and land the said John
pickard bought of William Law and vpon Topsfeild mens Land
the south part bounded by a litle peece of meadow belonging vnto
Robert Andrewes and by the fishing brooke the south east side
bounded by land laid out vnto Topsfeild men and also by land laid
out to Thomas dickinson also more to the said John pickard one
hundred acres bought of William Law the south east joyneing on
the foresaid foure hundred acres the Southwest and the Northwest
on land laid out to the foresaid Topsfeild men bounded on the North
by Thomas Dickinsons Land also more   Laid out vnto the said
John pickard Neere vnto Jonsons pond two hundred and fifty
acres be it more or lese Bounded on the North by the Line
deviding betweene the village Land and the Land called Mearrimacke Land bounded on the east by The Line that devideth
betweene the three Thoussand acres that belongeth to the towne of
Rowley and the other village Land the south bounded by Robert
Hezeltines and Gorge Hadleys meadow the west side is bounded by
common land against the midle part and at the southerly end by land
Laid out as the Right of micaell Hobkinsons lot and some others
and at the Northerly end by Land Laid out vnto Thomas Leauer
the Right of all this afforesaid Land laid out to John pickard was to
Richard Swans two acre lot two hundred acres Thomas Lilforth
acre and halfe lot sixty seauen acres Thomas Millers Lot sixty
seauen acres John Pallmers acre and halfe lot sixty seauen acres
John Scalles : (allias) John Jarrats two acre lot and his owne acre
and halfe lot two hundred and sixty seauen acres Isaac Coussins
acre and halfe lot sixty seauen acres Constance Crosbie two acre
lot two hundred acres the halfe Right of a two acre lot of m^r Joseph
Jewett one hundred acres and the halfe Right of a two acre lot
bought of William Law one hundred acres

    Laid out vnto Thomas Dickinson more one hundred acres be it
more or lese bounded on the east by John pickards Land on the
south by the land of John pickard bought of William Law bounded
one the west by William Stickneys and seuerall others vndeuied lands
bounded vpon the North by the minestryes farme Runing from a
tree that is at the side of the highway that goeth to Andever to a
tree that is on the North of a litle Round meadow commonly called
the Sedgy meadow and from thence to a tree that Standeth at the
southwest corner of the great pond

Laid out vnto the Topsfeild men Goodman Dorman Goodman Pebody and the Rest beinge sixe in all Twellue hundred acres of Land be it more or lese bounded one the south by the fishing Brooke vpon the east by Abell Langleys Land vpon the North by Ezekiell Northends Land Thomas Dickinsons Land and John pickards Land bounded vpon the west by John pickards Land

Ther was also laid out vnto Thomas Leauer as his Right of village Land sixty seauen acres of land be it more or lesse as it lyeth bounded by Jonsons pond on the North by John pickards Land on the east the south and west buting against common land the North west part of it is bounded by a litle Brooke vntill the said litle Brooke Isue into the pond

Laid out in the said village Land vnto m^r John Sandys as the Right of his father m^r Henory Sandys deceased two hundred Acres be it more or lese as it lyeth bounded on the westerly side by land laid out as the Right of m^r Nelsons lot the southerly end butting against land laid out to the Right of Micaell Hobkinsons lot and some others the Northerly end butting against a pond and the line that parts the village land and mearimacke land the easterly side lieing against land that Now is in common not yet laid out to any in pertickuler

Laid out vnto William Stickney William Tenney Thomas Pallmer John Burbanke Petter Cowper William Scalles to all these Sixty Seauen acres a peece and to Richard Longhorne one hundred acres of Land all these Seauen haue ther Land laid out together vndevided in pertickuler and it lyeth bounded on both sides of the high way that goeth from Ipswich to Andeuer that on the north side of the way Runeth from the high way at the head of the Elders pond takeing in that meadow that hath the litle pond in it and soe till it come to the ould high way that went from Andeuer to Newbery on the south side of the bald hills and then that path being its bounds on the north vnto a white oake tree that parts it and m^{rs} mary Rogers village Land that was the Right of Thomas Barker then the west side of it is bounded by the said m^{rs} mary Rogers land vntill it come to the high way that goeth betwixt Ipswich and Andeuer the east side is bounded by

that part of ther land that lyeth on the south side of the way is bounded on the east by Thomas Dickinsons land Runing from a tree that is Neere the fiue mille pond to a great pine tree in a swampe and from that pine tree to the north side of humphrays pond soe commonly called, about the midle of the pond to a plumpe of trees that is besides a Runell of watter that falls into the pond and from that plumpe of trees it is bounded on the west by the land of Thomas dorman John Commins and Robert Stilles the high way being the North bounds of it

Laid out for Thomas Dorman John Commins Robert Stilles foure hundred acres of Land on the east bounding on the land of William Stickney and the Rest the high way on the north that parts it and m^rs mary Rogers land and from against the south west corner of hir land it is bounded by the south ends of John Jonson Charles Browne and others lands till it come to a tree marked in the Line betwene Andeuer and Rowley and soe allonge by the line southerly the south side is bounded by a streight line from the plumpe of trees on the north side of humphrays pond that bounds William Stickney land and the Rest to a Tree marked in the line betwene this village land and Andeuer about fifty Rod from the great hill end all this

m^r
Nellsons
medow

land included in thes bounds was laid out to thes men, excepting a percell of meadow called fryes meadow that was laid out and that meadow wholly belongeth vnto m^r Nelsons village Land

Laid out vnto ffrancis Pebody Joseph Bexbie Abraham Redington and William ffoster Eight hundred acres of Land be it more or lesse Bounded by the land of dorman Commins and Stilles on the northwest on the south west by the Line betwixt Andever and us the south east bounded by Wades Brooke and by John pickards land the north east bounded by the small lots William Stickney William Tenney and the Rest all this vpland (the meadow excepted) within these bounds belongeth to the foresaid men ; the meadow that lyeth in This Tract of Land is Laid out one part of it to m^r Nelson the other part belongeth vnto the sixe Topsfeild men dorman pebody and the Rest (excepting a litle percell by Wads Brooke that is Laid out vnto Robert Andrews

That part that belongeth to m^r Nelson is one part of it in a meadow called Long meadow being estemated to be about eight acres be it more or lesse the other part of the said m^r Nelsons meadow lyeth on the south side of the high way betwixt topsfeild and andeuer called the maple meadow and all the Rest of the meadow on that south side of the way is his excepting the small percell that is before excepted belonging vnto Robert Andrewes

The other part of the meadow that lyeth in the aboue said Tract of Land was laid out vnto and belongeth vnto the aboue said sixe Topsfeild men Dorman pebody and the Rest to whom the first Twellue hundred acres of Land was laid out vnto

Laid out vnto m^rs mary Rogers as the Right of hir former husband Thomas Barker one Thoussand acres of Land bounded on the east by the line that parts it from the three thoussand acres of the townes land and by the land of the small Lots William Stickney William Tenney and the Rest the north side bounded by heseltines and hadley meadow the west side bounded by John Jonsons land the south bounded by the high way betwene Topsfeild and andever the meadow belonging vnto this land lyeth within the bounds of it

Laid out vnto John Jonson Sixty Seauen acres of Land be it more or lese lying on the west side of m^rs mary Rogers land the south end 58 Rod bounded by the land of dorman Commins and stilles the north end bounded by John Hezeltines meadow

To Charles Browne Sixty Seauen acres be it more or lese lying on the west side of John Jonsons land the South end being fifty three Rod wide buting against the foresaid dorman Commins and stilles there land the north end buting on the foresaid John Hezeltines meadow

To Richard Wickam Sixty Seauen acres be it more or lese lying on the west side of Charles Brownes land the southerly end being forty seauen Rod wide buting against the line betweene Andever and the village land the northerly end bounded by John hezeltines meadow and John pickards land

To John Spoferd Sixty Seauen Acres of land be it more or lese lying on the westerly side of Richard Wickams land the southerly end being forty seauen Rod wide bounded by the line betweene Andeuer and the said village land the north east end by John pickards land or a line that Runeth streight from a tree marked in John pickards line to tree that parts m^r Nelsons land and John Dresers land

To Richard Swan as the Right of Micaell Hobkinsons lot one hundred acres be it more or lese lying on the north west side of John Spoferds land the westerly end being seauenty two Rod and a halfe wide buting against the line the easterly end buting as the said Spoferd land doth

To Joseph Chapin as the Right of his father hugh Chapin lot Sixty Seauen acres be it more or lese lying on the north west side of the said micaell hobkinson land being at the westerly end fifty three Rod wide buting as the said hobkinsons land doth at both ends

To John Dresser Senior Sixty Seauen acres of land be it more or lese lying on the north west side of hugh Chaplins lot being at the westerly end fifty three Rod wide at both ends buting as the said Chaplins land doth the north west side bounded by m^r Nelsons land

To Robert Andrew there was laide out in the village about four or fiue Acres of meddow more or less liinge in two places. thre whereof doth ioine to his owne meddow bounded runing up on a spange to Abell Langleys meadow, bounded north and south as trees are marked the other two Acres liinge in land of leaftenant Remington being bounded round by vpland.

Laid out vnto m^r Nelson as his Right in the village land two Thoussand acres of land be it more or lese bounded by the Line betweene Andever and Rowley on the south west the line that parts mearrimacke land and the village land on the north west to a bound tree Neere the south west end of the litle pond the north east side bounded by land laid out vnto m^r John Sandys as the Right of his father m^r Henory Sandys the south end bounded by John dressers land all the meadow in this land belongeth to the said m^r Nelson (excepting) three percells that are Recorded laid out vnto m^r Joseph Jewets land in the neecke of land by mearrimacke and a small per-cell that lieth at the westerly end of that meadow by the pond at the south end of the foresaid land Next toward Andever line if it be soe that this litle percell fall with in the said land when the line of its knowne betwene John dresers land and it

To John Trumble as the right of an Acre and halfe lot there was laide out seauenty Acres by estimation be it more or less, liinge at the west side of John Pickards farme at Johnsons pond begininge at a white oake tree marked with · I · P · and · J · T · from thence southwest four score rod, to a white oake With · I · T · southerly of a great rock, from thence westerly to land laide out to Thomas Leauer bounded by a black oake marked with · I · T from thence northerly to a white oake marked with · T · L· I · T · which is the saide Leauers east corner bound.

	£
The Town Rate for this year 1668 is................	30 – 14 – 3
And the fines and debts coming to the Town.........	3 – 12 –10
The Totall is	34 – 7 – 1

At a Generall and legall Towne Meetinge held the 24 day of December 1668 it was agreed and uoted that m^r Philips should haue for the present yeare fourscore pounds for his worke that he had spent in the ministrye.

December: 30: 1668

for the better keepinge and preservinge of the trees in the streets of the Towne of Rowley, that they may be of that use and benefit to the towne, that they haue bene formerly intended for, it is from hence forth ordered and agreed that whatsoever person or persons shall any way barke girdle loppe or fall any tree in any of the towne streets, without the consent of the select men, they shall pay for euery tree that they shall barke loppe or girdell fiftene shillings to be improued to the use of the towne.

75   77   81   82   83   90   91   63   99   700   1701

These presents doe witnes that I John Bointon of Rowley in the County of Essex in New England doe owne my selfe to the indebted unto the Towne of Rowley the somme of eight pounds which some I doe bind my selfe my heirs or Assignes to pay unto the Towne of Rowley, or there Assignes, either in good cattell of the cowe kind, not to excede aboue seauen years of age, bulls and bullsegs exempted, or if not in cattell as before expressed, then in good merchantable English corne, and soe longe as I the saide John doe keepe the saide eight pounds in my hand I doe engage my selfe my heirs or Assignes to pay yearly eight shillings for the rent of the saide mony to the towne and to the true performance hereof I doe bind my selfe my heirs or Assignes as doth witnes my hand this: 7: day of January 1668

Read Signed and Deliuered   John boynton
    in the presence of us

Philip Nellson
Tho Leauer
John Dreser
James Dickinson

This bill was paid in to the hand of John Tod and he acknowledgeth himselfe debtor to the towne acording to the contents therof

John Tod payd of this bill by 1000 bords :........3 – 10 – 0
he payd to doctor benit for the towne ....1 – 10 – 0
John Tod payed of The bill or ingagementt aboue written in
    Seruice dun for The Towne thre pounds this seuenth day
    of ffeburwary 1681

These presents doe witnes that I George Killborne of Rowley
in the County of Essex in New England doe owe and am Debtor
vnto the Towne of Rowley the somme of one pound ten shillings to be payed to the Towne of Rowley, or there Assignes
either in a young beast of the cow kinde, or else in good marchant-
able English corne and soe longe as I the aforesaide George
Killborne doe keepe this thirty shillings in my hand I doe promis
to pay yearly eightene pence to the Towne of Rowley as Rent of
the saide money, and to the true performance hereof I bind my selfe
my heirs or Assignes unto the Towne of Rowley as doth witnes my
hand this :7: day of January (1668)

his
George K Killborne
marke

Read Signed and Deliuered
   in presence of us
Philip Nellson
Tho Leauer
John Dreser
James Dickinson

this £ 1 10 d 0 s in the hand of Gorge Kilborne was paid in to
the select men and by them let to Caleb Boynton the beginning of
may in the year 1672 for the towne
   Smith work dun by calleb boynton this + + + + +
cometh to + + + + +

At a Leagall Towne meeting held January the eight 1668.
   Ther was Chosen by the towne to serue as Constables for the
yeare ensueing Ezekiell Northend Abell Langley Also They are
chosen for towne marshalls to gather fines
   for Sellect men Samuell Plats Edward Hasen Leaonard Harriman Samuell Mighill Jonathan Plats
   Overseers for the east end of the Towne James Bayley John
Acie
   Overseers for the West end of the Towne James Dickinson
Ezekiell Mighill
   Pinder for the north east feilld on the east side of Satchwell
Brooke James Barker Junior Gorge White
   for the west side of Satchwell Brooke Richard Swan
   for Clarke to Call Towne Meetings Thomas Leaver
   for Judges to here the case of delinquents not comeing to
towne meetings

for the east end of the towne, James Bayley William Tenney

for the west end of the towne James Barker Senior Gorge Kilborne

for Seallers of Leather Maxemillion Jewet John Dresser Senior

At a Generall and legall Towne meetinge held the first day of February in the yeare one Thousand six hundred sixty and eight, it was agreed and uoted, that euery one that had gates upon the commons should haue liberty to keepe two sheepe upon euery gate if they did see cause so to doe besides other cattell that there gates were improued with, and that this liberty of keepinge two sheepe upon a Gate should continue for the space of four years.

desenters frō yᵉ voat vnles yᵉ may haue yᵉ same liberty for other catle Tho Leauer John Scails John Acie Tho Tenny John Grant

At a Leagall Towne meeting held the first of february 1668 it was granted That John pearson should haue foure Rod of land giuen him that lieth betwene his Tenters and the Riuer that soe he may fence it in to the Riuer to gether with the Rest of his land formerly granted

At the same Towne meeting it was Agreed and voted that the land belonging to the towne by the Warehouse Riuer should be fenced in by the towne in generall with a three Raile fence or that which is equiuelent

At the same towne meeting it was granted that William Boynton shall haue as much land on the north side of his house as he shall haue need of to set vp a conuenient leaneto to his house and when he hath set vp his leanto that then his fence to be streighned from the corners of his leanto both wayes as shallbe judged conuenient by John dreser senior Leaonard harriman and Samuell Brocklebanke who are chosen for + + + + + +

At a leagall Town meeting held the first of ffebewary in the year 1668 It was agreed that if any inhabetant of the Town of Rowley kill any wolues or woulue he shall haue Twenty shilings for euery woulfe he so kils within the bounds of the said Town

At a Leagall Town meeting houlden the 17 of feb: in 1668 It was granted That Joseph Boynton should haue as much land aded to his house of the comon as the bredth of his house for his mor conuenent diging of a seler vnder his house.

at the same Town meting it was agreed that if there apeared noo owner before the 26 of feb: in sam year to that lot comonly

caled Joseseph Horsly lot to mak and mayntayn the fence belong to
it the other proprieter of the fence should take up theire fence and
lay it to the comon

At a generall and legall Towne meetinge held the seauenteth
day of march, in the yeare one Thousand six hundred sixty eight,
it was agreed and uoted that John Spofforth if he would goe to the
thre thousand Acers that he shoulde haue the benifit of penninge
the cattell, for the terme of seauen years, he keepinge the herde of
the younge cattell as carefully and as cheape as any other should
doe.

Dated March :19: Anno Domini 1668 – 69

Be it knowne unto all men by these presents, that John Pickard, John Pearson Ezekiell Northen, Thom Leauer, John Dresser,
John Johnson, James Dickinson, and Philip Nellson all of us of
the Towne of Rowley, in the County of Essex in New England,
haue to farme lette by the order of the Towne of Rowley, unto
John Spoforth of the same Towne and County, his heirs and
Assignes thre score Acers of Land sittuate in Rowley aforesaide at
the Pen where the younge cattell of the Towne haue beene
hearded, this last yeare, called by the name of Grauelle plaine,
Bounded upon the South East neare to a thick swampe, upon the
North East, about twenty Rods below an old path, upon the Northwest by a greate rocke, upon the South west upon a red oake neare
to a Runlet of water, and allso thirty Acers of meddow more or less
liinge by the old path that goeth to Andever called by the name of
the halfe moon meddow

TO HAVE AND TO HOVLDe to the saide John Spoffoth
his heirs and Assignes, the saide sixty Acers of upland Bounded as
aforesaide, and allso the thirty Acers of meddow called Halfe moon
meddow, for the terme and space of twenty and one yeares the
terme of years to begin at the day of the date herof, the first fiue
years he is to pay no rent nor any rates to ministry or Towne
rates, exceptinge thre hundred of good white oake two inch planke,
sometime within two yeare, to be deliuered at the metinge house,
and the rest of the twenty and one years, he is to pay ten pounds
yearly, for the saide Land and meddow, and thirty shillings for all
stocke on land that he shall improue yearly, and is for the Gates of
the saide Land and stocke, and the ten pounds is yearly to be payed
at or before the nintenth of March, any where in Rowly, where the

select men that are yearly chosen shall appoint the one halfe of the saide rent is yearly to be payed in English corne at price currant, the other halfe in fat cattell or leane at price current as they shall be priced by indifferent men if he pay in leane cattell they are not to excede aboue seauen years of age, or in indian corne if he pleas, what he doth pay in fat cattell he is to pay at or before mihilmas, and he is to make use of any timber for building or other necessaryes for farminge, and he is to make use of by way of saile of no timber but to the Towne of Rowly, and he is to sell no hay excedinge aboue fiue loads yearly, and all dunge that shall be made yearly to be laide upon the saide Land, none to be giuen or sould and what buildings he shall erect upon the saide Land to uphold them, and leaue them tenantable, at the end of his lease, and allso all fences that he shall make to leaue them in good and tenantable repaire, he is to pay yearly cuntry rates. at the last yeare he is to liue in the house untill may day. that so he may spend his fother upon the saide land, and the Towne shall haue liberty upon the nineteenth of march to enter upon the saide Land or other necesaryes as entertainment into house and barne, for them and theirs, family and cattell, and to the true and sure performance hereof the saide John Spoforth hath hereunto set his hand and seale the day and yeare aboue written.

Read Sealed and Delivered,   John   his mark O   Spofard [seal]
    in the presence of us.
Philip Nellson
Thomas Leauer
John Dreser Seneor
John Johnson
James Dickinson

    I John Spofforth senior doe assigne ouer all my right and interest in this lease aboue written unto my two sons John Spofforth Junior and Samuell Spofforth this. 16.th of march 16 $\frac{77}{76}$ as doth witnes my hand

         John   his O marke   Spofforth senior

    We whose names are under written beinge appointed by the Towne of Rowley for to allter or change the conditions of the aboue saide lease, and to let it for longer time, we have agreed with John Spofforth and Samuell Spofforth, sons, and Assigns to John Spofforth senior that the time of there lease shall be lenghened out thre score years from the day of the date hereof, and that they are to pay yearly eight pounds in such pay as the lease aboue written doth specifie, and they are yearly to pay to the ministry rate for what stocke they keepe upon the saide land and for all broke up land, and unbroke land as the inhabitants of the Towne doe pay. they haue liberty to pay in porke there rent if they see cause. and duringe the times of the indians wars the rent is to be abated according to the iudgment of indifferent men, if they be hindered in carriinge on the saide farme. at the end of there lease they are to be allowed for all buildings on the said farme. to be uallued by indifferent men, soe that they are not to excede aboue twenty pounds, as doth witnes our hands : march :16 : 16 $\frac{77}{76}$

his
John   ⚛   Spofforth senior
marke

it was agreed at the lenghteninge of this lease to John Spofforth Junior and Samuell that they wase not to pay any Towne rates.

Ezekiell Northen	John Baly
Sammuell Plats Senior	Ezekiell Mighill
Philip Nellson	John Person
Daniell Wicom	John Pickard senior
Richard Holms	William Tenny

Receued the 10 of June 1669 of the cunstables of Rowly in full of theire Town proporsion to the cuntry rate for the year past ffiufty punds foure shiling and one peney I say receued in full of your warat acording to the generall courts order 50£ – 4ˢ – 1ᵖ

P mee Richard Rusell Treaserar

Its ordered that for this year that noe lot layers shall haue any power to Lay out any Lands within the Townshipe of Rowly but by vertue of some express grant in writing both for place and quantyty June 23 in 69   not Read for 77

+ + + 30 : 1669

At a Leigall Town meeting it was ordered and agreed that all the Inhabitants within our bounds dweling upon that land commonly caled the uilidg shall pay to all Rats as wee doe who dwell in the Towne. And that theire part of the Town Rate shall bee for the defraying all nessery charges about the said uilidg and the Remender shall be Imployed for puting that farm caled the ministers farm into a way of Improuement at the discresion of the select men

And It is further ordered that the benefit of the aforesaid farm shall belong to the Minister at that place when the haue an orthadox minister setled there And at all other times the benefit shall com to the vse of the Minister at the Town of Rowly

Red & voted the 2th of July in the Town meeting that this order should be a standing order till the Town see cause to alter it. 69 82 83

officers Chosen for the seruice of the towne for the Remaneing part of the yeare (69 and 70) this 10th of January 1669

for Constables Jeremiah Elseworth Richard Hollmes and marshalls

for Sellect men Ezekiell Northend Thomas Leuer John Pearson John Pickard Leaonard Harriman

Ouerseers for vuiing fences and hywayes and vuiin Chimneys Thomas Tene Edward Hasne James Dickinson Samuell Pallmer

It is ordered and this day declared that if any person whatsoeever shall fall cut out or lead away any tree of those y^t are within half a mill from the towne ends such person or persons shall pay fifteen shillings ten shillings to the informer & 5 to the towne

Aprill ye 4th 70   Read 1671 Red 72 80 88

its ordered further y^t all sheep that goe on ye Comans or be found ther at any time whill a sheeperd is in being shall pay to ye sheepard as if ye said sheep had been as if with him all ye tyme

The Towne Rate for the yeare 1670 is............... 7 – 10 – 2
The debts due by fines and for meadow and mony let and
    in the Constables hand is to the towne........ 4 – 13 – 9
the Charges of the Towne for the said yeare (70) is... 5 – 10 – 7

Receaued of Jeremiah Elsworth in full of his County Rate for the yeare 1670 the some of eight pounds one penney I say Receaued
                    P me Robert Paine Treassurer

Receaued the 7 of maie 1670 of the Towne of Rowley vpon account of ther Country rait the some of Thirty three pounds seuenteen shilings & two pence being in full of my warrant as by Court order : I say receued in full of the towne proportion for the yeer past of Jerimiah Elsworth.
                    By me Richard Rusell Treasurer

At a Leagall Towne meeting Held the 17th of January 1670
were chose by the towne for the yeare ensuing
    Constable Jeremiah Elsworth
    ffor Sellect men Thomas Tenney Samuell Brocklebanke John
Jonson John Trumble John Pallmer
    Overseers for west end of the Towne John Burbanke Danniell
Wickam
    ffor the east end Richard Hollmes John Acie
    Overseers for Newbery fence Mr Nelson John Grant
    Pinders for the North east field James Barker Junior Thomas
Wood and his son John Joseph Boynton
    Pinders for the west end of the towne Timothy Pallmer John
Boynton Junior

    At a leagall Towne meeting held the tenth of ffebruary 1670 it
was Agreed and voted and ther were chosen by the towne Sam
Brocklebanke Richard Swan and Ezekiell Northend for to consider
determine and set of what meadow John Lambert and seuerall
other of the neighbours to him did lay downe in crane meadow for
which the say they had salt marsh that soe the busines may be
setled and brough vpon Record
    at the same Towne meeting it was voated that william boynton
should stand a scoolemaster and the towne to giue him ten shillings
by the year

    Wheras it is apparent that ther was formerly some land and
meadow Laid out vnto William Boynton in and a bout the medow
Called litle meadow and not Recorded the Select men Considering
the omision ther of might be in Conuenient and truble some vpon
the best information of the Certanty of the bounds thereof gaue
order for the entry of it the claimes is for meadow he had laid out
ther. for amendment of meadow according to his neighbours, that
lieth at the oyster point meadows. and for his Riget acording to his
neighbours for land giuen them at the New plaine and for dreaineing
it through in the oxe pasture and it is bounded on the south and
south east by seuerall bounds where was formerly Set vp a fence
deviding it from the towne Common to a great maple tree with in
the Land Commonly Called oxe pasture Runing from that tree to a
stake in the meadow with in the said oxpasture and from the said
stake vnto the Corner of batcheler feild where it was aucuratly fixed

the said batcheler feild being the west bounds of it. ordered to be entered by the Sellect men

Thomas Tenney   John Jonson

John Pallmer   John Trumble

A Record of Merrimack lands suruayed by m^r Jonathan Danforth: Anno: 1670

To Faith Law widdow as the right of William Law there was laide out ninety Acres of Land, abatinge about thre acres for meadow of m^r Phillips laide out in it, it lyeth six hundred and sixty pole in length, and fourtene pole wide at the riuer, and seauentene pole wide at the midle range, and thirtie one pole wide at the uper end, the bound corners at that end is a great red oake at the southwest end, and a white oake stump at the southeast end.

To James Baley laid out to him eighty and Two acres of land (abatting about eight acres for meadow formerly laid out in it to m^r Rogers and m^r Phillips it is bounded by William Hutchins on the North east: by Joseph Pallmer on the south west; by the Riuer North west where it is fifteen polle wide a pine tree being his North west corner by the Riuer sidé at the midle Range he is about Thirteen polle wide and at the upper end Twenty and sixs pole wide his South east corner is a white oake his South west corner a great ash in the Swamp

To m^r Nelson 1 lot laid out to him Two hundred and fifteen Acres of land bounded on the : N : E : by Newbury line reaching from merimack Riuer to the brooke that coms out of Craine pond which is Three milles and : 140 pole : (only Nicolas Wallinton : interveins Near the : S : E : end : 82 : pole : one hundred and sixty Acres of the same lyeth with in the bounds of the first grant : being Twenty and two pole wide at the South east end : and Sixty seauen pole wide at the : N : W : end upon mirimake Riuer : and : 658 pole in length : bounded by Nicolas Wallinton on the South west : the hedge as it now stands being the bounds between them near the Riuer : there being an ash marked at the uper end of the hedge : and from this ash it runs in a streight line to the head bounds of the lotts as they weare at first layd out : Also fifteen Acres more of the same Number Adjoyning to the former land at the : N : E : end and bounded by Newbury line as before on the North east by Nicolas Wallinton : on the South west the line continueing streight between them from the ash at the hedge 136 : beyound the head of the lotts unto a wallnut Tree marked about Thirty pole before you com at the first meadow

Also Twenty and sixs Acres more lying onward toward the South east bounded by Newbury line as before : 140 pole: by his own meadow on the South east: Twenty four pole : at that end bounded by Nicolas Wallington on the South west and by his former land : 15 pole : Nicolas Wallington : 15 pole : Joseph Baley seauen pole : all the North west it being: 37 pole wide : in all at that end

Also fourteen acres of wood land of the former Number lying the farthest from the Riuer : and Ajoyning to the former brooke being bounded by Newbury line as before : eighty Two pole there being a white oake marked in Newbury line and from that a range of trees marked from Newbery line to the brooke aforesaid: So that all these four perticulars containe the first Number of Two hundred and fifteen Acres

Also at the same time the meadow that lyeth on the North east side of craine pond brooke was deuided between: mr Nelson and Nicolas Wallinton: And all that part of the medow: that lyeth lowest toward the south east and untill you com up to the Narowest part of the meadow : i : e : where the brook coms the nearest the upland (where there is a stake set downe by the brook side and a white marked with : N : W : at the nearest point of the upland) belongs to mr Nelson which containes thirteen Acres more or less the which the said Nelson accepted as his half of the meadow on that side of the brooke : the rest remained to Nicolas Wallington

Also there was layd out to the said mr Nelson one hundred and Twenty seauen Acres of land more : it being the fourth lott from Newbury line : (abatting about sixs Acres for which is taken from it by meadow laid out formerly to James Baley this lott is bounded by Joseph Baley: North east: by Thomas Tennee South west: by his own and Nicolas Wallington on the South east: by the riuer on the North west being fifteen pole wide at the riuer and Twenty one pole wide aboue the plow land at the stake in the midle range of markt trees: and thirty six pole wide at the uper range of trees: and Elm being the South west corner bounds: between Thomas Tenne and himself: a littel white oake upon a great Rock being the South east bound of this percill at the uper range

Also nineteen Acres of the former number lyeth beyound the uper range of trees: being one hundred thirty sixs pole in length and Twenty three pole wide at the south east end where it is bounded by Nicolas Wallington a walnutt tree markt at the east corner and so runs euen with the ridg of hills acording to bound markt trees: and it js Twenty fiue pole wide at the: N: W: end: about one half of the width of it spreading upon the head of Joseph Baley lott the : N: W : corner of this percill is a white oake standing and ould markt in that uper range of trees Twenty three pole short easterly of the afore said Elm

Also at the same time it was agreed between m^r Nelson and Nicolas Wallington that the rest of the meadow lying on the south side of crane pond brooke should be equally deuided between them after wards: also so farr as after ward there should apear any meadow either in m^r Nelsons first lott: or in Nicolas Wallington lot it should be equally deuided between them acording to couenant

Merrimack: 10th: 12^m: 1670

The bounds of seuerall abutments in the saide Towne :

Laide out to widow Mighill of Rowley two hundred and fiftene acres of land, bounded by Merrimack riuer on the North, by Thomas Kimball, and partly by Johnsons pond on the East, by the commons of Rowley on the south, by John Watsons on the west, it is seauenty and two pole wide upon Merrimack riuer, the Northwest corner is a birch by the side of Merrimack riuer. from thence it runs one hundred forty thre pole, to a white oake, from thence the line continnues, four hundred and twenty pole, to the southwest corner, which is seauenty pole wide from Johnsons pond, the northeast corner is a pine tree with a heape of stones, from thenc· it runs one hundred forty and four pole, to a white oake, at this place it is fifty and six pole wide, from this white oake it runs thre hundred and thirtie thre pole, to a great white oake at Jonnsons pond, allso there is an angle in each side, onely it runs in a direct line from angle to angle as aforesaide.

Laide out to John Watson in right of Thomas Abbot, fiftie Acres of land bounded by John and Robert Hazeltine on the west, by the widdow Mighill on the east, by Rowley land south, by Merrimack riuer on the North, his northeast corner is a birch, from thence it runs one hundred fortie and thre pole to a white oake, from thence the line turns a littell· westward, and runs four hundred forty and four pole to a heape of stones which is the Southeast corner, the Northwest corner is a white oake, by Merrimack riuer, from thence it runs one hundred fortie and thre pole, to a red oake, from thence the line turns a littell westward, and runs four hundred and thirtie pole to a great white oake marked

with : W : H : which is the southwest corner, it is twenty two pole
wide at the south end, and a leauen pole wide at the North end,
and thirtiene pole wide at the elbowe in the runinge lines.

Laid out to widdow Hobson two hundred and sixty acres of
land bounded on Merrimack riuer on the north, forty and four pole
by Thomas Kimball on the west, and partly by Johnsons pond, by
Edward Hazen on the east, thre hundred and sixtie and fiue pole in
one direct line, and partly by Johnsons brooke on the east, one
hundred and eight pole, it is bounded by a maple standinge by
Johnsons brooke, which is the northwest corner of Hazens land, the
west line is a littell crooked, at one hundred and fortie and four pole
from Merrimack, where it is bounded by a dead blacke oake, it is
one hundred and thre pole wide at the southend, runninge cross
Johnsons brooke, the southwest corner a pine stub, the southeast
corner is a white oake marked with : H : H :

laide out by Jonathan Danforth suruaer.

Laide out to John Hazeltine one hundred and thirtie Acres of
land bounded by Robert Hazeltine east, thre hundred and eightene
pole, by the uillage line south : seauenty foure pole. by land undis-
posed of on the west, thre hundred and forty pole : by Beniamin
Kimball North, sixty six pole. the Northeast corner in a small white
oake marked : H : K : R : H : it beinge an angle for thre lots. in
this line which is on the east side, there is a white oake marked :
H : H : twelue pole short of the South east corner : the Northwest
corner is a great white oake marked : I : H : and forty six pole
short of the Southwest corner, there is a white oake marked in the
runninge line with : I : H : allso I find upon the worke, in allowance for meadow that fell within these lines.

This was by order of the select men in the yeare 1679 sent to
me to be recorded.

Laide out to William Sticknee as his owne right, and the right
of Richard Wicom, ninety and three Acres. these lots beinge the
nintenth, and twentieth in order, and is bounded on James Barker
on the west : 691 : poles, and by Land of Thomas Weston the east :
709 : poles. by the uillage south. by the riuer North, where it is :
26 : poles wide upon a leuell line, yet but : 21 : pole and a halfe
perpendicular, the Northwest Angle is a basswood tree, the North
east angle a popler, and the southe end is twenty two pole, at the
head upon a leuell, and twenty one pole and a halfe perpendicular,
he Southwest angle is an old tree, the southeast angle is an oake
tree

Laid out to Thomas Pallmor fiftie and six Acres of Land, it beginneth at the Elders pond, at the North end of that pond, where a littell brooke runeth into it, and from thence it runs south, eight degrees west, one hundred and eightie pole, which runneth to the highway that goeth from Ipswitch to Andeuer, and bounded by the saide highway, seauentie eight pole: the southeast corner is a white oake, this lot is but seauenty six pole wide upon a square, and from the brooke at the head of the Elders pond aforesaide it runes in a direct line to a nother high way, that was the old high way from Andeuer to Newbury, on the south side of the bald hills. and is bounded by that high way twenty four pole. the west side of it is bounded by Deacon Tenny, and the line betwene them runs upon the same point of the compus, with the other, that is, from the path, it runs north, eight degrees east. and all the meadow contained within the saide line, belongeth to this lot, and the whole is well bounded by markt trees.

Laide out more to him sixty and eight Acres liinge on the sout side of the former highway, that goeth from Ipswitch to Andeuer, begininge nere a pond, that lieth by the path side, at a white oake marked and runneth south, 36 degree west: one hundred fortie six to a great pine. the west end is seauenty pole wide, and both the sides are parralells: it is bounded on the southeast by and on the southwest by Deacon Tenny, one hundred fifty two pole, the other side line, is one hundred eightie pole, it lieth seauenty pole wid upon the highway. this is the right of Thomas Pallmor sen, and John Borebanks lot.

Laid out to Deacon William Tenny, twenty and eight Acres, on the north side of the high way that goeth from Ipswitch to Andeuer. and is bounded on the south by Thomas Pallmor, and by the aforesaide highway, southwest twenty nine pole; and by Sammuell Cooper northwest, and by the old high way that goeth from Andeuer to Newbury; on the North east twenty six pole and a halfe, and the meadow contained in it, doth belong to this lot.

Laide out allso unto him thrtie and fiue Acres more, on the south side of the former high way, that goeth from Ipswitch to Andeuer, it lieth forty two pole wide upon the high way, and is of the same width through out, it runs from the high way south thirtie six degrees west: one hundred and fifty pole: it is bounded by Thomas Pallmor south, by Sammuell Cooper North, and both the side lines are parrelells.

Allso there is a small angle of land, that lieth betwene the path and the pond, right against the former lot of Thomas Pallmor; so far as untill you come to a marked white oake by the pond side, and takes some small Ispangs of meadow in it, allso the meadow that lieth at the Northeast end of this diuision belongeth unto it, and taketh a littell part of that meadow that lieth against Sammuell Coopers lot, accordinge to the bounds, which is a white oake on the south side of the meadow, then runinge ouer the first coaue to a wallnut tree, then turnes to the side of the high ridge, leauing all the meadow west of it to Sammuel Cooper, then takes all the meadow, betwene the saide ridge and the pond, till you come to Thomas Stickneis meadow, who bounds it on the North.

Laide out to Sammuell Cooper twenty and eight Acres of land, on the North side of the highway, that goeth from Andeuer to Ipswitch and is bounded on the North by Deacon Tenny, bounded by the high ways at each end, beinge twenty six pole wide upon a square through out, but it is twenty eight pole wide upon the high way, at the south end; bounded on the Northwest upon Thomas Stickney.

Laide out allso to him thirtie four Acres more liinge on the south side of Ipswitch roade aforesaide, liinge forty eight pole wide upon the high way, the line runs from the saide high way south, thirty six degrees west. and both the side lines are parralells, bounded on the southeast by Deacon Tenny, and by Thomas Stickney on the north west. and by Humphries pond mostly on the west. allso the meadow at the east end of the lot belongeth to it, from a white oake on the southside of the coue, to a wallnut tree on the North, and so to the high ridge, takinge all the meadow westward to the bounds of m^rs Rogers and Thomas Stickney on the North.

Laide out to Thomas Stickney, as the right of his father William Stickney, and the right of William Scales fifty and six Acres of land on the North side of the high way that goeth from Ipswitch to Andeuer, bounded by the saide high way sixty two pole, bounded by Sammuell Cooper on the southeast, the line betwene them runs from the former high way north, eight degrees east, unto a nother old high way that goeth from Andeuer to Newburie, and is bounded by the saide roade untill you come to a white oake, which is the corner of m^rs Mary Rogers Land, called uillage land, and is bounded by the saide Rogers on the Northwest. untill you come to a stake standinge on the side of the brooke in the meadow, then from that stake alonge by the saide brooke to a narrow neck betwene two hills, and then by two

littell maples marked, untill you come to the pond, and on this end
of the pond, it is bounded on the west by Deacon Tenny, and
Sammuell Cooper

    Laide out more to him sixty six Acres of land on the south side
of Ipswitch roade aforesaide, bounded by the saide highway, one
hundred and sixty pole, the south east corner is a black oake, the
most northerly angle is a white oake, and from that white oake it
runneth one hundred seauenty two pole to an ash by Humphries
pond, bounded by the saide pond on the southwest it is bounded
southerly by Sammuell Cooper, and his line betwene them runs
from the path south thirtie six degrees west unto Humphries pond

    To Ezekiell Jewett, laide out to him one hundred forty and
fiue Acres as part of his father Parrats right, and part of Richard
Thurrells right bounded by John Tenny North east, by m͏ʳ Worsters
on the south west by the riuer North west it is twenty pole
wide, and at the middell range, twenty and four pole wide,
and at the upper end forty seauen pole and a
15 Lot: half wide, Allso there is added a parcell of
common land and meadow at the end of his
lot, untill he come to land laide out to John Pallmor runninge upon
a streite line or the same line that m͏ʳ Danforth hath run.

    To M͏ʳ Sammuell Worster laide out to him three hundred thirty
and one Acrees, bounded by Ezekiell Jewet on the North east; by
Sammuell Sticknee on the Southwest. by the riuer northwest where
it is sixty pole wide, and sixty four pole wide at the middell range
of trees, beinge about seauen hundred and twelue pole in length,
and at the upper end it is ninety and nine pole wide, Allso there is
added a parcell of common land and meadow at the end of his lot
the whole breadth of it untill it come to land laide out to John
Pallmor, runninge parrallell upon the saide lines run by m͏ʳ Jonathan
Danforth.

    March: 1671 A Record of seuerall Allotments, granted by
the Towne of Rowley to seuerall there inhabitants liinge
aboue the Hazeltines lands begininge next m͏ʳ Glouers
farme at that time suruayed and well bounded by m͏ʳ
Jonathan Danforth.

    To Joseph Chaplin there was laide out thirtie and fiue Acres
of land, beinge the first lot in order, bounded by m͏ʳ Glouers farme
on the west. by the widdow Coopers on the east, by the uillage

line south, by merimacke riuer north, where it is eleuen pole and a
halfe wide at the riuer, but nine pole wide perpendiculer, the west
line is fiue hundred fiftie five pole long, at the south end it is eleuen
pole wide, the southwest angle is a wallnut tree, the south east angle
is a blacke oake, and at the riuer each corner trees are blacke oakes.

To John Simmons laide out to him as the right that was widdow
Cooper fortie and two Acres of land, beinge the second lot in that
order, bounded by Joseph Chaplin west, by John Burbanke east,
uilledge line south. the riuer north. by the riuer it is twelue pole
wide perpendiculer, but ten each corner, there are black oakes: his
west line is one hundred sixtie and fiue pole in length. at the south
end it is fourtene pole wide. its south west angle is a black oake.
its south east angle is the stub of a broken downe tree.

To Abraham Fauster as the right of John Burbanke there was
laide out thirtie and seauen Acres of land, beinge the third lot in
order from the west end, bounded by John Simmons on the west,
by John Simmons on the east. by the uilledge line south, and by
merrimacke riuer on the North. where it is twelue pole wide by
the riuer but ten pole wide perpendiculer. the northwest angle is a
blacke oake, the most northerlie angle is a poppell, the west angle
is fiue hundred and seauentie two pole long. at the south end it is
twelue pole wide. the southwest angle is a broken stub the south
east angle is a black oake bounded with B and·C·

To John Simmons as the right of Thomas Pallmor there was
laide out thirtie and six Acres of land, being the fourth lot in that
order, bounded by Abraham Fauster on the west. by his owne land
on the east. by the uilledge line on the south. by merrimack riuer
on the North. where it is allmost fourtene pole wide by the riuer.
yet it is but ten pole perpendiculer, the northwest angle is a popler,
the most northerly angle is a stake, standinge at the mouth of a
brooke. on the east side of it, the west line is fiue hundred seauentie
and seauen pole long. at the south end it is eleuen pole and one
quarter wide: yet but ten perpendiculer. the southwest angle is a
black oake. the south east angle a great white oake, marked with
·P·S·

To John Simmons as the right of William Wild and William
Jackson sixtie and six acres of land bounded by his owne land on
the west. by land that he purchased of Sammuell Smith on the east,
by the uilledge line on the south, by merrimake riuer on the north,
where it is twentie and seauen pole wide, yet it is but eightene
pole perpendiculer, the northwest angle is a stake standinge at the

mouth of a brooke, on the east side of it, the most northerlie corner is a blacke oake. the west line is fiue hundred and eightie thre pole in length. at the south end it is twentie and two pole and a halfe wide, yet it is but eightene pole perpendiculer., the southwest angle or rather the most southerly angle is a great white oake bounded with · S · P · the south angle is a bass wood tree.

To John Simmons as the right of Hugh Smith there was laide out twentie and eight acres of land, beinge the seauenth lot in order, bounded by his owne land west. by michaell Hopkinson east. by the uilledge line on the south by merrimake riuer on the north. where it is twelue pole and thre quarters wide. by the riuer side, yet it is but six pole and a halfe perpendiculer. both the corner trees at that end are blacke oakes. at the south end it is ten pole and thre quarters wide upon a leuell line ; and nine pole perpendicular, the south west angle is a bass wood tree, and the southeast angle a black oake the westerlie line is fiue hundred and eightie six pole, and the easterly line fiue hundred and eightie nine pole.

To Jonathan Hopkinson as the right of Michaell hopkinson, there was laide out thirtie and two Acres of land, beinge the eight lot in order, and is bounded by land of Hugh Smith on the west. fiue hundred and eightie nine pole : and by John Eastmans on the east six hundred and four pole : and by the uilledge line on the south. by the riuer on the north, where it is but fiue pole and a halfe wide perpendiculer, yet fourtene pole upon a leuell line by the riuer side. the northwest corner is a blacke oake : and the northeast corner is a birch, at the south end it is fourtene pole upon the leuell line and thirtene perpendidular ; the southwest angle is a black oake and the southeast angle an ash.

To Sammuell Boswell as the right of William and John Bointon ther was laide out fiftie and thre acres of land, beinge the ninth and tenth lot in that order, bounded by Jonathan Hopkinson on the west : six hundred and four pole by Thomas Dickinson on the east six hundred and twelue pole, by the uillage line south : by the riuer north. at the riuer it is twentie four pole and a half wide by the riuer side : yet upon a sqare it is but nine pole wide. the west angle is a birch, the north east angle is a black stub, the south end it is twentie pole and ¾ upon a leuell line, yet but ninetene pole perpendiculer the south west angle is a birch : the southeast angle is a wallnut tree.

To James Dickinson as the right of Thomas Dickinson there was laide out fiftie and seauen Acres of land beinge the eleuenth lot in order, and is bounded by Samınuell Boswell on the west: six hundred and twelue pole : and by Mazemillion Jewett on the east sixtie two pole : by the uilledge line on the south. twentie pole and thre quarters, yet it is but eightene pole upon the square. the west angle is a wallnut free : the southeast angle a stake and stones. at the north end it is bounded by the riuer, twentie thre pole, yet perpendiculer but thirtene pole, the northwest angle is a birch. the north east angle a black stub.

To Deacon Jewett as his owne right and the right of John Spofforth, there was laide out ninete and fiue acres of land beinge the twelfth and thirtenth lots in order, and is bounded by Thomas Dickinson on the west. by m^{rs} Kimbals lot on the east : six hundred and twentie two pole by the riuer on the North : it beinge thirtie and one poles and a halfe wide by the riuer side : yet but twentie four poles perpendiculer, each angle by the riuer are bounded by stubs. at the south end it is bounded by the uilledge line twentie six pole and ¾ yet it is but twentie and fiue pole perpendiculer : the south west angle is a stake and stones, the south east angle is a white oake.

To Mistres Kimball of Boston as the right of Leaftenant John Remington and George Killborne there was laide out as the right of these two lots to her, one hundred and two Acres of land, beinge the fourtenth and fiftenth lot in order, and is bounded by land of Deacon Jewett on the west. and by land of James Barker on the east, six hundred and thirtie two poles : and by the riuer on the north : thirtie pole and a halfe : yet it is but twentie fiue pole perpendiculer : the northwest angle is a great stub : the northeast angle is a wallnut tree, at the south end it is bounded by the uilledge line, thirtie pole and a halfe : upon a perpendiculer line : twentie nine pole and a halfe the southwest angle is a white oake : the southeast angle an ash.

To James Cannida and James Barker, as the right of James Barker William Sticknee, and George Abbot laide out as the right of these thre lots one hundred and eleauen Acres, they beinge the sixtenth seauentethth and eightenth lott : and is bounded by m^{rs} Kimball on the west six hundred fiftie eight pole, and by William Scales now the right of Andrew Sticknee on the east six hundred ninete one poles : it is bounded on the North by the riuer : thirtie thre poles and a halfe perpendiculer ; twentie and fiue poles, the northwest angle is a wallnut tree, the north east angle bass wood : by the uillage line on the south ; twentie nine poles, perpendiculer twentie and fiue poles, the southwest angle is an ash. the south east angle is an old tree.

To John Bointon as the right of William Scales and Richard Wicom : there was laide out ninetee and thre Acres these beinge the ninetenth and twentith lots in order : and is bounded by James Barker on the west : six hundred ninety one poles. and by on the east : seauen hundred and nine poles. by the uillage south. by the uillage north, where it is twentie six pole wide upon a leuell line : yet but twentie one pole and a halfe perpendiculer : the north west angle is a bass wood tree. the northeast angle is a popler : at the south angle it is twentie two pole, at the head upon a leuell, and twentie one pole and a halfe perpendiculer : the southwest angle is an old tree the south east angle is an oake.

A Record of the Diuision of the remainder of the land not formerly diuided done by the ioint consent of the proprieters.

To Joseph Chaplen there was laide out seauen acres of land, at the north end of the littell pond : bounded by John Griffens land west : by John Burbanke east : by the pond south, beinge six pole wide at the pond : and thirtene pole wide at the north end, there it is bounded by the ministers land.

To Abraham Fauster there was laide out fiue acres of land, beinge six pole wide at the south end, and ten pole wide the north end it is bounded by the pond south ; Joseph Chaplen west : Thomas Pallmer east : ministers land north.

To John Simmons there was laide out eightene Acres, twentie eight pole wide at the south end ; and thirtie two pole at the north end : bounded by the ministers land north : by the pond south by thomas Pallmer west : Hugh Smith east.

To John Simmons as the right of Thomas Pallmor, there was laide out six Acres of land eight rod wide at the south end : and eleuen wide at the North end. bounded by his owne land east : Abraham Fauster west : pond south, ministers land north.

To John Simmons as the right of Hugh Smith there was laide out fourtene Acres of land. bounded by the pond on the south : by his owne land west Jonathan Hopkinson south east : the ministers lot north : at which end he is fortie and thre pole wide, but narrow at the south end.

To Jonathan Hopkinson as the right of Michaell Hopkinson there was laide out thirtie and one Acres of land, bounded by John

Simmons west, by John Eastman east. by George Killborne and the pond on the south, by the ministers land north : beinge thirtie two pole wide at the west end.

To James Dickinson as the right of John Eastman there was laide out, thirtie and one Acres by George Killborne south : by Jonathan Hopkinson west : by James Dickinson in the east, by the ministers Land on the North. beinge fortie pole wide at the north end, and twentie thre pole and a halfe wide at the south end.

To James Dickinson there was allso more laide out twentie and seauen Acres of Land, bouuded by his owne Land that he had of John Eastman west : by land of Deacon Jewett East by George Killborne south. the ministers land north, being thirtie four pole wide at the North end, and twentie thre pole and a halfe wide at the south end.

To Mazemillion Jewet the Deacon there was laide out thirtie and one Acres of land, be it more or less, bounded by James Dickinson on the west : by Jonathan Remington east, by the ministers land north, by George Killborn south being fortie rods and a half wide at the north end and twentie fiue wide at the south end.

To Jonathan Remington there was laide out to him (in his fathers right.) sixtene acres of land, bounded by Deacon Jewett, by John Hazeltine east : by the ministers land north. by George Killborne south, beinge sixtene pole wide at the South end; and twentie pole wide at the north end : the side line on the east side, is one hundred sixtie and six in length.

To Joseph Killborne as the right of George Killborne, there was laide out eight acres liinge a crosse at the head of the four former lots, bounded by Jonathan Remington, Deacon Jewett, James Dickinson and John Eastman, Jonathan Hopkinson all on the north, and by John Hazeltine east : by the pond west. beinge fiftene pole wide through out the whole lot. bounded by James Barker south.

To James Cannida and James Barker iunior there was laide fiftene Acres, bounded by John Hazeltine on the south east fortie and thre poles. and by leaftenant Brocklebanke on the south. by George Killborne on the North, by the pond on the south west : allso his side lines are parralels.

To Captaine Brocklebanke there was laide out eight acres of land, being the last and most southerly lot. in that angle of land, liinge sixtie pole in length. beinge bounded on the south east by John Hazeltine : and on the south by the uillage line. and on the west by the pond. and on the north by iames Barker.

At the same time by the ioint consent of the foresaide persons proprieters then present, there was laide out fortie acres of land, ioyning to the north end of the former par-
To   cells of land. liinge twentie and eight pole
Ministry   wide at the east end, and twentie and six at the west end, bounded by John Hazeltine on the east. by land formerly belonginge to John Griffinge on.the west. and by Jonathan Remington Deacon Jewett, James Dickinson John Eastman. Jonathan Hopkinson Hugh Smith. John Simmons Thomas Pallmer. Abraham Fauster Joseph Chaplin, all of them on the south. and by land claimed by Beniamin Kimball on the north. .and it was granted by the proprietors aforesaide, that the foresaide fortie Acres should from time, and at all times for euer here after be for the use of the ministrie in that towne of merrimacke. and that it should neuer be the proper and peculier right of any person or or persons, any longer or further than while he or they were the orderly ministers of the aforesaide towne of merimacke.

At a towne meeting held the ffift of Aprill 1671 it was Agreed and voated that John Pickard and Ezekiell Northend were chosen by the towne to joyne with some of the villagers to lay out a high way betweene the towne and the village

At the same towne meeting it was Agreed by vote that what Right the towne might expect to haue in an Iland that lieth in mearrimacke Riuer against the neeke of land m^r Jewett had of the towne : they did giue all there Right to sarjant John Gage

Receaued the 17th of may 1671 of Jeremiah Elsworth Constable of Rowley for the Townes proportion of the halfe Rate for the yeare 1670 the some of sixteene pounds two pence : and for the Colledge proportion two pounds eightteene shillings eight pence I say Receaued in full —— 18 — 18 — 10

By me Richard Russell Treasurer

At a towne meeting held the 24th of nouember 1671 it was Agreed and voted that John Pickard Ezekiell Northend Richard Swan Thomas Leauer and Samuell Brocklebanke should be as a commite in the behalfe of the towne to Treate with a commite chosen by the towne of Topsfeild about our villagers joyneing with them for a certaine time for the mantinance of ther minestry

At the same towne meeting ther was chosen by the towne as survayers of the meeting house John Pickard John Pearson and Daniell Wickam to see if it were sound and firme soe as to incurage the towne to make an addision vnto it

At a Leagall Towne meeting held the fift of december 1671 it was granted by vote that Caleb Boynton shall haue the benifit of two gates on the commons for eatage and firing and two acres of fresh meadow wher it maybe most conuenient and commodious for his use. and that he haue both the gates and medow : the use and benifit of both dureing such time as he is seruiceable vnto the towne in his calling of a smith

and also the towne doe further grant that if any of his son or sons if he haue any doe suckseed him in the said traide of a smith that then the same priuelige of the benifit of the two gates and two acres of meadow shalbe continued vnto them dureing such time as he or they remaine to be seruicable vnto the towne in the said trade of a smith

Desenter from The aboue said act Tho : Leauer John dreser Junior

At a Leagall Towne meeting helld the 27ᵗʰ of december 1671 it was Agreed and votted that Mᴿ Samuell Phillips should haue allowed for the said pᴿsent yeare (which Isueth according to our ordenary account at the next may after the date of this :) for incuragment for his great worke of being allone that he shall haue after the some of ninty pounds by the yeare. for soe much of the yeare as he hath or doth the wholle worke of the minestry alone

John Pearley makeing a proposision vnto the towne for The exchainge of some Land and it being attended acording vnto order at three seuerall Towne meetings at the third in January 1671 it was granted to be considered of and men chosen for that end (viz) John Pickard Ezekiell Northend and Samuell Brockelbanke that at the charge of the said Pearley they should vew the same and acording vnto ther descresion if they found it for the good of the towne to agree with him and exchange it and what they should doe in the townes be halfe to be a vallid act

a bill of fines for defects of fence giuen since into Constables hand dated 7 of September 1671 amounting to. . . . .– 1 – 15 – 4

8 11 71 Reconed with the Constable and ther remains due in his hand. . . . . .4 – 4 – o

1 – 2 – 10 he is to pay to the treasuer for the defraying of an ould debt of 3 – 6 – o   John Pickard promised to pay haueing alredy paid out of the Rate he had in his hand 1 – 10 – 8 the Rest of 4 – 4 he Remaines debtor to the towne to pay in the next towne Rate for the yeare 1671 which is. . . . . .3 – 1 – 8

one pound fiftene shillings and foure pence he returned in a bill of fines that he had ingaged the partyes conserned in it to pay in at the next towne Rate the same Constable Jeremiah Elsworth being chosen for the ensueing yeare had the bill returned againe besides in a bill of more fines put into his hand to defray publicke charges o – 9 – 4 and for grase let o – 13 – o besides one from John Tod vpon consideration of money Lent o – 8 – o and of gorge Kilborne o – 1 – 6 besides a Rate Laid on the seuerall inhabitants of the said towne for the defraying of the Charge of the publicke consernment of the towne amounting to. . . . .–10£ – 3ˢ – 4ᵈ:
the wholle put in to his hand amounting vnto. . . . . . . 14£ –15 – 10
The bill for publicke chaige that is to be defrayed
    out of amounting vnto. . . . . 14£ – 9ˢ – 3ᵈ

The bill of the Country Rate put into the Constable Jeremiah Elsworths hand for the yeare 1671 is 34 – 14ˢ – 9ᵈ out of which the Treasurer warrant of Twenty foure pounds is to be satisfied the Remander of the abouesaid bill of Rate is to be disbursed for the procureing of pouder to an addission of the Towne stocke according vnto Law

at a Leagall Towne Meeting Held the 16ᵗʰ of January 1671 for the year ensueing
    for Constable Jeremiah Elseworth
    Sellectmen Samuell Brocklebanke John Pickard Jonathan Plats Samuell Plats John Grant
    Ouerseers at the west end of the towne John Burbanke Daniell Wickam
    at the east end James Bayley Thomas Tenney
    Pinders for the northeast feild John Watson Timothy Pallmer John Wood
    for that part of fleld toward oxe pasture gate Joseph Boynton

at a Legall Towne meeting This 15 1 mth : $\frac{80}{81}$: This order below was declared by the Towne not to be in force

At a Leagall Towne meeting held the 30th of January 1671 it was agreed by the towne that what orders are in the booke and

The interlining between the 3 and 4 line was agreed vpon in a legall towne meeting 29 of March 1678 by a vote

Read by the Sellect men from yeare to yeare shalbe be of force *till the time of publishing orders by the select men of next yeare* and all other orders that tho they be writen in the booke shalbe of noe force if not Read and those that are Read to be of force to be date according to the date of the Select men of that yeare : Voated

Daniel Wakam doth desent from this order 75 76

at a leagall meeting held the fifteenth day of march this order aboue written was declared to be null and of no efect

At a Leagall Towne meeting held the 13th of february 1671 it Agreed and voated that deacon maxemillion Jewett should be moderator for the yeare ensueing   Chossen again 1672

At a Leagall Towne meeting held the 13th of february it was agreed and by a voate declared that what gates any in the Towne or other. that haue them Recorded in the entry of gates they are accounted and owned that those gates that any one claimes in either end oxe pasture are part of those gates that are Recorded and claimed vpon noe other account but as those gates that are Recorded and euery one in the said meeting voated the affirmetive

Those who haue nôe oxe gates and desire to haue Conueinent accomadation for the pastareing of them as well may be the towne grants to John Tod 2   voated

The act was pased by the maior part of the towne in february 1671

At a Leagall Towne meeting held the 20th of february 1671 it was agreed and voated that the towne would accept of one one quarter part of ther Rates vnto the minestry of our neighbours lieuing vpon the Land commonly called the village land being Rated according vnto ther estates as they in the towne are by the select men of the towne and that it shalbe in the liberty of the Select men to chuse one two three or more of them of the village whose Rates may amount vnto the one quarter part to bringe ther Rates vnto the towne such as they shall thinke meet provided that none of them that are chosen to bringe that quarter part to the towne for the minestry shalbe by the select men be apointed two yeares together

that soe they be not twice burthened together to bringe to the towne
And also that ther shall be apointed from time to time one that
shall have powre to destrane for the said Rate that is not dully paid
according to appointment that soe the minestry where they orde-
naryly heare may haue the other thre parts and this agreement
to continue vntill the towne and our neighbours of the village do
other wayes agree

To the towne of Rowley or the freemen Therof or whom it may
concerne meet to gether about publicke ocations this 13 of march
1671 or 72

Margery fflint excequtorix to the Last will of Mr Samuell
Shepard craueth the Liberty of the Law page 50 Tituled Libertyes
common to moue a mottion to whom of you it may concerne
humbly craueing your Answer either in a joynt concurrance or else
by a pertickuler signement of your Names here vnto either in con-
senting or dissenting to the said motion as your wisdome shall see
meet that soe I may make Returne therof to this next County Court
and therin discharge the duty incombant vppon me both from the
Lord and the honnored County Court Trust commited to my care
and Trust

The motion is that the farme Granted by your sellues to the
abouesaid Mr Samuell Shepard and by some considerable persons
amonge you put into the inventory of the said Mr Shepards Estate
and Returned into the Records of this County Court for the benifit
of the proper heire thereof — maybe Speedyly Laid out according
to the grant or an order granted from you to me soe to doe — I
shall waite for your answer desireing it may be in writing according as is premised and Rest as euer affectionate of all your good
and welfare according to my power

Margery fflint

At a Legall Towne meeting held march the 13th 1671 or 72 In
Answer to M^{rs} fflintt conserneing a farme said to be Granted to the
Late Reuerend pastor of this place Mr Samuell Shepard yet not soe
cleare to many some saying it was granted and yet many douting of
the Legallety thereof yet for composeing the differance there about
in the towne and for satisfaction to those who are concerned it was
Agreed and voated that a farme of one hundred acres should be vnto
the Child of the said Mr Samuell Shepard if it Liue and attaine
vnto twenty one yeares of Age and to that end conuenient Care
shalbe had that it be Laid out and bounded that soe it may be
Recorded

Some ther was that when this was voated intended to enter ther dissent and not haueing then open twnety entered the next meeting vpon the 19ᵗʰ of the aboue said march at the same meeting disclamed ther desent and are not entered in thes booke

Whereas it is aparent by experience that diuers persons haue fenced of there gates from the Common with a fiue Raille fence intending to preserue them from swine and other small cattell and yet they haue considerable Numbers of swine and sheepe and such small creatures goeing vpon the Commons where *Read* other mens wholle share lieth in Common vn- *March* fenced it is therfor ordered that the owners of *71 or 72* all such pastures shall only be secured by ther fence and shall Recouer noe dammage nor poundage by swine nor other small cattell except the owner of such swine or other small cattell be knowne to put them in or any by there order and if any be knowne soe to doe they shall pay for euery such swine or other small beast six pence a head besides just dammage

According vnto an agreement made with John Ellathrope as he was an atturney vnto his mother brother and sisters for Land belonging vnto the Right of Thomas Sumner his acre and halfe lot for devissionall lands alredy laid out at the village mearimacke or elsewhere and for Charges of Court as full satisfaction vnto the judgement of the Court held march 26ᵗʰ 1672

Ther is Laid out by John Pickard and Samuell Brocklebanke acording vnto the said agreement: vnto the said John Ellathrope foure score and sixteene acres of Land be it more or lese as it lyeth bounded on the north by land of widdow mighill John watson Robert Heseltine and part against John Heseltines land being the head of ther merrimacke devission of land the east end buting against Johnsons pond the south side and west end lying against land vndevided the bound by the pond at the south east corner being a white oake tree marked with I E the south west corner being also a great white oake Tree marked with I E Runing at the west end by a Reed oake Tree neere about the midle bredth marked on the south and north sides to the end of John Heseltines land

Work done for Samuel person in yᵉ war

Jo Hares oxen 1 day plowing betwene yᵉ corne

James Tenny 1 day Thomas Hasen and Edward each a day

Nathaniel browne a day William Tenny & Samuel Tenny each a day

Josepth Horsley in ye war work done for him

William Tenny 1 day mr phi plowing & Richard lattens boy

There being some differance betwixt the towne and Thomas Lambert conserneing the Right of the Creeke & Thach banke at at the end of Thomas Barkers planting lot the Select men or the maior part of them in the name of the towne haue Agreed with the said Thomas Lambert for the Rest of this yeare from the fifth of September vntill the feild be broken that vpon his disclaimeing of any Right to it by vertue of the said lot as his owne : That he shall haue the vse and benefit of the said Thach banke for the afforesaid time he paying vnto the towne three shillings for the said time and and the Select men Thus agreeing doe ingage for themsellues and in the behalfe of the towne that the said fence that at p^rsent incloseth it shall not any way be remoued for the afforesaid time by them or any other by ther appointment and they further mutually agree that after this p^rsent yeare the said Thomas Lambert or whom it may conserne shall and will Remoue the said fence that at p^rsent seemes to impropriate it to the afforesaid lot that was formerly Thomas Barkers vnto the place wher the said lot is butted by Record except the towne doe otherwise Agree vnto this as a mutuall Agrement of the partyes aboue mentioned they haue set ther hands this 5th of September 1672

wittnes   Samuell Brocklebanke
Abraham Jewett   Thomas Lambert
Jane Pickard·   John Pickard
                                  Jonathan Plats

At a Leagall Towne meeting held the 15th of January 1672 weere chosen for the yeare ensuing

for Constable John Jonson

for Select men Ezekiell Northend James Bayley Gorge Kilborne John Dresser Leaonard Harriman

for ouerseers at east end of the towne Thomas Tenney John Pallmer

for ouerseers at The west end of the Towne Samuell Pallmer John Hobkinson

for ouerseers for Newbery fence Mr Phillip Nelson Henory Royley for pinders for the northeast feild and farme Joseph Boynton Timothy Pallmer Andrew Hidden John Wood

At a Generall and Legall Towne meetinge held January the fiftenth one Thousand six hundred seauenty and two, in refference to a grant made·march the thirtenth, seuenty one or two, of a parcell of Land and meddow, of about an Hundred Acres liinge neere unto Craine medow, which was granted unto the child of Mr Sammuell Shepard upon condition, that it did liue to the age of twenty and one years, the Towne doth hereby take away the saide Condition, and grant it absolutely, and freely to be at present the saide Childs his heirs, and Assigns for euer.

Att a leagall towne meeting held the 22 of January 1672 Richard Swan Mr Phillip Nelson and John Pickard and leiuetenant brucklebanke was chosen by the towne to deuide and proportion newbery fence

att a leagall towne meeting held the 11 day of March 167⅔ itt was agreed and voated that the upland and marsh should bear an eaquall prorortion of fence

Att a leagall towne meeting held the 21 offebbruary 1672 'John person sen John pickard thomas wood and daniell wickam was chossen by the towne to Join with the Select men to considder which might the best way to Repair the meeting house

Att a leagall towne meeting held the 21 of febbruary 1672 itt was agreed and uoated that newbury fence should be deuided and proportioned acording to the land and meadow in the farm that is not fenced by creeks

at a leagall towne meeting held the 21 of febbruary 1672 leiuetenant brucklebanke Richard Swan and Ezekiell northen was chossen to lay out the farm that was granted to Mr Samuell Shepherds child

at a leagall towne meeting held the 21 day of febbruary 1672 itt was agreed and uoated thatt Joseph bointan should haue a peice of land lying on the north side of his hous nott exceeding forty Rod and Leiuetenant brucklebanke thomas tene and John Jonson was chosen to lay itt out

att the same towne meeting itt was agreed and uoated that daued benit should haue a·parcell of land nott exceeding thre acres on the north side of Richard Swans pasture on the west end of the aboue said land granted to Joseph bointan and to be laid out by thos men chosen to lay out Joseph bointans land upon condition that if the aboue said doctor benitt leaue the towne before he die the said land shall Return to the towne the towne paying him all nessesary charges of fenceing and building on the said land

The land laid out to doctor benit be accounted of as being fully satisfied therwith in liew of that which was granted him by the Towne

According vnto a grant of the towne in the yeare 1672 made vnto dauid Bennet of three acres of land to build vpon vppon the condissions in that grant expresed it was laid out by the men then appointed for to lay it out and it lyeth on the north side of the pasture land of Richard Swan the east end and North side of it lyeth against the common the west end of it buteth against land laid out to William Scalles William Stickney and James Barker and John Jarrats pollipod lots only ther is resserued a high way through the said land at the west end of it to goe crose it for John Scalles Samuell Plats or others that have necessety of a carting way into the said pollipod lots

Vppon The Devission of Nubery fence The Agreement made by Those men appointed by the Towne with John Poore Junior; was, that the abouesaid John Poore his heires and sucksesers for euer should haue that peece of vpland on our side against his house he takeing of all and maintaineing sufficiently betwixt the towne and it the fence vnto the Corner of the meadow that cometh to the fence vpon Condission that the Townes land and meadow and William Tenney and all others that lyeth on the north side of the Cowbridge Creeke haue free libertie to haue A way for Carting theire hay to the towne ouer the said land by the inside of the fence or Line that parts Nubery land and ours in case that they or any of them be prohibited from cominge through Newberry Common about the aboue said Poores land into the highway with in the gate. memorandum it is heereby vnderstood that the way that the aboue said men are to haue is from The place where it was formerly Agreed with John Poore Senior that they should come to the fence to goe into Nubery common to the corner of meadow where the towne fence and his joyne Together and that those that haue need to use it are to make it and maintaine it for there owne Conueniency he being at noe other charge but allowing the land to goe vppon : vnto this as

a mutuall agreement of the partyes concerned: The set to ther
hands the 14th of march 1672 or 73

> John Poore Junior
> Samuell Brocklebanke
> Richard Swan
> John Pickard

Truly Copyed out of the orriginall paper to stand vpon Record
here as a wittnes

According vnto the appoyntment of the Towne for the devission of Nebery fence by Richard Swan John Pickard and Samuell
Brocklebanke They according vnto the best light and Instruction
that they could get for the equall proportioning of it devided it
vpon the 14th of march 1672 or 73 as followeth begining at the
creeke and euery one ending at ther seuerall markes

In primis begineth	Rods	foots	inches	Markes
Samuell Mighill	1	4	6	I
Richard Hollmes	1	11	6	II
John Grant	1	7	3	III
John Harris	0	9	4	IIII
John Pallmer	2	15	0	V
John Tod	0	9	4	VI
Sam̄ & Abell Plats	1	2	8	VII
James Barker Jū.	0	4	8	VIII
Simon Chapman	0	14	0	VIIII
Edward Sawyer	0	4	8	X
Abram Hezeltine and his sisters Longhornes	1	2	8	XI
James and John Bayley	0	14	0	XII
William Tenney	1	0	0	XIII
Marke Prime	0	4	8	XIIII
Abell Langley	1	0	0	XV
Charles Browne	0	7	0	XVI
John Lamberts	1	12	6	XVII
Tho Remington and Parrats Childeren	2	5	4	XVIII
John Jonson	2	12	6	XVIIII
ffaith Law	1	0	0	XX
m[rs] Crosbie	0	14	0	I
Thomas Burkbie	0	4	8	II
Richard Swan	1	7	4	III

Thomas Leauer	0 –	12 –	0		IIII
Thomas Tenney	1 –	2 –	0		V
John Scalles	1 –	12 –	0		VI
Will & John Acie	1 –	2 –	8		VII
m^r Phillips	1 –	3 –	0		VIII
Edward Hazen	0 –	4 –	8		VIIII
Henory Royley	2 –	14 –	6		X
Thomas Wood	1 –	15 –	0		XI
Ezekiell Northend	3 –	8 –	0		XII
m^r Phillip Nelson	9 –	0 –	2		XIII
Thomas Nelson	1 –	6	2		XIIII
m^{rs} Rogers	13 –	11 –	8		XV
Thomas Lambert	7 –	4 –	4		XVI
Ann Hobson	5 –	10 –	0		XVII
hir Capt farme	4 –	8 –	0		XVIII
Ezekiell Mighill	2 –	11 –	0		XVIIII
Daniel Wickam	0 –	7 –	0		XX
John Sam̄ dreser	3 –	2 –	4		I
William Boynton	0 –	7 –	0		II
Sam̄ Brocklebanke	1 –	6 –	10		III
John Pickard	1 –	6 –	10		IIII
William Scalles	0 –	4 –	8		V
John Stickney	0 –	4 –	8		VI
James Barker Se	2 –	13 –	4		VII
Birzilla Barker	1 –	6 –	10		VIII
Gorge, Kilborne	0 –	7 –	0		VIIII
Leaonard Harriman	2 –	8 –	8		X
John Wickam	1 –	11 –	6		XI
Deacon Jewett	2 –	6 –	4		XII
James Dickinson	1 –	6 –	10		XIII
John & Joseph Boynton	0 –	14 –	0		XIIII
John & Jonathan Hobkinson	1 –	14 –	0		XV
Jeremiah Elsworth	1 –	0 –	0		XVI
William Jacksom	0 –	14 –	0		XVII

Joseph Chaplin betwixt the tree & gate
Samuell Pallmer from from the gate post

To the marke	1 –	2 –	6		XVIII
John Burbanke	0 –	9 –	4		XVIIII
Samuell Cooper	0 –	11 –	6		XX
Richard Clarke	0 –	14 –	0		I
Ezekiell Jewett	0 –	19 –	2		II

Abraham Jewett.............. 2 – 0 – 0 III
John Trumble............... 0 – 4 – 8 IIII
Jonathan Plats............. 0 – 11 – 0 V
John Pearson Seni.......... 0 – 14 – 0 VI
Nehemiah Jewett............ 1 – 6 – 0 ending against

John Poors fence

A List of the fence of the Common feild that lieth betwixt the oxpasture and it as it begineth at the Rocke by the Riuer and soe to the oxepasture part homeward and soe begining againe against the Comon on this side next to the towne

In primis	Rods	foots	Ending at Number
John Tod begineth at the rock and is in proportion.	34 –	8	I
widdow hobson	23 –	8	II
Thomas Lambert	21 –	15	III
mrs Rogers	2 –	1	IIII
Thomas Nelson	12 –	10	V
Towns land Tho Wood	23 –	13	VI
mr Phillip Nelson	7 –	13	VII
John Pearson Senior	6 –	13	VIII
Edward Hazen	8 –	5	VIIII
Ezekiell Northend	15 –	5	X
mr Phillips	0 –	14	XI
Henory Royley	3 –	9	XII
John Acie	14 –	14	XIII
John Scalles	9 –	14	XIIII
Thomas Tenney	6 –	9	XV
Thomas Leauer	8 –	3	XVI
Richard Swan	6 –	12	XVII
Thomas Burkbie	6 –	12	XVIII
mrs Crosbie	7 –	6	XIX
francis Parrats Land	9 –	7	XX
ffaith Law	13 –	1	XXI
John Jonson	two Lengthes		XXII

and the street and gate at his house

At the oxe pasture gate begineth Richard Swan and hath the bredth
of his land ending at   Number I

	Rods	foots	
Thomas Remington	6 –	5	II
John Lamberts land	13 –	4	III
Charles Browne	1 –	1	IIII
Abell Langley	8 –	2	V
Marke Prime	7 –	3	VI
James Bayley	10 –	1	VII
William Tenney	11 –	3	VIII
Edward Sawyer	3 –	1	VIIII
Abraham Hezeltine	4 –	12	X
Simon Chapman	7 –	13	XI
Andrew Hidden	1 –	9	XII
Rebecka Law and hir sisters	4 –	13	XIII
Samuell Plats	6 –	11	XIIII
Nehemiah Jewet a litle	2 –	0	

peece ending at m^rs Crosbies Crosse fence

Ther being a mistake in the meassure of Samuell Plats fence
and he not doeing it vp to Nehemiah Jewetts and it apeareing
that Marke Prime haueing noe fence for his oyster point marsh it
was aloted to the said Prime and ther is of it sixteene foot and
thirteene Inches lying at the south end of Sam Plats fence.

The other part of the fence betwixt Mosses Broadstreets farme
and the feild begineth at the bound tree   ending at Number

	Rods	foots	inches	
Jonathan Hobkinson	0 –	6 –	9	I
John Clarke	0 –	3 –	0	II
Ezekiell Jewet	0 –	10 –	3	III
Joseph Chaplin	0 –	6 –	9	IIII
John Dreser and Samuell	4 –	12 –	0	V
Samuell Couper	0 –	6 –	9	VI
Abraham Jewett	0 –	13 –	0	VII
John Burbanke	0 –	13 –	0	VIII
John Pickard	0 –	6 –	9	VIIII
Samuell Pallmer	1 –	3 –	9	X
John Trumble	4 –	2 –	0	XI
William Jackson	1 –	3 –	9	XII
Jeremiah Elsworth	0 –	6 –	9	XIII

John Boynton . . . .   0 – 13 – 0   XIIII
James Dickinsin . . . .   0 – 13 – 0   XV
Deacon Jewett . . . .   0 – 10 – 3   XVI
James Barker Senior . . . .   1 – 14 – 0   XVII
Gorge Kilborne . . . .   0 – 6 – 9   XVIII
John Stickney . . . .   4 – 0 – 0   XIX
Leaonard Harriman . . . .   2 – 1 – 9   XX
William Scalles . . . .   0 – 13 – 0   XXI
John Wickam . . . .   0 – 6 – 9   XXII
Sam Brocklebanke . . . .   2 – 7 – 0   XXIII
William Boynton . . . .   0 – 13 – 0   XXIIII
Ezekiell Mighill . . . .   4 – 15 – 0   XXV
John Pallmer . . . .   14 – 8 – 0   XXVI
John Harris . . . .   12 – 1 – 0   XXVII
John Grant . . . .   6 – 2 – 0   XXVIII
Richard Holmes . . . .   15 – 6 – 0   XXIX
Warehous parture . . . .   15 – 8 – 0   XXX
John Pearson Jun . . . .   0 – 13 – 0   below the
     lower end of the great Rocke in the ware house pasture
Samuell Mighill hath the gate and the crose fence for his share

*At the Annual Meeting of the town of Rowley, held
12th day of March, 1894, it was unanimously voted:*

*"The thanks of the town are due and are hereby
tendered George B. Blodgette, esquire, for his services,
gratuitously rendered, in copying our records for
printing the first volume of printed records of the
town."*

INDEX TO NAMES IN THE RECORD.

REMINGTON—*continued.*
83, 84, 86, 89, 90, 93, 96, 97,
100, 114, 125, 126, 127, 141,
180, 190, 191, 192, 198, 216.
Jonathan—218, 219.
Thomas—112, 127, 132, 137,
157, 170, 178, 228, 231.
————59, 128.

REYNER, (Rainer)
Humphrey (also Elder)—1, 4,
10. 14. 18, 24, 26, 30, 33,
34, 36, 37, 51, 52, 53, 54,
59, 62, 68, 84, 97, 98, 100,
112, 115, 116, 126, 131, 140,
193.
Jachin—109, 125, 131, 133,
140, 163, 169, 173, 190.

RILEY, (Rila, Royley)
Henry—59, 90, 94, 100, 109,
114, 132, 136, 144, 146, 159,
162, 165, 170, 176, 177, 182,
186, 225, 229, 230.

ROGERS,
Ezekiel (also Mr.)—4, 9, 10,
12, 18, 25, 26, 31, 35,
36, 46, 47, 51, 52, 53, 54,
59, 60, 61, 63, 64, 79, 93,
94, 97, 100, 101, 102, 103,
107, 108, 109, 110, 111, 113,
115, 117. 118, 126, 128, 129,
145, 148, 149, 150, 151, 159,
170, 172, 191, 207,
Ezekiel of Ipswich—109, 110,
115, 144,
Mary (also Mrs.)—106, 112,
116, 117, 118, 125, 128, 133,
139, 150, 151, 153, 154, 158,
168, 175, 177, 182, 183, 184,
191, 195, 196, 197, 212, 229,
230.

ROGERS—*continued.*
Robert—133.

ROUSE,
Daniel—59, 122.

RUSSELL,
Richard—164, 170. 185, 204,
205, 219.

SANDYS, (Sands)
Henry—4, 9, 13, 18, 20, 24,
195, 198.
John—195, 198.
————128.

SAWYER, (Sawier)
Edward—40, 41, 51, 53, 59,
62, 75, 93, 103, 123, 132,
136, 143, 168, 170, 174, 186,
187, 228, 231.
Thomas—41.

SCALES, (Skales, Sales)
John—33, 37, 43, 48, 51, 52,
53, 59, 60, 61, 63, 64, 65,
70, 73, 125, 132, 138, 158,
163, 167, 168, 169, 170, 176,
185, 187, 188, 194, 201, 227,
229, 230.
William—3, 8, 12, 17, 20, 24,
36, 37, 50, 51, 53, 61, 65,
82, 84, 87, 125, 133, 138,
140, 169, 170, 173, 188, 195,
212, 216, 217, 227, 229, 232.
————128.

SCOTT,
Benjamin—132, 150.

SEWALL, (Shewell, Seawell)
Henry (also Mr.)—62, 63,
64, 119.

SHEPARD,
Samuel (also Mr.)—158, 159,
170, 175, 183, 223, 226.

INDEX TO PLACES AND SUBJECTS.

Note.—During the period covered by this record, Bradford, Boxford, Groveland and Georgetown were parts of Rowley.
Bradford in this record is called Merrimack.
Boxford is mentioned as The Village and
Georgetown as Pentucket.

www.ingramcontent.com/pod-product-compliance
Lightning Source LLC
Chambersburg PA
CBHW061721270326
41928CB00011B/2068